RAGNAR E

ACTION CAREERS

EMPLOYMENT IN THE HIGH-RISK JOB MARKET

CITADEL PRESS
SECAUCUS, NEW JERSEY

Published 1988 by Citadel Press
A division of Lyle Stuart Inc.
120 Enterprise Ave., Secaucus, N.J. 07094
In Canada: Musson Book Company
A division of General Publishing Co. Limited
Don Mills, Ontario

Published by arrangement with Paladin Press.

ISBN: 0-8065-1079-X
Printed in the United States of America

Contents

Introduction

Americans, of all people, do not have to be stuck in mundane, uninteresting, nine-to-five jobs. There are dozens of exciting action careers for those who crave something more exciting than frying burgers, installing rear ends or counting beans.

All it takes to get into an interesting, fast-paced action career is the intense desire not to live a humdrum, conventional nine-to-five existence. Combine this will to live on the ragged edge with a long-range plan and ready willingness to take risks and face uncertainties, and virtually anyone can put it together. In addition to the strong need to live in the intense lane, one must be alert to the possibilities available and then be willing to work like hell to make an action career plan a reality.

For those who really want action careers, America is truly a land of opportunity. Even otherwise dull, stodgy accountants and engineers can become industrial or political spies. The very exciting job of process server, for instance, is available in virtually every community -- without training and often with very little overhead.

In some places in the States, the services of explosives handlers are not only needed, they are vital. Certainly that is true of process servers and bounty hunters.

This book is dedicated to those men of adventure who feel there are never any guarantees and who feel that living life in the rut may be steady and certain, but it is also a terminal drag.

Everyone will, in his lifetime, at least have a chance to get involved in something exciting. Most men don't take that chance because they think they must see past the immediate future. They want more of a guarantee than just the excitement of the moment. Those who really, truly want action in their lives will have to decide early on that they will give up what few certainties life has in exchange for the excitement it can provide. Those in action careers will find their work is not only fun, but it is always interesting. The most others have to look forward to is work that is interesting.

This book describes some of the many jobs that are available to action-oriented men. They all entail risk. Some entail *great* risk. Rodeo riders, for instance, are notorious for getting busted up. Gunrunners go broke, get shot -- or make a million.

The rewards are often great. There is a good living to be made, plus there is the realization that one is not out there scratching shit with the chickens. Rodeo riders, for example, can make $250,000 per year or more. The average starting salary of an FBI agent is $30,000 per year, with a top limit of $75,000. Stuntmen can expect to make about $40,000.

Most men who have thought about it, wish they had elected to go for an action career. The woods are full of people who hate what they are doing and wish they would have twisted when they dodged and would have gone for the brass ring. Certainty and a steady career path be damned, they say. But many men feel it is too late.

Perhaps not. There is always the industrial or political spy, or even the Peace Corps. (It may not be all that exciting, but the Peace Corps does open a million doors to a whole world of opportunity for anyone who is halfway innovative.)

Perhaps the theme of this book should be "let's go for it." There is really little to lose but boredom. Most of the jobs are really not as dangerous as they first seem to outsiders. But who cares? Who can even predict? To a great extent, it's how you live it. Politicians are notorious for colon cancer. Accountants get ulcers. Even newspaper reporters get the shit kicked out of them at times. Most gunrunners I know, guys who really know what they're doing, have never gotten the shit kicked out of them.

Bodyguard

Kidnappings, assaults, extortion, and political revenge, along with a large dose of plain old garden-variety fanatical craziness, have dramatically increased the opportunities for action careers guarding other people's lives, property, and loved ones.

Providing security for the various VIPs who find they need this sort of protection should furnish enough action for the average man to last several lifetimes.

Supplying acceptable, competent services as a bodyguard requires a strange and unusual mix of high intelligence, attention to detail, commitment, and self-control that is seldom found in the average citizen who is also willing to stand between a client and trouble.

People with these characteristics often gravitate to other, easier and less-exciting lines of work simply because the talents of a good bodyguard are just thrown away. A bodyguard is, after all, only someone who must be killed or neutralized so that one can get to the main target, i.e., the VIP the bodyguard protects.

Knowing that he or she is little more than cannon fodder does not appeal to most normal people. Persons seeking action careers are not generally considered normal in our society anyway, making the fit a good one.

People who require and can also afford to pay for personal protection include some executives exployed in high-tech or high-risk fields, entertainers, a few domestic politicians, visiting foreign politicians, and politically sensitive political exiles living in the United States.

The degree and kind of protection required does, of course, vary considerably from individual to individual.

Most people want bodyguards who more or less blend into the woodwork. The exception are entertainers who may need semi-friendly goons to act as a physical buffer between well-meaning fans and themselves.

Business executives often need people with some knowledge of electronics who can provide guarantees that the executive's phones are not being monitored by the competition.

Deposed political types may require protection from fanatical home-front survivors who come with quasi-official sanction from the new bosses at home, armed with high-tech weapons and a fanatical desire to send their target straight to Valhalla.

Mob types can be very nasty if they decide to go after one's client, usually a business person who has stumbled onto the mob's turf or an ex-mob type who has given information pertaining to his former buddies! In this latter case, his only permanent help is some sort of government protection program, including relocation to a remote region with a new I.D.

BGs are often hired to watch people targeted by the IRA, KGB, Armenian nationalists, or other political groups.

A bodyguard must be physically fit, possess a high degree of physical presence, and not be prone to use violence or lose his temper. Professional BGs never attempt to substitute throw-weight for skill. The term they use in the business is "presence." A good BG has lots of presence.

Many years ago during a time when I was managing a then-extremely popular discotheque, I met a bodyguard who had what I thought was presence. This one night was wet-T-shirt-contest night. One of the contestants, a local budding actress, brought along her professional bodyguard. Later in the evening, I got into an altercation at the gate with a 6'6" university lineman. Although I am not small myself, the situation was rapidly going out of my control.

"My God," I thought, "I am going to have to mace this guy or he is going to run right over the top of me and start some real trouble inside." I didn't really want to escalate the situation to that point, but at the time I didn't see that I had much choice.

Just in the nick of time, the little chickadee's main man came waltzing up.

"Any problem here?" he asked.

"No. None at all," the footballer blurted out as he turned to leave.

It was an unforgettable demonstration of presence that I will always remember. The bodyguard was, at most, 5'11", but, no matter, he looked like he could handle anything. In this case he did it, without discussion or even the slightest show of force.

In the trade, bodyguards are known to possess a fair working knowledge of martial arts and a high degree of skill with small arms. Universally they agree that if they have to resort to use of weapons, they have materially failed to provide a professional level of protection to their clients. Military or police training is essential for a BG. A university education is helpful in terms of gaining some knowledge of the maneuvers and interests of the people whom he will guard.

Ex-Secret Service agents make good bodyguards but sometimes are not used because they tend to rely on an unreasonably extensive back-up system.

Secret Service agents come from British,

French, Italian, U.S., and even Soviet agencies. All can be well trained depending on the personal devotion to duty and professional sense of responsibility that each carries to the assignment. Pay scales for bodyguards are OK but not fantastic. Depending on the exact assignment, daily rates run from $200 to $250. Contracts are negotiated that are essentially based on these day rates times the number of days and people required to get the job done.

Duties range from being what the industry refers to as a wrangler, or person who is personally responsible for getting the client safely from place to place, to a driver, electronics wizard, protection-team captain, trainer, close-in specialist, female assistant who will sweep -- or check out -- places off limits to other members of the team, and others.

Sometimes the driver will double as the wrangler, an impossible situation if the principal is genuinely at risk and truly wants to be protected.

There are, then, a minimum of two jobs guarding every person: the bodyguard and the driver. The driver must be able to perform his job under stress and to drive his client out of a tight situation, if the need occurs.

Most drivers must get this training at specialized defensive driving schools.

Wranglers usually get their initial training on the job either by working as drivers or for highly qualified team captains. Most have some idea what is expected if they've had some military background.

Military training as an MP or in counterespionage or counterterrorist fields is OK, but no guarantee that one can make it as a bodyguard. Often these people are thought of as too macho and too tough without the requisite intelligence to stay away from bad situations in the first place.

Most often bodyguards start their careers by going to work for a friend in the business or for an expanding company offering bodyguard services. If they like the work, they generally do well. In a few years, the by-now trained BG will start thinking about setting up his own company.

Professional BGs carry weapons, but always say they try to avoid a shoot-out if possible. There is general agreement that the first-line weapon of the professional bodyguard should be a fairly small and reliable automatic pistol having a large magazine capacity. Most suggest the Browning Hi-Power as being pretty near ideal.

Most BGs carry a second large pistol of the same caliber, as well as a Detonics MC-1 or MK VI type of pistol that becomes their hideaway weapon.

As a matter of convention, a knife is also recommended.

Beyond the basic pistols, the issue of armament becomes clouded. Some professionals like submachine guns, while others think submachine guns are too tough to shoot well and recommend carbines or shotguns.

To a great extent, the choice of weapons depends on the client and where one will be operating. (Many BGs hire out in foreign countries where the choice of weapons is radically different than in the United States.)

About the only points of agreement in regard to weapons are:

1. Keep your client out of situations where weapons might be needed, and
2. Professional bodyguards don't use revolvers.

A bodyguard not only need to have a nose for dangerous situations, he also has to be able to watch for attacks with explosives. Assassination by bomb has become very common worldwide. Good BGs know where to look for bombs and are sensitive to situations that expose their clients to the threat of bomb attacks.

Military training in handling and use of explosives is often vital to the career of the bodyguard.

Companies or individuals offering BG services are often called on to design complete, fully integrated security systems for homes and estates of those they protect. Performing these services can range all the way from speccing a custom-hardened limo to designing closed-circuit TV and contracting for perimeter fencing. It will almost always include bringing in other members of a security team, such as dog handlers, electronics people, drivers, and gate guards.

Bodyguards usually start in the trade by knowing what the job entails, matching their qualifications and training to what is required, and offering their skills to a potential client. An especially qualified person may approach an existing bodyguard service about possible employment. After building contacts in the industry, it is often possible to start one's own company.

As a general rule, bodyguard services are more in demand in the difficult, disagreeable places such as New York, Washington, D.C., and Miami, where it is tough to own weapons, practice shooting, and generally live a fairly "normal" life.

How You Can Do It

1. Survey the situation in your area to see if there is a need for a bodyguard service.
2. Get any specialized military training available including firearms, martial arts, MP, and special police work.
3. Work as a local cop if possible.
4. Locate an existing bodyguard service to see

if you can get on as an apprentice. Sometimes it helps if you can bring in a client.

5. Electronics wizards can often start work as bodyguards, and it isn't all on-the-job training. People skilled with listening devices and bugs should learn the business before trying to contract out their services.

6. Learning to be a driver can be a way to break into the business of being a bodyguard.

7. Go to a driving school if possible.

8. Work as an explosives handler in order to become familiar with explosives.

9. After working for someone else for a few years, plan to start your own company.

10. Buy business cards and an answering device, and develop a fee schedule.

11. Put together a brochure listing your terms, services, and qualifications.

12. In many cases, a team can be made up of people whom you know are available and whom you can call upon to help out with an assignment.

13. Inventory the local market for BGs. Go visit the people whom you have identified as potential buyers of your services.

14. Handle all contracts perfectly and professionally.

15. Develop "presence" and an eye for trouble and detail.

Border Patrol Officer

As a general rule, almost any law enforcement job is of interest to men who are looking for action careers.

The enforcement agency that has the best record for continuous action has got to be the U.S. Border Patrol. As agents for the Immigration and Naturalization Service in the U.S. Department of Justice, these men have traditionally seen more firefights than the FBI, Secret Service, and the BATF (Bureau of Alcohol, Tobacco and Firearms) rolled into one.

Charles Askins glamorized the service to a great extent by reason of his excellent ability to detail midnight encounters with shotgun-toting Mexican desperadoes. Partly as a result of Mr. Askins' graphic accounts, the Border Patrol has acquired the reputation of being one of the most hard-core macho branches of our enforcement agencies.

The statement has been made that members

of the Border Patrol expect shoot-outs and that they are surprised when they don't occur.

The intensity of these border encounters seems to fluctuate on a wide scale depending to a great extent on laws in the United States and the basic economy of Mexico.

During the twenties and early thirties, for instance, rum and booze runners made big money by bringing bottles across to a Prohibition thirsty nation. By the early thirties, the Border Patrol became much better organized while the Mexicans became more desperate, as the worldwide recession destroyed what little ability they had to make a living by any means other than smuggling.

Furious gun battles were reported that would have been more in keeping with popular tales of the Old West than of a rapidly modernizing America of the thirties. In the late eighties, the issues are drugs and illegal aliens. Dealing in illegal drugs attracts truly huge amounts of money. As in times past, Mexico is going through a horrible depression, and it is oftentimes impossible to earn a subsistence living in Mexico.

As a result, entrepreneurs either go for the bucks in drugs or try to smuggle themselves over to "Yanqui land" where they can get a job. Professional and often brutal, smugglers are a huge headache for the Border Patrol.

The challenges for the 4,500-member Border Patrol force are obvious. It must watch the borders and, insofar as possible, cut down on the blatant abuses. In some cases, its operations take on the aura of military patrols rather than routine police actions.

Against this backdrop, the Immigration and Naturalization Service is actually out hiring people for the Border Patrol, claiming there are 400 openings per year. Total applications usually are many times 400, but apparently there have been some problems recruiting qualified men. Recently, ads for the service have appeared in many of the larger papers in the West.

Obviously not all the applications for employment that are received are valid, but working in an action-filled Border Patrol job definitely should be on an action-career-oriented man's agenda.

Criteria for a Border Patrol job are unique. Applicants must pass a fairly rigorous medical examination, given at agency expense, that will give reason to believe the applicant can withstand the "rigorous environmental" conditions under which he will be working.

In addition, applicants must demonstrate that they possess the following qualities:

1. The ability to take charge, maintain composure, and make sound decisions in stressful situations.

2. The ability to learn law-enforcement

regulations, methods, and techniques through classroom training or on-the-job instruction.

3. The ability to establish, maintain, and improve interpersonal relationships with a wide variety of people in all walks of life.

4. The ability to gather factual information through questioning, observation, and examination of documents and records.

5. The ability to speak and read Spanish.

Item number 5 is very important. Spanish is taught as part of the training program, but some competence level is desirable right from the first interview.

The aspiring action-career-oriented men can make initial and preliminary contact with the Border Patrol by contacting their nearest Federal Job Information Office and, if there is one, its testing office. These offices are to be found under the listing "U.S. Government" in metropolitan phone books.

Secure from the Federal Job Information Office Form 5000AB and the address of the nearest Office of Personnel Management. Also, ask where the nearest Federal Test Station is located.

Complete Form 5000AB and send it to the Office of Personnel Management that is located closest to a convenient test station. The Federal Job Information Office can and should help you sort all of this out. At times, several offices and test stations are combined at one location, so it can get a bit confusing. (The idea is to apply for a Border Patrol position in a manner that will allow you to take the required tests and interviews with a minimum of hassle; since few federal employment offices are located at or near Border Patrol duty locations, the agency tries to schedule the application process and all subsequent follow-up in as convenient a location as possible.)

Form 5000AB is a very simple, eleven question pre-application form. It functions as an application for the application.

At the time that the agency receives your 5000AB, it will send you a significantly more detailed employment application. This document is called a Standard Form 171. It includes space to put down information on virtually one's entire life history. At the same time, a notice is sent telling you when and where the employment written test will be given. This information will include a date and the name of the person to contact.

As a general rule, pre-applications for Form 171 and the written test are made during November and December of each year. Form 5000AB pre-aps are not usually accepted outside of this November/December annual period. The local Federal Job Information Office will have specific data regarding this requirement.

The written exam is usually given in the month of January. People who have taken it say it is very comprehensive, including questions regarding everything from job aptitude to IQ.

Previous job experience is also important, of course, with a good ability to read and write Spanish. Examiners also look for extensive past experience in law enforcement totaling at least one year, which can be as a paid officer in another governmental agency. Completion of a college education will qualify a man as long as he is deemed to have the other pertinent leadership, language, and physical qualities. Experience as an unpaid volunteer in a police auxiliary will count for the needed experience.

Travel to the testing office and to the interview site must be done at the applicant's expense. All applicants are expected to have a valid driver's license.

Applicants must be at least twenty-one years old but no older than thirty-five. In some cases where an applicant is transferring from another federal enforcement agency, the thirty-five-year cap is waived. This is a special situation that is best discussed in person with the Border Patrol recruiting officer.

Candidates who do poorly on the written exam can take it again after waiting a year.

As a practical matter, it takes about eight

weeks for the test results and job interview evaluation to be processed. A rating of 70 or above is required to be eligible. Assuming a successful outcome of the test and interview, actual training does not usually start for another six to eight months!

Candidates are selected from the top of the rating list on down till a sufficient number have been recruited or there are no more remaining applicants who qualify.

Then background and extensive referral checks are run on all acceptable applicants. Because this process and test grading take considerable time, applicants are advised right up front to stay "interested and available." Like most other enforcement agencies, the Border Patrol is looking for agents who are street smart. They want men who have been exposed to crime but who have not personally participated because of strong inner moral conviction.

All new recruits are hired on a one-year probationary basis. Entry-level salaries are at the GS-5 level, or about $14,390 per annum. The top salary paid by the Border Patrol is $21,804 per annum, with a level of GS-9. Advancements in salary usually come on a yearly basis.

The new recruits are batched together and sent to the Border Patrol Academy at the Federal Law Enforcement Training Center in

Glynco, Georgia. They receive an extremely intense seventeen-week training course. It isn't Army boot camp but, because of the extensive duties involving physical exertion under very rigorous environmental conditions, there is heavy emphasis on physical training.

The course includes sections on the history and legislatively mandated responsibilities of the service, immigration and other applicable national laws, marksmanship, interrogation, investigation, public relations, and written and spoken Spanish.

There is an especially heavy emphasis on weapons training. Excellent firearms proficiency must be demonstrated within six months of appointment. Failure to do so will result in summary dismissal, as will failure in any other part of the training program.

In times past, agents were allowed to use their personal weapons. Standard-issue M16s and Remington 1100s are now de rigueur for the service.

After Border Patrol Academy, novice trainees are placed in a probationary program. Additional exams related to their advance from probationary status are given at six-and-a-half months and at ten months.

Postings during this time are generally at larger offices where the new recruits can get a bit of on-the-job training. These posts are often in California, New Mexico, or Texas.

After the training and probation periods, agents may be assigned to small, isolated border communities in Arizona, California, New Mexico, and Texas.

Recruiters say that the prospect of service in these places turns many recruits off and that some drop out of the program when they find out what it's really like to live in these remote border towns.

After assignment to such a town, it is 99 percent sheer boredom as the agent spends hour after hour in his pickup patrolling sleepy, weary stretches of border, usually during the wee hours of the morning.

The one percent that is interesting occurs when the agent encounters a tough hombre bringing a load of drugs, illegal workers, or women across the border. Sometimes the shooting starts before the agent can get on his radio and call for help.

Other duties involve cooperative projects with the Drug Enforcement Agency (DEA), FBI, BATF, or similar undercover agency to expose and subsequently bring to justice those engaged in large-scale illegal organized activities.

The cases might sometimes make the papers, but generally it's drudge work, pitting one's ability to do detail work against the bad guys' desire and ability to do the same thing.

How You Can Do It

1. Attend college or get a junior college degree.
2. Learn to read and write Spanish.
3. Get a job in the police auxiliary on a voluntary basis.
4. Look in the telephone directory of a larger metropolitan city for the number of the nearest Federal Job Information Center.
5. Find out where the nearest testing center is located.
6. Fill out and submit the Form 5000AB.
7. Get Standard Form 171 and fill it out.
8. Submit this form in November or December and get a schedule to take the lengthy Border Patrol written exam and job interview.
9. Score high on the written and oral tests.
10. Accept employment.
11. Stay available and interested till a training class is formed.
12. Go to Border Patrol Academy at Glynco, Georgia. Work hard and complete the academy in a satisfactory fashion.
13. Start work on a probationary basis.
14. Make a career out of the Border Patrol.

Bounty Hunter

Experts in the business of bounty hunting claim that the occupation is open to anyone. Anyone who weighs 250 pounds and is as agile as an NFL offensive end, has an IQ of at least 140, and can maintain his or her composure and decorum like a seasoned diplomat.

Of all the action careers available to the average person, that of the bounty hunter is probably the most physically demanding and dangerous. Depending on the number and nature of the cases one handles, it will probably be the most immediately exciting.

Few occupations in the twentieth century have remained as unchanged as bounty hunting. The business is a direct throwback to the Wild West when wanted criminals were recaptured via a reward system and anyone bringing them in could claim the reward. As in the past, bounty hunters are individuals who pursue and arrest bail jumpers wherever they might try to hide.

Good estimates by experts in the industry indicate that there are only twelve to twenty people in the States who make a full-time living at this sort of business. Quite a few bondsmen round up their own "runners." Some have developed an awesome reputation for never losing a man to bail-jumping. Yet, although the opportunity is there, few people pursue this line of work on a full-time basis, indicating the field is either wide open or too tough to consider, depending on one's perspective.

Given the rising crime rate and the long time it takes to get one's day in court, the incidence of people who skip out is apparently rising dramatically. Bounty hunting in the United States is a growth industry with good financial potential.

Anyone arrested in the States for the commission of a crime is entitled to bail except in some cases of capital offense. All but the most heinous crimes allow for the defendant to be released on bail. In return for the bail bondsman posting the stipulated amount of bail, the person charged is released from jail. He is not "free." The prisoner is in the custody of the bondsman. To secure the bail to the bondsman, the prisoner pays the bondsman a fee, usually 10 percent of the posted bail amount. If the bond is set at $50,000, the prisoner must pony up 10 percent in cash, or about $5,000--an important concept to keep in mind later when negotiating fees and expenses to bring a man in. Bondsmen will often give up their profit (10 percent) on a deal to save the remainder of their money, giving the bounty hunter some idea how much money he might have to work with.

Often bail is secured with property or real estate pledged by the prisoner's family or friends. Depending on the prisoner's ability to pay, the process of getting him out of the slammer can take hours or even days. The purpose of the bail is both to guarantee the prisoner's court appearance and to allow him a shot at a normal life while awaiting trial.

Should the defendant skip, electing not to show up for his court appearance, the judge will issue a bench warrant for his arrest. Some states give the bondsman up to six months to get his man or woman back once the warrant is issued. If during that period the police do not pick up the defendant, the bondsman will usually get worried. At the end of this time, the court will expect the bondsman to hand over either the defendant or some fairly substantial amount of money.

Other worriers include the friends and family who have pledged their homes and other real property for the runner. Often they have as much or more to lose than the bondsman and will cooperate with the bounty hunter and his attempts to find the missing defendant.

Every state has code sections dealing with the right of the bondsman or his agent to pursue and arrest the fleeing principal.

Most court decisions related to this subject date from the 1800s. The issue has been so well litigated that it is no longer brought before the courts in this day and age. Any bondsman can appoint any agent (bounty hunter) he deems to be competent to go out and find the defendant and haul his ass back to the court of jurisdiction. All that is needed is a certified copy of the bail agreement and an understanding with the bondsman regarding fees.

Fees, in many cases, can be fairly substantial. Not only must you, the bounty hunter, find the defendant, you must also bring him back to the jurisdiction from which he has fled. All this can cost a lot of money.

The Supreme Court ruling which upheld state law in the matter of bounty hunting makes interesting reading:

[The Bondsman] Wherever they choose to do so, may seize him [the fugitive] and deliver him up in their discharge; and if this cannot be done at once, they may imprison him until it can be done. They may pursue him to another state, may arrest him on the Sabbath and, if necessary, may break and enter his house for that purpose. The seizure is not made by virtue of new process. None is needed. It is legally similar to the rearrest by the sheriff of an escap-

ing convict.

The cutting edge of the bounty hunting business is skip tracing. Theoretically the bondsman could, if he knew exactly where his ward had run to, call the local sheriff and have the guy picked up; but it is seldom that easy.

It usually takes a smart, hard-working person to locate a skip -- but not a genius. Having the sheriff pick the guy up once he is located is often cumbersome because of state extradition laws. Usually it is cleaner, easier, and also cheaper to hire a bounty hunter to do the job.

The truth that good skip tracers keep in mind while going about their business is that somebody always knows where their skip is located: the skip's parent, sibling, or other relative; ex-girlfriend; his bartender; ex-employer; doctor; bank; or attorney. Somebody always knows. The challenge for the skip tracer is to find out who this someone is and provide the proper motivation for that person to tell what he knows.

People who are about to lose their property as bond guarantors will often have some ideas whom to call. The bondsman will usually have a list of relatives, friends, and acquaintances for you to work on. It isn't cold turkey--but it can be awfully damn tough.

Bondsmen hire bounty hunters to do two things they cannot or do not want to do: go out and find the skip and forcibly bring him back to stand trial.

By using the phone, a professional bounty hunter can get a pretty good idea where his guy is. This is the cheap part.

After that, it gets expensive. The bounty hunter must go to the city and place where he believes the fugitive is hiding, make absolutely positive identification, and pick the guy up.

No professional bounty hunter makes the pickup alone, because this is the part of the job where arms get broken, shots are fired, teeth are knocked out, and things generally get pretty hairy.

Almost all bounty hunters go out armed. They maintain, however, that their most important tool is a pair of handcuffs with which to restrain the fugitive. They insist that their duty is to bring the person back in reasonably good condition for a court appearance, not to shoot the skip or beat him.

Getting started in this business is like other action careers. One must be in the right place at the right time. Old-timers recommend that the novice befriend a successful full-time bounty hunter and go out with the guy eight or ten times, perhaps on a pro-bono basis. Remember that the idea at this point is to establish credentials and to see whether the occupation suits one's interests.

After that, the newcomer might visit all of the bondsmen in the area, offering to bring back a few lesser criminals on an expenses-only basis in order to prove interest in the job and not in knuckling heads.

Those who do well will get more and more contracts until they can build up their own full-time business. Professional incomes of around $50,000 per year are about the standard.

Like private pilots and coon hunters, bounty hunters enjoy telling stories about some of the people they have picked up. My favorite involves a runner who otherwise worked as a lumberjack. He was, they claim, 6'8" in all directions, solid muscle, and mean as a bag of snakes.

The lumberjack was a skip out of Seattle where he was wanted on charges of battering his wife. The fee to bring the guy in was a relatively measly $3,000. This included finding him someplace in North California, taking him into custody, and bringing him back to Seattle.

By calling the power company, the bounty hunters were able to get a fix on the guy. They verified his supposed address by calling the only local logging company. Most skips are not smart enough to realize someone will probably come after them.

Finally the time came to make the pickup. With much fear and trepidation, the two bounty hunters drove to rural McCloud, California -- sure that they faced the battle of their lives.

Later on both privately admitted to me that they fully expected to get stuffed in a bowling bag.

Sometime after dark, they located the small rural house where Mr. Tough Guy lived. Mercifully he wasn't home. They parked their van across the gravel street and waited. At 1:15 a.m., the runner and two friends showed up, drunk as skunks. The wait continued.

When the two friends left at 3:30, the bounty hunters figured their time had come. In many cases in this business, positive identification is a vital problem. Because of the guy's huge size, there was no question in either of the bounty hunters' minds that they had the right guy.

With knees knocking and hearts pounding, they stepped up on the old wooden porch and rapped on the door.

After a bit, the hulk came swaggering out on the porch. They hadn't discussed in specific detail what they were going to do with him once they found him. Both carried stun guns (police department paraphernalia that throw shot-filled beanbags at a fairly high velocity). Apparently their nerve failed at this point and both pulled up and almost simultaneously discharged their stun guns into the hulk.

The lumberjack had been drinking and took the broadside in a very relaxed and unsuspecting mode. The impact threw him back through the screen door into the kitchen, creating a shambles of the entranceway. The bounty hunters quickly swarmed over the guy, who had actually sustained the equivalent of two very heavy punches to the chest, and cuffed him up securely. By using three sets of standard wrist cuffs, they also manacled his legs.

Now the real work began. The guy started feeling better and reacted by fighting the restraints. His captors found that carrying a thrashing, twisting bundle of irate muscle to their van was no easy task. To make matters worse, the fellow was bleeding heavily from cuts on his arms and shoulders that he had received crunching through his own screen and wooden front door.

There were apparently some serious questions being raised regarding the breaking strength of the handcuffs.

By the time the skip got to Seattle, he was really a mess. The jailers at the county joint refused to believe the two bounty hunters had not subdued the guy in a free-for-all.

I met the pair in a bar as they were seriously discussing other alternate action careers in which they could profitably engage.

How You Can Do It

1. Read as much on the subject as possible and talk to as many people about it as possible.
2. Go to visit all of the bail bondsmen in your

region. Find out how they handle runners and see if you can get a job as backup or a helper in order to bring in a runner.

3. Buy a couple sets of handcuffs and a can of industrial-strength mace.
4. Work on needed skills as a skip tracer. Develop a system. Learn to use the phone.
5. Identify any bounty hunters working in the region. Hire on as an apprentice if possible. Do so on a pro-bono basis, if necessary.
6. If the job turns you on, expand and take on increasingly tough contracts of your own.
7. Print cards, buy a telephone answering machine, and go into the business.
8. Carefully evaluate your fees so as to get as much as possible out of each runner.
9. Don't plan to shoot the runners that you are after.
10. Develop a working knowledge of, and business relationship with, the sheriffs with whom you will be working.
11. Start working out a system with a buddy who will work with you as a backup.
12. Take care to bring in your first few runners in a timely, seemingly effortless manner so as to impress the bail bondsmen who have given you the assignments.
13. Be cautious of long-distance moves involving expensive plane tickets.
14. Be wary of any international bounty hunting assignments. Check with the authorities.

Explosives Handler

A person who has the background, training, and inclination can carve out a fairly good living in many places in this country handling explosives.

The need for this type of service is growing and will probably remain fairly strong for several years to come for reasons not always completely obvious to people outside the business.

Statistically, bombings are decreasing within our society. An explosives handler will probably not be called on to handle bomb threats or to defuse and/or remove bombs planted by terrorists to any great extent! He may, after a bomb is found, advise that the situation is serious and that the law-enforcement people with whom he is dealing had better call in experts either from the FBI or from a nearby military base. There isn't much billable work in this aspect of the business.

Most explosives work for the freelancer

occurs in smaller communities around the United States where the local police do not have anyone on board who knows anything about explosives and ordnance. Problems for these communities arise when war souvenirs, such as rifle grenades and M-79 rounds, turn up in somebody's garage or attic. The questions needing an immediate answer are how dangerous such souvenirs are and how can the stuff be moved.

Law-enforcement people tell me that the incidence of stray, unexploded serviceable 105 rounds, hand grenades, and mortar rounds is greater around military bases. But as a general rule, military people are more than anxious to be good neighbors and to police up their leavings and mistakes. Depending on the circumstances, they will dispatch a crew of ordnance experts on a moment's notice.

A freelance explosives expert has the best opportunity for employment if he can contact a number of smaller communities away from military bases to make it known that his services are available should the need arise. Should the police department get a call regarding explosives that it feels is too mundane to bother the military with, the freelance explosives expert can go and be the one who removes the old dynamite or artillery round and destroys it.

For a negotiated fee, you, as a resident

explosives expert, can examine the potential risk and advise the police as to the best course of action (i.e., you may inform them, for example, that it is a live HE artillery round and it is very dangerous). You may recommend that it not be moved farther than the front yard where a sandbag revetment can be built and the souvenir exploded rather harmlessly. You may advise calling the army in immediately if, for instance, there are six or eight live rounds to contend with.

In some cases, the expert may advise that the FBI or perhaps another government bomb squad be called in. This advice is probably given on the basis of intent. When you or the police suspect malice of intent, it becomes more than a routine disposal chore.

Many explosives-handling incidents I have looked at are nothing more than PR gestures. Recently, we detonated a Civil War Parrott projectile, a black-powder round, by shooting it with a stick of dynamite. The TV crews we called to document the event thought the dynamite was the projectile. We didn't tell them differently.

Assignments are most frequently handled on a one-time, negotiated basis. The local police will call an explosives handler they trust when they get an inquiry. There might be a billable fee for showing up as an adviser with a greater negotiated fee should you, the expert, decide to remove and dispose of the ordnance yourself.

People who contemplate this type of adventure career obviously should have a broad military and commercial background in dealing with explosives. Because so much of what is done involves commercial explosives, the expert had best understand this part of the business very thoroughly. It is very common to be called out on a few sticks of dynamite found in a basement or garage.

11 The credible expert who intends to make a living at this business should have a strong academic and street background in explosives chemistry. A good working knowledge of electronic timers and mechanical detonating devices is also indispensable. One must also know how to safely deactivate explosive devices and to determine when and if dangerous chemicals can be moved.

A big obstacle for the explosives freelancer is to find a storage and disposal area -- a place where dynamite and detonators can be safely and legally stored and where that Claymore or block of C-4 you pick up can be safely detonated.

In the eastern United States, a suitable location in an old gravel pit or open field may be very tough to find.

A close friend of mine, who is in the business, got a call from a local refuse-removal company. It came through the municipal police who first got it, I guess, through the state police. It seems that some cartridges that looked suspiciously like dynamite turned up at the landfill.

My friend ran out to the landfill for a look. Based on his regular fee schedule, he billed fifty dollars for that much work.

The cartridges appeared to be dynamite, so he negotiated another contract to dispose of them. For another $150, or a total of $200, he agreed to get rid of the explosives. The fees were payable by the refuse company -- a much more straightforward deal than trying to bill a local municipality. (In many places in the States, municipal or county work must be bid. It is wise to check out how billing systems work so you know what's the fastest way to get paid for your services.)

My friend first evacuated everyone from the landfill site and then carefully raked the sticks together, dumping kerosene on them. There is relatively little danger in burning the explosives this way, but the guy didn't want anyone to know that so he issued the evacuation order.

The sticky part of this line of work is getting liability insurance. Most municipalities don't check on the credentials of explosives handlers but do insist on being indemnified by the man they call. In that regard, one becomes more than just an explosives expert. People in the explosives removal-and-disposal business become the ones the small municipalities can blame if something goes wrong.

At the time of this writing, property-damage liability insurance is extremely tough for anyone to get, much less an explosives person. The only way to determine whether one is insurable and at what price is to ask for quotes from larger indemnitors.

Another time, my friend was called in to look at a 105 projectile that was found in a garage by a new home owner.

Having called the previous owner, my friend found out that the unexploded round had been picked up in a desert artillery range as a souvenir. The expert determined that it was live and lethal. He recommended carefully moving the projectile no farther than the front yard, where he built a four-sided sandbag enclosure. Using commercial dynamite, he shot the projectile in place with only very minor damage to the surrounding homes.

For that caper he billed $1,500. It is an excellent example of an incident that perhaps should have been handled by the Army. The previous owner kept insisting it was no sweat. ("I brought the damn thing home in my pickup truck," he said, "let's just take it away the same way!") In the meantime, the neighbors, police, and new home owners were getting extremely edgy.

Another acquaintance of mine, named Don, did explosives work on assignment for contractors in a four-state area. He basically stayed away from municipal ordnance disposal that required costly, hard-to-obtain insurance. He mostly sold dynamite -- under federal and state permit -- to people who wanted it for their own use. Other jobs involved hiring out for $200 per day plus expenses to set the charges and do the actual blasting.

His best day was when a local businessman who had purchased an old mining claim for a summer-house site found two-thirds of a case of badly deteriorated dynamite in a little shack on the property.

I went along with Don to look at the stuff. The cartridges were worn white with age and looked tattered. All of the prills in the powder had melted and slicked into the carrier material. In many cases, the cartridges were open and exposed. Many were torn. Our hearts started to race when we examined the pile, signaling the fact that it was nitro-based material with which we were dealing.

Don simply backed out of the little board outbuilding and told the owner it was "a hell of a mess." He said that, for two thousand bucks, payable in advance, he would clean it up. The owner must have wanted badly to put his summer house in because, to my extreme shock, he agreed. Don evacuated the property, and had the owner take anything of value with him.

It wasn't really that bad, but it made it look like good old Don was really earning his money.

Don went back to his truck, got four quarts of 10 weight oil, opened the cans, and poured the contents all over the dynamite.

After talking to me for an hour, he went in and very carefully slid the cartridges onto a snow shovel and carried them outside to a generally open area. We piled the oily mess up and doused it with kerosene. After lighting the kerosene, it took about two minutes for the stuff to burn to ashes.

Next, he went in and pried out the shelf boards that the dynamite had rested on for those many years and burned them as well.

It was as nice a two-grand pop as I've ever seen anyone make in my years around people in action careers.

Federal and state environment protection rules stipulate that, in the process of destroying an explosive, no residue can remain. Picric acid and some nitric acid compounds are so dangerous that they are best transported only a few blocks by foot and then blown in place.

Not possible, the EPA (Environmental Protection Agency) types often say, creating a situation far more dangerous than if they simply let the stuff be detonated in an empty ball field or old stone quarry.

A call to the local EPA for the latest information regarding explosives, including laws on the topic, would be vital before actually hanging out one's shingle. Federal laws regulate the purchase and storage of explosives often needed to detonate excess and abandoned explosives. State laws generally mirror federal laws but at times are much more stringent. Municipal laws generally prohibit ownership of explosives, but this doesn't help the poor, unsuspecting guy who finds an old 88 round in his attic. There are no federal or state laws licensing explosives handlers that I have encountered.

People who are in the business of handling explosives and disposing of ordnance live roller-coaster lives. They must be on call virtually twenty-four hours per day. Sometimes weeks go by and there are no calls; then a couple will come in, allowing the technician to get back to his $2,200 to $2,500 per month billing range that is typical for the business.

To make a living at this profession requires that one have contacts at state police headquarters and in all of the municipal police departments in at least a three- or four-state region.

Getting into the business can be more expensive than one would at first suppose. The handler will need a good reference library on military ordnance, including as much information as possible on foreign ordnance. As previously mentioned, a disposal site is an absolute must. Sometimes a local farmer will cooperate by leasing an old quarry.

A good, solid background in chemistry is necessary if one contemplates disposing of dangerous explosive chemicals and/or very many homemade bombs.

How You Can Do It

1. Take an interest in explosives and common ordnance.
2. Get as much military training as possible in explosives.
3. Have an extensive library of pertinent information.
4. Print up business cards.
5. Install a telephone-answering machine.
6. Visit the municipal police chiefs in the region in which you intend to operate. Leave cards and, if possible, a mimeographed list of services and charges.
7. Be sure to check with state and federal EPA authorities to find out what their requirements are.
8. Do perform as much commercial explosives work as possible.
9. Contract for a disposal site.
10. Do necessary state and federal paperwork to allow you to own and use commercial

explosives.

11. In the case of municipal work, secure liability insurance.
12. Keep checking in with the local police groups to be sure they know you are around.
13. Handle the first few cases with as much PR as possible. Call the TV station and newspapers if the authorities will allow you to do so.
14. Research the local laws regarding the dollar amounts one can charge before running afoul of the bidding laws.
15. Keep updating your file on foreign military ordnance.
16. Work with military ordnance people as much as possible.

FBI Agent

For an outfit that holds itself out to be 99 percent investigative, the FBI gets into a hell of a lot of shoot-outs.

A recent story on the AP wire tells about a fifteen-minute firefight between a reinforced detail of FBI and a gang of armed robbers. It's something right out of "Miami Vice," occurring, ironically, in a suburb of Miami, Florida.

It seems that a carload of agents spotted a van that matched the description of one reported at the scene of a recent armored car holdup. The agents, prudent souls that they were, called for help which included firepower from an FBI SWAT team. The heavily armed outfit attempted to pull the van over, wrecking five cars in the process.

A furious gun battle broke out at a major intersection. Shotguns, submachine guns, assault rifles, and pistols were emptied up and down the street. Unsuspecting motorists drove through the battle zone, picking up hits on their vehicles.

Two FBI agents were killed and five were wounded. Two of the robbery suspects were also killed.

At this writing, one of the FBI agents lies in South Miami Hospital, hovering between life and death.

Not a bad engagement for an outfit that, until the mid-fifties, hired only law school and accounting grads to do its "investigations."

The FBI, like other organizations, mirrors the times with its hiring policy. When J. Edgar Hoover took the directorship in the mid-thirties, the biggest problem facing the nation was organized crime. Because of the complexity of federal law and the complex nature of certain financial-type crimes, only lawyers and accountants were hired.

Then, during the forties, duties dealt with counter-espionage. Traditional agents handled this well, so there was little change in policy regarding employment and procedure.

During the fifties, the emphasis was shifted to organized and white-collar crime. The FBI started to think about using computers to keep track of files and to evaluate evidence.

The era of the sixties brought a need to monitor anti-American groups and to bring in draft dodger/deserter types. Open acts of espionage gave FBI agents additional work. This was the era, no doubt, when the Bureau kept busy watching Jane Fonda types.

Agents from the FBI monitor activities of Soviet intelligence officers throughout the United States, as well as spies from Eastern bloc countries, Cuba, and such violence-prone countries as Libya and North Korea.

During the eighties, computer programmers; electronics radio specialists; electrical, mechanical, or chemical engineers; explosives experts; photographers; systems analysts; metallurgists; spectroscopy operators; and those who can speak Spanish, Vietnamese, Chinese, and Russian are sought. Lawyers and CPAs are still in demand.

In general, applicants choose one of five entrance-level programs if they wish to become a special agent. Typists, clerks, and technicians (of which the FBI has many) are known as non-agents.

Law graduates can go into the law program. College graduates with a degree in accounting go into the accounting program, while those who have a degree in language may elect the language program. A modified program allows the college graduate with three years of experience in police work to qualify.

The science program is for those college graduates who have an M.S., B.S., or Ph.D. in physics, toxicology, mathematics, engineering, business or public administration, computer science, computer systems, chemistry, or biological sciences.

Within those general requirements, a prospective agent must, in the case of biological sciences, have completed a minimum of sixteen semester hours in chemistry (including organic) and eight semester hours in physics.

Applicants who have expertise as firearms examiners, explorers and ordnance experts, document examiners, and fingerprint specialists may also qualify under the science program.

Like all federal policing agencies, employment requirements change with the times. About the only long-term trend is one toward men with special computer abilities. Other obscure talents (some sort of unique training) are also in demand from time to time.

Starting pay is about $30,000 per year. This includes a $6,000 annual bonus for normal overtime and working odd hours. This scale is certainly competitive with what an attorney just out of law school or CPA would make in private industry. On the down side, some attorneys and CPAs find the odd hours and uncertain weekends to be completely unacceptable. Assignments often involve long hours and are extremely tedious by just about anyone's standard.

Duties for FBI agents in the eighties still mostly concern evidence-gathering pertaining to the ever-growing list of federal crimes.

Duties include dealing with bombers, bank robbers, and subversives; doing laboratory analysis in support of state and local police; and being an expert witness as needed by these local entities.

Financially pressed municipalities appreciate these services because they are provided on a no-cost basis.

Monitoring the activities of KGB operatives constitutes a growing part of the FBI's current mission. The Bureau also monitors Chinese and Bulgarian diplomats who, like the Soviets, are under severe travel restrictions; it is the duty of the agency to determine whether such restrictions are followed.

Electrical engineers may be called on to design new television and/or radio systems for use by field personnel. The FBI does seem to have a place for the innovative and creative wire-head.

To work in the crime lab in Washington, D.C., requires that one be knowledgeable in chemistry, biology, and microbiology, including hair and fiber exchange, paint analysis, soils and metals analysis, firearms and ballistics, document examination, cryptoanalysis, graphic arts, mathematics, translation and interpretation, study and evaluation of body fluids, and the identification of both type and use of illegal narcotics.

Law-enforcement agencies trying to identify

suspect fingerprints will use the FBI's fingerprint files, since the agency is the single repository for fingerprints in the United States.

Because of the extensive record keeping conducted by the FBI, thousands of file clerks, typists, and stenographers are employed by the agency. Most of these positions are available in Washington, D.C., although some clerical personnel work in the fifty field offices. These positions are not considered to be field-agent positions, pay fairly well, and are definitely career jobs.

In addition to the large number of science-related fields for which it is responsible, the FBI has an extensive training mission to fulfill. It puts thousands of law-enforcement officers from the local level -- mostly administrators -- through a twelve-week course in investigative procedures at its national academy in Quantico, Virginia. Outstanding teachers who don't want conventional careers should consider applying at the FBI.

Technical specialists and clerical workers are considered to be on a non-agent career path. Policy regarding these people and their training is shifting. Apparently, it is best (but not essential) that technical specialists do some field agent training before settling down to their analytical calling.

Any potential employees having the abovementioned skills or training are urged to at least apply. The FBI is said to be a large, diverse organization in which one can find competitive pay and benefits as well as many opportunities for advancement.

Applications can be secured from the field offices located in most cities of medium to large size.

After filling out the application, most potential recruits who have any chance with the Bureau are given an extensive interview. Because the FBI is by its own admission a very autocratic organization requiring many different arbitrary duty assignments, people from some related military and police backgrounds are given preferential consideration. Applicants from the needed scientific disciplines who have three years of work experience also get better consideration.

Like the CIA or the Secret Service, the FBI does an extensive security check on applicants. They also like to talk to a person who has been around and who has become street smart, without being sullied by the experience. The background investigation takes from one to six months and includes contacting former and current employers, references, social acquaintances, and neighbors.

School credits, as well as arrest, medical, and military records, are reviewed. A polygraph examination may also be required. Audiometric tests (used to detect hearing deficiencies) are administered to all candidates. A security check may go back as far as ten to twelve years, depending on the circumstances.

FBI physical requirements are strict. Agent candidates must be in excellent physical condition, with no impairments that would interfere in firearms use, raids, or defensive use of martial arts. Uncorrected vision must be no less than 20/200, corrected to 20/20. Color blindness is unacceptable.

Mandatory retirement is set at age fifty-five, and an average career spans twenty or more years. As a result, only those in the age bracket of twenty-three to thirty-five years are normally considered.

Training at the Quantico Marine base is notorious for its intensity, being both highly physical and extremely academic. Perhaps because of the intense prescreening, the dropout rate is a modest three percent. (The physical portion includes running, calisthenics, push-ups, and the world-famous FBI firearms course.)

New agents learn to fire pistols, submachine guns, and shotguns on a range that teaches instantaneous target recognition and prioritization, tied to consideration for the well-being of innocent bystanders.

Martial arts are taught for the purposes of self-defense and evasion. The stress is on how to keep from getting hurt and how to handle people, not on getting a black belt.

In order to teach a recruit safe arrest procedure and effective investigative techniques and conduct, practical problems are rehearsed in a play-acting context; specific crimes are dramatized for the agent's instruction.

Agents are taught to interrogate a witness, as well as how to observe, find, and evaluate evidence.

A great deal of time is spent learning how to write reports, testify in court, and conduct effective surveillance. The role of expert witness is considered to be central to the FBI's reason for existence.

There are about 240 federal crimes that the 9,500 FBI agents are in charge of monitoring. It takes several weeks of intensive schooling just to see to it that the recruit is aware of all of these specific crimes and their numerous peculiarities.

At the end of the sixteen-week session, the new agent is generally posted to a smaller regional office for a period of two to four years. Apparently, some attempt is made to post the agent in the area from which he first joined the bureau. Pay is given for the sixteen-week training session.

During the time the new agent is posted to a "local" office, he is still considered to be in training and is expected to work as a partner with another agent.

After successfully completing the twenty-four- to thirty-six-month mentoring period, the agent is posted to a Big 12 office in a place such as Miami, Chicago, or New York.

Even many agents who join the Bureau knowing they are destined to a life performing lab analyses are sometimes expected to work five years as a field agent. The experience supposedly makes the lab people better scientific and analytical investigators, as well as more credible expert witnesses.

The budget for the FBI is published, and amounted to one billion dollars in 1985.

The FBI is often instrumental in putting together various types of crime-solving task force groups. As previously mentioned, priorities change. Currently, there are groups operating in cooperation with the DEA to deal with members of organized crime groups trafficking in drugs; postal inspectors are tracking down bombers; the BATF is looking for illegal guns; the Border Patrol is tracking down illegal immigrants; the Secret Service is tracking down counterfeiters; and the CIA is keeping track of various nefarious Soviet activities.

As the FBI recruiting brochure says, the work is seldom routine. It is often exciting, dangerous, and full of pressures.

More than one would ever suppose, FBI agents are stationed all over the United States.

Unsuspecting citizens are often surprised to find so many living among them. Almost anyone would expect that a crime-ridden place like New York City would require the services of 1,400 agents, but three in Pocatello, Idaho, for God's sake?

One of the Bureau's recent assignments has been to neutralize the efforts of members of the Aryan Nations. These guys originated in northern Idaho and rural eastern Washington.

FBI recruiters visit virtually every college campus during the course of a year. Campus placement offices usually have application forms even if their office is not on the regular visitation schedule. A call to a local FBI office (which can be found in the yellow pages) or to the local police will turn up an application form. As previously mentioned, virtually anyone who is smart, clean, and highly motivated could be considered as a potential FBI agent.

How You Can Do It

1. Check with the placement office at your local college or university for a list of skills and disciplines currently in demand by the FBI.
2. Major in the appropriate courses in college.
3. Work hard and graduate in the top half of your class.
4. ROTC and/or regular army service can be a help when applying. Consider enlisting or serving on the local police auxiliary while in

school.

5. Work for three years in one of the currently desired fields.

6. Secure an application from a regional FBI office and apply.

7. Undergo the extensive FBI background check.

8. Go through the agent training period until you are posted to a central office to do the analytical scientific work for which you were trained.

Fire Fighter

As a young child, I vividly remember sitting with friends in the shade of a big old sycamore tree in the front yard discussing what we planned to be when we grew up.

Artie Crumm said he wanted to be an insurance underwriter like his dad. None of us had the dreamiest idea what an insurance underwriter did, but Art is now a plumber. Even ignorant farm kids know what plumbers do.

David Hancock said he intended to be a doctor. Today he clerks in a computer store.

Lisa Bierd said she would be happy to be a housewife. In real life, Lisa is a classy waitress in an exclusive restaurant. She probably has had more chances for more real action than either Artie or David.

Franky was going to be a farmer; Sean said he intended to become an accountant. Mike Sharp opted for the life of a heating man. Today he is still bending metal for a living.

It was great fun going around the circle finding out what everyone's career plans were.

To this day, I still find it fascinating that so many of us had such clearly defined goals so early in life. Perhaps it was due to our rural upbringing. Under those circumstances it was almost immoral to admit that we did not know what we were going to plant in the field of life.

Certainly there were many slips between the cup and the mouth. Typically life's circumstances did not allow many of us to harvest or even to plant the crop we intended.

Of the entire group, the one fellow I admired most was little Ralph Metzger. Ralph steadfastly maintained that he was going to be a fireman.

Like all the other careers, we didn't really know what firemen did except the obvious. We knew they tore around in big flashy trucks and made lots of noise coming and going. Being practical farm kids, we reasoned firemen had to polish their red trucks a lot.

But the important point was that, without being more definitive than is reasonable at the age of ten, Ralph was admitting that he didn't have everything worked out and that he didn't want to live a dull, ordinary life. He was opting for a life of action.

Although the days of just grabbing a hose have passed forever, the occupation of fireman can and does put some action in the lives of some otherwise pretty dull people. Volunteers who are normally clerks, cooks, paper shufflers, and bean counters can, when the whistle blows, legitimately drop everything, run off, and risk their lives in a wild, uncontrolled atmosphere. The adrenaline rush from the experience seems to appeal to these sorts of people.

The career is open to just about anyone in reasonable physical shape. Those who start young can add as much money, glamour, and action as they feel they can handle.

Today my little friend Ralph Metzger is the respected and honored chief of a smallish suburban fire department. He makes about $40,000 per year and lives with his family in a nice suburban house. On the average of 120 times a year when the call comes in, he goes screaming off to save the lives and property of terrified and ultimately very thankful citizens.

I asked him one time why he didn't go the whole route and become a smoke jumper. Ralph said he was happy living in one place with his wife and kids and that anything more would have been more excitement than he cared to sign up for.

Action careerists who think they want to give the fireman idea a whirl need do little more than stop down at the local fire station and ask to talk to the chief. Most cities have a volunteer auxiliary to augment the staff of full-time professionals. It is still quite common in rural areas for the entire fire department to be comprised of volunteers other than the chief.

In general, volunteers need know very little about fighting fires. They are simply agreeing to come down to the station house two or three days a week to be part of the standby crew, or to call in to the dispatcher if the fire whistle blows. In this latter case, their commitment is to jump in their own vehicle and run out to the fire to help.

Some volunteers in some departments are paid a nominal amount for the time they actually spend fighting fires which usually amounts to little more than five or six dollars an hour. The majority of volunteers still have their equipment furnished to them as well as being eligible for workers' compensation insurance in case of injury on the job. Full-time paid professionals are usually provided with insurance plans or have the option of buying their own coverage at nominal rates.

Most departments ask volunteers to pass a simple agility test. The intensity of the test is a function of that department's current need for new volunteers. As a rule, volunteers must be nineteen to thirty-four years of age.

The agility test will generally involve a quarter-mile run, the demonstrated ability to carry or drag a sixty- to eighty-pound hose section, and the ability to walk across a four-inch beam twenty feet in length.

Smoke jumpers and regular department professionals must pass a more rigorous physical test. Usually this comes later after the volunteer has decided that the flashing lights, smoke, heat, and collapsing walls really get his adrenaline going.

Many departments try to rate and qualify volunteers on the basis of sincerity. The meaning here seems to be an honest desire to assist the community by putting out its fires, rather than equipping one's pickup truck with flashing lights and being a hero at the fireman's ball.

Chiefs do not seem to like volunteers who join up for the glamour, who simply display their volunteer decals but seldom show up for training or for duty assignments, especially on tough, dangerous fires.

A volunteer will be expected to supply his own work clothes but will be issued special boots, jackets, fire-retardant suspender work pants, hard hats, gloves, and, as appropriate, portable breathing apparatus. Depending on state law, some departments expect volunteers to buy vehicle lights.

It is quite common for volunteers who make the job into an all-consuming hobby to turn their pickup trucks into private fire wagons.

Having volunteered, the rookie fireman is expected to take an active interest in his work and to begin what can become a fairly lengthy home-study qualification process.

Old-timers caution that the novice volunteer had best be sure that all of the reading and study material, as well as short courses he takes, lead to permanent, nationally certified and nationally recognized fire ratings.

The plan for those who like this kind of life is to do the study program with an eye to either moving up in the department or going to another department as a full-time paid professional. Clerks and merchants in small cities who are pulling volunteer service as a kind of civic duty won't get heavily engrossed with this part of the program, but for the full-timer or action-career type, it is a must.

Probably the first test or learning session will be learning how to drive the big trucks. Farm boys who have driven grain trucks have an edge here, but, depending on the type of equipment a specific department has, the test can be very tough. (Overconfident truckers with previous experience have been known to have to take the driving test two or three times.)

Driving instruction and the test are generally given by either the chief or the department dispatcher. Instruction takes about eight to ten hours. The test, which usually lasts two hours, consists of successfully driving the various fire trucks through a series of pylons.

In some cases, with large hook and ladder

rigs, the equipment is so unusual that it takes lots of practice before one is ready to try the driving test.

The second in-house training session will almost invariably be on the care and use of the self-contained breathing apparatus. Most chiefs around the country now say that their men will not go into or on a burning building without a breathing apparatus.

Several state colleges in the United States offer courses leading to a degree in fire science. Of these, the University of Maryland is considered to be the flagship. Quite a lot of the course work, which includes required hours in chemistry, physics, English, and business management, is standard academic fare applicable to many different degrees.

High-paid professional chiefs in medium- and large-sized cities will invariably have at least one degree.

For starters, however, the gung-ho volunteer will learn to run the trucks, use self-contained breathing apparatus, and then begin to take short courses that lead to National Fire Protection Association skill ratings.

Some states don't offer these ratings through correspondence schools or self-study. In their place, they have a series of short courses and seminars that the volunteer will be expected to attend. These seminars will be given at central locations around the state and are usually organized by the state fire marshal's office. It is common for a city or fire department to pay travel, lodging, and meal expenses for those attending the sessions.

Firefighters who like to travel and teach may eventually work themselves into jobs conducting these types of training sessions.

In addition to these seminars and self-help, correspondence-type study programs, many states offer special fire-training classes through their vo-tec educational system.

These ratings, or certifications, run I (the lowest) through III. A Class III firefighter implies a working knowledge of hydraulics, including the ability to calculate water pressure, volume, and delivery. This person will best know how to battle various types of chemical and electrical fires and have a good knowledge of the danger from fumes from various types of combustibles.

Progress through the various ratings can be rapid, depending on one's desire and ability to handle these types of academic endeavors.

Some especially sincere volunteers are then selected to go to Emmetsburg, Maryland, to a two-week, federally run National Fire Academy, where, upon completion, they receive a nationally recognized certificate.

Volunteers find that small-town experience is easier to acquire and is considered valuable. Small-town fire fighters do not get to go to as many fires, but the fires they go to tend to be more diverse and include types that some big-city firemen seldom see. They include ag chemical fires, ground fires, petroleum fires, and, of course, the occasional furniture store, body shop, and truck and car fires.

Full-time and experienced professional fire fighters in medium to large cities make about $17,000 to $20,000 per year. A fire chief in San Francisco or Chicago will make $75,000 to $100,000 per year. Obviously, an action careerist must really enjoy this kind of business to be able to claw his way up through the ranks from volunteer to professional to chief.

As a general rule, chiefs not only have a fire science degree, they will also have a degree in business administration.

In recent years, as the large and medium cities around the United States have been squeezed financially, they have opted to hire more professionally oriented fire people rather than political hacks.

Still, there is quite a bit of politics involved in getting a chief's job in most U.S. cities. For those who do not want to go the political route, there is always private industry. A well-qualified chief who sets up a special fire-fighting unit in a factory, large shop, mill, or hospital will make about $50,000 per year. There are more of these types of jobs around than the novice could ever have supposed.

The action careerist who wants to go for the brass ring in fire fighting should consider smoke jumping.

Smoke jumpers are the guys who bail out of planes onto forest fires in remote mountainous regions. Their job is to contain the fire or to call in more ground personnel and equipment to help with the blaze.

A smoke jumper will often stay with the contained fire for a few days to a week to make sure it doesn't flare up again.

They are expected to sleep on the ground at the burn site, eat field rations, and walk out when the danger is past. It's a tough game that few people in this day and age know very much about.

As a practical matter, this dangerous and exciting action career is only open in the West for men who are willing to live nomadic lives while working for the U.S. Forest Service.

The slots are generally filled by teachers and students who otherwise have their summers free. Previous jump training is marginally helpful; experience as a city volunteer is helpful but not necessarily a certain route to a job as a smoke jumper.

Military training for either a smoke jumper or a volunteer for a city fire fighter position is not particularly important unless one has received specific training regarding certain materials or in relation to certain fires that the chief judges to be a current threat.

Smoke jumpers are almost all trained by the Forest Service. Many Forest Service jumpers say they made their first jump in the military, but this seems to be more coincidence than anything else.

Schools for smoke jumpers are held in Redding, California; McCall, Idaho; Redmond, Oregon; Missoula, Montana; and Fairbanks, Alaska. The Fairbanks school is the only one not run by the Forest Service. It is a Bureau of Land Management school.

Application for these schools is made by contacting the nearest Forest Service or Bureau of Land Management regional office. People living east of the Mississippi should write to the U.S. Forest Service in Washington, D.C., or contact their nearest land-grant state college for the name of the nearest Forest Service representative.

Applicants must be between the ages of nineteen and thirty-four and must pass an aerobic fitness test. This test includes running one-and-a-half miles in eleven minutes, doing seven pull-ups in two minutes, and forty-five situps and twenty-five push-ups in three minutes. Depending on the projected need for jumpers that year, about 108 from a group of 500 applicants will be chosen for the school.

Training lasts for three weeks and usually starts in late May or early June. Of those who start school, virtually all will graduate. The purpose of the school is to qualify jumpers and not to wash people out through an endurance process.

Graduates are certified to be smoke jumpers for one year. As a rule, they work that summer and then reapply for the following year's jump school. Most only work five or six seasons before they find something better to do with their summers.

Graduates are assigned to camps located in the West in areas where there are large Forest Service holdings that are thought likely to have forest fires. They may work in Idaho and Montana for a few weeks and then be transferred to Alaska.

Smoke jumpers are paid a flat $6.90 hourly while waiting for a fire on which to jump. During this time of waiting, they are assigned general Forest Service project work which includes routine maintenance on buildings and of the grounds. During an especially slow fire season, smoke jumpers will mostly paint buildings and repair roads and trails.

When they do go out on a fire, they are paid straight time plus an additional bonus of 25 percent called hazard pay. They receive this pay until the fire is contained or controlled.

Their duty, once the fire is identified, is to be the first on the scene to try to contain and minimize the fire. They will also provide the initial coordination of the ground crews who might be called in to assist their efforts if they can reach the site.

Smoke jumpers also direct planes flying in borate, water, and flame retardants.

Smoke jumpers must always be prepared to jump from fixed-wing DC-3- or Beech 99-type of aircraft. They use WW II type parabolic military chutes supplied by the Forest Service. These chutes are somewhat steerable, but jumpers must often walk several miles over rough terrain to their final destinations.

Whenever it has been possible, the Forest Service in recent years has been contracting for helicopters to take jumpers into the fire. This added expense is justified where the distances are not too great because the landing can be better controlled and coordinated.

As a general rule, jumpers are sent in in teams of four or five or more. It is not uncommon for as many as twenty jumpers to be sent to an especially serious-looking fire. Stories of heroism on the part of individual jumpers abound, but are mostly apocryphal, coming for the most part from an era when there were fewer, less-organized jumpers and a great deal more bravado.

Action careerists who want to increase their chances of being selected for jump school should plan to spend a couple of seasons working on Forest Service ground crews.

Ground-crew personnel are hired by the regional Forest Service office to be part of a fire-fighting crew that is kept on permanent standby during the dry summer months. Like the smoke jumpers, these guys mostly paint, rake, and conduct repairs until a fire breaks out.

After the alarm is sounded, they are transported in troop trucks to the scene of the fire. In some cases, roads are built by bulldozer crews hired on contract for the occasion by the Forest Service.

Ground crews are paid $6.16 per hour throughout the season. While on the fire line, they receive food from a common mess and sleep on the ground in sleeping bags supplied by the Forest Service.

Jumpers and ground crews are expected to supply their own inner work garments and suitable boots. (In the case of the jumper, boots can be a significant expense.)

Because Forest Service employees are moved around so much, the job is often not a viable one except for the young, unattached male.

Working as a volunteer fireman in a small town or suburb is, of course, very possible for the now-sedentary family man who wants to put some action into his life or otherwise explore a second career; both jobs entail risk and a desire to get out and around where the action is.

Several years ago, I was involved with a forest fire in the Uinta Mountains in Utah. It started at the 1,300-foot level from a lightning strike and quickly spread into a box canyon where it was considered to be extremely dangerous.

Being good citizens in need of a well-paying, short-term job, a friend and I walked up the mountain to the fire and asked the supervisor if we could work. He said we couldn't since we didn't have hard hats and the fire was too dangerous for anyone to go down into the box canyon. Besides, he said, a special group of fire fighters from the Utah State Prison were on the way. They were all convicted murderers, the supervisor said, and would be sent into the canyon because they were expendable.

The convicts arrived in their special vehicles, and about thirty of them went immediately into the canyon. We ambled down off the mountain and drove on into Talmage where we stayed overnight.

Around ten the next morning, word came down that the murderers had fought the fire for twenty hours straight and had succeeded in containing it. They were due into town about four that afternoon, it was said.

The whole town turned out to see these strange men, who came rumbling by in specially equipped fire-fighting trucks. On arrival and seeing the large crowd lined up to look at them, the crew foreman announced that it was their afternoon workout time and that the men would spend an hour keeping in condition lifting weights.

The crowd couldn't believe it. After twenty hours on a desperate fire line, the prisoners rummaged through their trucks and pulled out their weights! For an hour, they worked out in front of the amazed and apprehensive group of citizens. It was the most macho display I have ever seen in my life!

How You Can Do It

1. Stop by your local fire station and talk to the chief about enlisting as a volunteer fire fighter.
2. Join your local volunteer organization. If there is a choice, pick the group that pays a small amount for actual work done.
3. Take a fire-fighter home-study program. If such a program is not available, work toward being able to attend regional and national seminars.
4. Be sure all the certificates you earn are nationally recognized.
5. Learn to drive the necessary vehicles.
6. Get certified in the use of self-contained breathing apparatus.
7. Strive to move up in the department.
8. Seek and find work as a full-time fire fighter in a bigger city.

9. Consider taking college course work in fire science.
10. Keep working to get National Fire Protection Association ratings.
11. Become a big city chief or go to work for private industry.
12. Those in excellent physical condition having free summers should consider smoke jumping.
13. Contact the U.S. Forest Service or a Bureau of Land Management office about working on their fire crews.
14. After a couple of summers' experience, apply to one of the five smoke jumping schools.
15. Buy the necessary boots.
16. Go to jump school.
17. Travel around with the fire service fire crews.

Gunrunner

I arrived in Frankfurt, Germany, on Friday and wanted to drive to Liege, Belgium, before the weekend started. My contact would, I felt, work over the weekend if he were certain I was on the scene.

Traffic moves fast on German highways. Liege, just inside the Belgian border, was only a three-hour drive.

I found my contact at his little office on an obscure street after hiring a taxi to lead me down the many twisting, narrow streets for which this sprawling, dingy city is famous.

Yes, my contact assured me, he had five million rounds of 7.62 NATO ammo available for immediate shipment. All was first-quality, private-manufacturing company overrun produced in Belgium, he said.

The price at eighty U.S. dollars per thousand was astronomically high for the late sixties. By way of reference, a week before this transaction, I had purchased a mixture of surplus 8 mm Lebel and 7.35 Terni for twenty U.S. dollars per thousand and had handled it all by phone!

I had the crates spray-painted, covering any previous marks, and stenciled markings in French to indicate that the contents were spare parts for printing presses.

On Monday afternoon, we moved the stuff to port. I engaged space on a container ship and had my cargo stuffed into containers. (The limit is twenty-two metric tons per container, so even though my containers were not packed full, I had to pay for a total of five containers!)

Different people remember different trivia. I vividly recall that the freight charges from Antwerp to Capetown were $475.00 per container. At the time, I thought this was an outrageous rip-off.

Once the container was stuffed and sealed, the shipping company took my word for the fact that the contents were printing-press gears and shafts. I did this by having a phony bill of lading that detailed dozens of parts that were included in the shipment prepared by the trucking company. The steamship line took the trucking company document at face value. No inspections were made.

From Frankfurt, I flew to Nairobi and stayed only a couple of days before leaving for Lusaka, Zambia. The Zambians spotted my then-Rhodesian visa and ordered me out of the country in twenty-four hours. So, on the following day, I took a short flight from Lusaka to Livingston, then a bus to the bridge over the Zambezi, where I walked to freedom.

Upon arriving in Rhodesia, I called my client in Salisbury to let him know I was on my way. (He already knew about the shipment since my transshipper in Capetown had alerted them.)

It took three weeks for the freight to arrive in Capetown. As agreed, the South Africans put everything on trucks and sent it north through Johannesburg to Bulawayo.

The interval gave me time to check out the sources of my money and to be sure it was, in fact, in a South African bank dollar account.

I sold the stuff for $180 per thousand, delivered, or CIF, as it is known in the trade. In this one instance, I broke one of my cardinal rules and gave the Rhodesians a very good deal because I believed so strongly in what they were doing.

Gunrunning, or engaging in the international trafficking of armaments, is an incredibly attractive business for many really ambitious adventurers. Its lure is in part due to the attraction to the unknown. For others, it's a chance to permanently alter the course of history. For still others, it's the jingle of the cash register. Practical gunrunners point out that the net proceeds from one small deal can easily run half-a-million dollars. In that regard, most gunrunners are in the business for the money and the travel that often takes them to such remote, out-of-the-way places that no hotels can be found.

Gunrunning is an industry of huge potential. In terms of dollar volume, there is no other single class of manufactured goods traded internationally that is larger than armament. On a worldwide basis, annual expenditures for weapons is almost one trillion dollars. That may be more money than is spent for the import and export of food commodities worldwide and is certainly more than is spent for cars and trucks.

Trouble spots where armaments are in intense demand are many. The locations change a bit from time to time, but the world always seems able to support a consistent number of troubles on a reasonably steady basis. Because most of the world is disarmed, the timely delivery of even a few weapons and a small quantity of ammo often has tremendous long-term political ramifications.

The gunrunner has three basic challenges. He must buy his supplies someplace reasonable and then deliver them to the end-user who, in turn, must often be persuaded to pay up in a timely sort of way in a usable currency.

Securing supplies always has political considerations and traditionally has been tough. More and more new supplier countries (such as Korea, China, Thailand, and Turkey) have come on the scene, making it easier to get ahold of armaments than way back when only the Soviet Union and the United States dominated world supplies. As recently as fifteen years ago, the freelance gunrunner had little chance of success without CIA or KGB backing.

To make sourcing easier, Soviet weapons shipments around the world have been huge. Bulging warehouses full of reasonably good Soviet weapons spotted around the globe give the gunrunner a source of supply unavailable until fairly recently. Whenever the gunrunner needs weapons, he can almost always find someone who will sell Soviet stuff from some obscure warehouse someplace or other.

As with any business, the trick for the gunrunner is to match the source of supply with an effective transportation system.

To locate new or surplus supplies, the gunrunner must be on the scene and do a lot of traveling. He must travel constantly and quickly, making contact with the appropriate manufacturers and users so that he can continually update his assessment of who has what for sale, and who is looking for what particular items. The business usually involves a huge overhead that will quickly scare off the poorly financed or financially timid person. Some private gunrunners use Falcon 50s to get around, and won't touch a deal involving less than fifty million U.S. dollars.

At this writing, the neophyte gunrunners can virtually always secure something that will work for their client revolutionaries by contacting one of the following manufacturers: the Pusan Munitions Works (with offices in Pusan or Seoul, Korea); Norinco (Beijing, China); the Turkish government (contact the Turkish export office in Istanbul), and the Argentine National Manufacturing Plant, Fabrica Militar de Armes (at Rosario, Santa Fe, Argentina).

Other than the Chinese, these sellers will generally have weapons that are characterized as small arms, which include pistols, rifles, assault rifles, submachine guns, grenades, and mortars. As a general rule, bush league revolutionaries can get along on this range of items and will seldom have money to buy much more.

There are many other suppliers, but the companies mentioned above are the major new players who will often sell to customers without asking an insurmountable number of embarrassing questions.

Other increasingly sophisticated weapons might come from Spain (tanks), Singapore (SAMs), Czechoslovakia (cheap AKs and ammo), and France (helicopters and jet fighters).

The movement of goods in the more sophisticated end of the business is extremely tough. It is seldom done without official sanction on both ends.

Unlike the relatively simple machine guns, mortars, anti-tank weapons, grenades and most artillery, sophisticated state-of-the-art supplies are closely held by a relatively limited number of governments.

It takes skill and experience to put a deal together that involves scarce, high-tech armaments, but it is where the big money is in this day and age.

As with so many action careers, a military background is helpful, but not essential, for the gunrunner. At times, military training or a past commission is the entree needed to be able to walk in and talk to foreign military purchasers. Also, many modern weapons systems are now so complex that the gunrunner must either have specialized training or take appropriate experts with him when either buying or selling, no matter how smart or how clever he may be about buying and shipping weapons in general. Buying or selling aircraft, radar-controlled systems, track vehicles, electronic gear, or missiles usually requires a team approach.

In most cases, the tough problem is arranging for sources of supply in countries that may not want weapons manufactured within their borders delivered to your specific end-user. China and Korea are notoriously selective.

France will almost always allow shipments to anyone who pays.

Making cold calls on potential customers is, in my opinion, more of an art than a science, although I do have a formula for locating potential buyers.

Shipping weapons, the second part of the puzzle, can tax the ability of the brightest people in the world. Delivery is really the core element of the business. Experts in armament often team up with shipping people in an attempt to put a usable system together.

Most world freight moves by water. Loading the boxes and crates on an old scow that will eventually be beached and abandoned in your customer's territory is often the cheapest and best idea, provided the buyer has a safe coastal area on which to beach the vessel.

In an emergency, small arms and ammo can be moved by air. Moving weapons by air is immediate and positive and initially somewhat less risky. Because air freight involves less risk than other methods, it is often the method specified by the end-user. On the other hand, air freight is so breathtakingly expensive that it is unbelievable.

Other means of movement include common smuggling or working the goods through a regular official port by hiding them in sacks of rice, a hold full of grain, or in containers of frozen food. My original example how ammo was moved into Rhodesia is an excellent case study of what can be done using friendly neighbors who will agree to look the other way.

Developing a delivery system is easier if the buyer is well enough established to have sympathizers in high places. This always requires close cooperation between the indigenous buyer and the gunrunner. In spite of claims to the contrary on the part of the buyer, this type of cooperation is usually only a pipe dream.

Like everything else in the gunrunning business, the successful operator has got to be continually on the scene. He must have a nose for trouble zones and be willing to visit them regularly. Frequent contacts with the end-user are not only important, they are absolutely vital.

Making contacts with reclusive, idealistic revolutionaries can be a hairy experience. Good gunrunners develop their contact skills to a fine point, or their overhead will break them in a year or two. They learn to find out where revolutionary headquarters are located and how to make contact with the leaders in the shortest time possible.

Try the following when attempting to make contact with potential buyers with whom you have not previously had any contact.

1. Read the local papers and talk to local military officials, police, and interested citizens

to find out who is leading the opposition and where they are generally located.

2. Make the effort to go to that region of the country even if the districts are closed to outsiders by the central government.

3. Talk to every bellboy, taxi driver, bartender, and hotel employee who can speak enough English to comprehend that you make your living dealing in arms. Point out that you would like to talk about weapons to commander "what's-his-name."

4. Leave your business cards around, making sure that such people as bellboys and waiters each have one.

5. Be patient but active; talk to a dozen new people or more per day.

6. Stay in the same hotel and wait. Emissaries from the bad guy's camp will generally contact you by the fourth day if they are in the area. Usually this contact will occur in a crowded bar or restaurant and will consist of instructions to meet some other busy place.

7. Explain to the emissaries with whom you meet what you are doing and point out that you come into town regularly. Offer to meet with them the next time you are in town.

8. Come back on schedule and open a dialogue with the revolutionaries. Eventually you will meet the main man if the go-betweens are convinced you can deliver.

Dealing guns is big business -- definitely not

a game that the fainthearted should play. Overhead, including the cost of delivery, can at times be truly outrageous. Markups must be almost unconscionably large. A good rule of thumb is to always strive to get every possible cent the market will bear and that your buyer currently possesses. Sympathy for the cause or other politics must never be a factor.

In most cases the fee may not be enough to cover the items the customer says he wants, but that is up to the buyer and seller to negotiate. Most buyers will talk to two or three gunrunners in an attempt to work out the best possible deal. Even if no one else is on the scene, buyers will usually maintain the fiction that they are shopping around.

Getting paid is a problem for the gunrunner. Unless there is a spot market for the commodity, it is best to stay away from trade goods such as tankers of crude oil, packages of heroin, scores of voluptuous maidens, and other similar goods.

It is not at all uncommon for revolutionaries to have dollars or gold coins to turn over at the time of delivery which are on deposit in bank accounts in the United States. Professional gunrunners spell all this out in detail so they know beyond any shadow of a doubt when and how they will get paid when the deal is consummated.

Professionals also warn against accepting

currency of the realm. Most paper money is not freely convertible in world markets. Gunrunners who want to stay in business must be sure the money they agree to accept has value. Almost all weapons deals are denominated in U.S. dollars.

The seasoned gunrunner never assumes his buyers won't have enough money. Examples are numerous. Traditionally, the Muslim National Liberation Front, operating on central Mindanao in the Philippines, was penniless. At this writing, following the Marcos/Aquino election, they are in the process of an incredible arms-buying program.

Saudi and Libyan money is said to be pouring into Moro coffers which, in turn, is being spent in the world armament market. The plan is to have the Moros armed to the teeth in time for a 1988 general insurrection directed at the Aquino regime.

The gunrunner can trade for, or buy, old and obsolete weapons. Weapons trading occurs quite often as countries update their systems and hardware and are often anxious to put their old stuff out for whatever the market will bear.

Historically, these sorts of upgrades have been regional in nature, rolling over the countries involved in waves. Competition and national pride are the principal causes of this "buy modern" syndrome.

Packing and crating are two additional skills the gunrunner must possess. My rule of thumb is to pack for the product and only occasionally for the end-user.

The crate must be strong enough and be designed well enough to adequately protect the goods, be they mortar rounds or sophisticated radios and avionics. Should the end-user require three rockets per case instead of four in order to best load his pack mules, that is up to him. Endeavor only to deliver in good, usable shape -- not to provide mule-sized loads.

Often, but not always, the current owner will have packing crates left from the time when the goods were originally purchased and delivered. Storage may have been done down through the years in those same old crates.

Using the old as a sample, new crates can be built as required. People who have been in the business gain a sense for what will work and what won't, depending on the conditions at the point of delivery. A small amount of experience goes a long way at this point.

Weapons that will spend three weeks at sea and then perhaps go to land through the surf must be packed much differently than those moved by air.

Getting started as a gunrunner is costly. At a minimum, one should figure $70,000 to $100,000 in expenses for the first year.

It is much easier if the fledgling has a deal

when he starts, but this is seldom possible. If the terms are cash on the Jeep hood, the gunrunner really has his work cut out negotiating operating credit. The age-old dilemma is how to finance the deal so as to pay an anxious seller and not scare off the buyer.

Keep in mind that there is always some way to put a deal together. It's part of the skill a gunrunner must possess.

It is very expensive to deal weapons. Small arms orders, including delivery, are never for less than a quarter of a million dollars; just a few tanks, pieces of artillery, or APCs (armored personnel carriers) will run eight to ten million dollars. A small helicopter deal will start at fifteen million. Expenses are less if the gunrunner acts as a broker or agent. But profits, as well as outright opportunities, are greatly reduced as compared to owning the stuff yourself and reselling it.

Experts say to include a huge markup on every deal and not to overlook more mundane items such as supplying rations, shoes, and uniforms. Medical supplies, for instance, can be easy-to-finance, yet especially lucrative, items for gunrunners.

People in the gunrunning business sometimes forget to remain professionals. The old-timers strongly urge that the gunrunner not ever become part of the cause. Sell to both sides if need be, but never, never succumb to the urge to grab a rifle and head for the bush -- no matter how bad the injustices may appear. Those who do so are not gunrunners but rather soldiers of fortune, another action career covered elsewhere in this book.

How You Can Do It

1. Learn at least one segment of the weapons industry, i.e., night-vision devices, heavy machine guns, armored personnel carriers, etc.
2. Collect information as to what small wars are being fought where.
3. Travel endlessly and talk to people. Develop contacts among potential end-users.
4. Study the international shipping business so as to develop a knack for moving big, heavy items under difficult circumstances.
5. Travel extensively so as to develop contacts among the world's armament suppliers.
6. Negotiate a contract with an armament buyer. Often smaller deals in obscure places are more doable than going for the big time supplying jet fighter parts to Iran, for instance.
7. Be extremely creative, competent, and timely about delivering the goods.
8. Price the stuff to allow for excellent profits necessary to cover large overhead.
9. Handle spare parts, medical supplies, and other related items at the start as a means of breaking into the business and staying solvent.

Don't:

1. Ever become part of the cause.
2. Fail to ask the locals for help dealing with customs and port officials when smuggling arms through regular port facilities.
3. Ever take currency that is not fully convertible.
4. Ever trade for goods that are not immediately salable.
5. Ever offer very much for used, old, or obsolete items.
6. Neglect the repair and reconditioning part of the business.
7. Fail to sell to both sides if possible.
8. Fail to grease the generals' palms when necessary.
9. Plan for crating, loading, and shipping to move along without a hitch. If anything can get screwed up, it probably will.
10. Expect the business to run without you on the local scene to make it happen.
11. Try to buy complex, modern systems without really good, knowledgeable people on your team to help.
12. Be afraid to break in by dealing for unexciting items such as food, clothing, and medicine.

Hunting and Fishing Guide

Working as a guide may only qualify as an action career for those who have not been close to the business. Many times there isn't much action to the work. Burned out, retired action-career types make ideal fishing guides.

I say this in spite of the fact that I have had horses fall off mountains and kill themselves, gotten stuck unexpectedly in the high country by storms for two weeks at a clip, had bears attack my clients, lost clients for two days in the woods, and tipped my canoe over in a huge reservoir fourteen miles from the nearest road.

The life of a guide is generally an easy, uneventful one, riding around on horses or in Jeeps, running boats on peaceful lakes, sleeping in tents or nice lodges, enjoying the scenery, and eating fairly good food. The livin' is easy, but it isn't action packed.

The big myth in all of this is that a guide has to know anything about fish and game or the country in which he works. It is absolutely essential that hunting and fishing guides know quite a lot about human nature and dealing with people, but a knowledge of game is absolutely not required. Anyone with the right temperament who is in reasonably good physical condition can be a hunting or fishing guide, provided he is even half smart and plausibly intelligent. At best, only a rudimentary knowledge of the outdoors and camping is required. Many otherwise qualified people commit a gross error whey they do not consider guiding because they feel they are not five-star game scouts.

While I personally think that guiding is boring for the most part, it is an occupation that at least should be considered by the person who wants a low-key, easy-living action career. The business is fun and interesting, but the adrenaline high that most action careerists want to live on may not be there.

A few years back, I took a businessman and industrial psychologist out on a hunt in the mountains of Montana. They were both from Boston. The following account is typical of what usually happens.

We made camp at the 7,500-foot level. The first day, I woke them early. As is typical, they were most fearful of getting lost, so they paid close attention to my maps and drawings and didn't try to go outside of the agreed-on area in which we were hunting.

By the third day, the combination of the thin, mountain air, strenuous exercise, and their generally borderline physical condition had taken its toll.

After that, all these guys wanted to do was sleep. They came in at midday. I fixed them a big lunch, and they slept all afternoon. At night, they thought they would die from exhaustion.

Hunting guides most generally work for an outfitter or hunting promoter who has leased or purchased the right to take hunters out in a certain area. This area can range from hundreds of sections in the West to a few acres of good quail cover in the South.

Hunting guides are not expected to shoot -- the clients do that -- so they do not have to be especially competent with firearms. Similar rules apply to handling a fishing rod, but a fishing guide must know how to handle a net or gaff very skillfully.

Guides must be generally cool and unflappable, and in a general sense big-game guides must be able to track wounded animals and to determine how they might have been hit by an erratic hunter. I have found that most people who live in game areas have enough skill to pull this part of it off.

A rudimentary knowledge of the game in one's area is helpful. However, most clients like to think they know quite a bit about the business themselves. An in-depth working knowledge of deer or elk habits, for instance, is often a waste for the guide.

Perhaps I unduly depreciate the skills required to be a guide, but I have worked for a number of promoters who offer hunting packages and always found out enough about the game and the immediate area from them and my first reconnaissance over the country to get by with my clients.

Readers must remember that the days of actually taking dudes out to shoot game are gone forever. In most cases it isn't even expected; after all, it is not a foregone conclusion that game will be spotted.

I have also gone out with a considerable number of professional guides, most of whom didn't really know very much about game or the country they were in. All were basically commonsense outdoorsmen, and their mode of operation, I found, was very similar to my own.

One thing the guide has got to know how to do is field-dress and haul out the catch, no matter what it is or where. No city hunter is going to know how to do this, nor will they want to do it. Field-dressing larger elk and moose is tough, but packing it out is where the real work starts. Hunting guides must be prepared to handle this business. (Fishing guides are often evaluated on the basis of how well they handle the catch.)

Getting started in this occupation depends to a great extent on being at the right place at the right time. One must either work for the guy with the hunting block or be at a place where a block is available to take over. Owners of hunting resorts and lodges are always on the lookout for people who can play the part of a guide. Guides generally work only three or four months a year so the line to get into the business is not a very long one.

Some guides think in terms of eventually buying out an operational outfit or starting their own hunting camp. My general rule is that no hunting concession is worth paying for. There simply is not enough profit in modern hunting or fishing deals to make paying for a hunting right worthwhile.

Sometimes a hunting promoter might have a stock truck, horses and tack, or perhaps even a base-camp building that is worth some money, but beware. This becomes more of a hotel-restaurant management situation. Under these circumstances, you may be looking for a guide or two yourself in a few years. You may also find yourself being more interested in the weenie and mustard inventory than hunting and fishing.

In many places in the southern and western United States, a knowledge of horse packing helps. The last hunt promoter I worked for had stock. He learned all he did about packing by reading a book or two and then packing himself around on his own territory the summer before he started. In the fall, he had twenty elk hunters at $1,500 each, but still went broke. As I remember, we only got four or five trophies, but that wasn't the reason he couldn't make it. His expenses (which included bills for feed, gas, and saddles) were just too high, even at $1,500 per hunter.

A relatively low-risk way to get started is to put a hunt idea together yourself. Line up the land over which you will hunt (check with the Bureau of Land Management). Put together a small brochure and advertise in the various hunting magazines.

Some magazines have guiding/hunter promoter qualifications, but most just want the money with the ad copy.

When the dudes answer, write back to them on letterhead stationery. Usually it takes a couple of letters before a date is set and they send the required 50 percent deposit. Guides are not expected to use typewriters.

Under the correct circumstances, all this can be done for $1,500 out-of-pocket, including ads in most of the popular hunting magazines.

Many, many hunts these days are done on foot from a lodge or base camp. Sometimes the hunt is done from a boat. An average alert American who even begins to contemplate an action career certainly can quickly learn to run a boat. The boat can be leased rather than purchased if money is a severe problem.

My rule of thumb when taking people out is to give them as tough an experience as they can endure. That way even if they get no game, they have the ordeal to recount with their friends back home. Americans are so soft and lazy that even at my advanced age, it is not difficult for me to give them a tough time.

Sometimes dudes request an exotic fly-in hunting or fishing trip or hunt. I have often done these, more as an arranger than anything. Just be sure to add your 20-percent commission to everything when pricing such trips to the clients.

A close friend who promotes both hunting and fishing trips believes that the key to success is food. He budgets huge amounts of money for steaks and other delectables. His plan was to substitute culinary skills for hunting skills.

Tented base camps have passed from the scene in the States for the most part. Some camping skills are occasionally required of the hunting guide, yet most hunting nowadays is done from warm, waterproof lodges and cabins. For the most part, Jeeps have replaced horses. Many times a motel owner will work with you and allow you to put together a package using his facility.

Camping skill levels are about what the average adventurer will naturally have as a result of the life he leads.

Fishing guides have a much easier life. At most, there will be but one or two proven methods of catching fish in any given body of water. Anyone who is halfway interested can pick these up in a week or two.

About the biggest problem for the guide involves the heavy drinker and the intolerable braggart. Both are difficult to contend with for seven to ten days in a lodge or small base camp (or worst yet, in a fishing boat.)

People who want an action career should be alert to the possibilities. Being a guide is much easier than a novice would ever assume. It is also one of the least profitable action careers. Some guides make more, but generally guides are paid about the same as cowboys. Two hundred dollars per week is on the high side. As a general rule, fishing guides make more than hunting guides. This always seemed strange to me because it takes slightly more skill to pass oneself off as a hunting guide.

Guides have many chances to make money on the side. Savvy readers will immediately think of the all-night poker games they got into with guides they have hired for hunting trips, or perhaps the tales of the guide on the Lochsa in Idaho who brought a couple of unattached lady cooks into the camps.

I am referring, though, to things like running a trap line and catching and selling fish commercially when they were coming in fairly well.

How You Can Do It

1. Look around your general area to see whether there are any hunting or fishing possibilities. Don't overlook any possibilities (even the chance to land lunker carp will appeal to some city people.)
2. Find out if there are any hunting or fishing package promotions in your area and whether or not they need guides.
3. Go out hunting or fishing with the local promoters, or fish with some locals to get a handle as to how they do it in that particular area.
4. Learn how to field-dress or clean local game, becoming proficient at it.
5. Go back to local hunting and fishing promoters and offer to guide for them on a contingency basis.
6. Be wary of starting a hunting service, fishing camp, or buying an existing outfit since you may find yourself working as a restaurant operator and hotel owner rather than as a hunting guide.
7. If no existing concession holders hire you, put out a small brochure, run a few ads, and see if anyone is attracted to the area.
8. Place ads in sporting magazines.

9. Be alert to other activities to get into while guiding.

International Courier

Perhaps a dozen different people during the last twenty years have come to me and suggested that we jointly start an international courier service.

There are some people who make nice supplementary incomes as couriers but most don't engage in the business openly.

The idea, for the guy who simply wants to hang out his shingle and have business and government people call him with orders to take a packet of money or papers overseas, is a non-starter. In the real world there isn't much of a market for this kind of service.

Professional international delivery services such as DHL or International Express Mail will take up to two pounds of paper virtually anyplace overseas. They charge about thirty-five dollars for guaranteed twenty-four-hour delivery to Tokyo, Jidda, Bangkok, Hong Kong, Djakarta, or just about anywhere in the world.

The only way I know to compete with these

guys is to offer better service. Generally this means going to more places, faster service, or cheaper prices -- probably an impossibility under the circumstances.

The established couriers use computers to pick the best and fastest route and then put the documents in a locked aluminum box that such commercial airlines as Pan Am, United, or Northwest Orient haul on their regularly scheduled flights. The pilots themselves are responsible for the parcel. Contracts for this service are negotiated by airline management and the delivery service people. It is not done on a freelance basis.

At the other end of the line, the courier's service agent will pick the box up, deliver the envelopes by motorcycle, pick up the outgoing packets, restock the box and deliver the box back to the airline. It may leave again on the same plane that it came in on.

Because the delivery services want to avoid customs hassles at all costs, they allow absolutely nothing in the packets but papers. They will not haul even a small bottle of chemical, a tiny parcel, or a machine part. There would seem to be an opening here for the entrepreneur, but, if there is one, it is not very large.

Regular established delivery services are inexpensive and reliable. Due to the volume of material they transport, most companies carry to almost anyplace in the world on very short notice.

An individual courier who intends to buy a plane ticket to Singapore or Nairobi and personally hand-carry papers for large companies or the government will find that it is exceedingly difficult to compete with such courier services. In many cases, personal couriers wouldn't even be able to obtain visas fast enough to match the service offered by established services, even if price were no object and the company were desperate.

But price can be immaterial to businessmen and in some cases to governmental people. An economy-class plane ticket to Calcutta will run about $2,800. This does not include the courier's time and expense.

I have worked in the field of international business for many years and have yet to run into the first situation where anyone has been willing to spend this kind of money to send anything overseas. It is possible that a small bottle of chemicals or machine parts may be in such demand that it would be worth the price of a special trip, but I have not seen it to be the case.

In this day and age of increasingly sophisticated telex and FAX machines, the need for actual physical delivery of contracts or other papers is becoming obsolete.

At times the U.S. government will send a pouch over to an embassy or from an embassy on an emergency basis. The contents may be sensitive documents. It doesn't happen as often as one would suppose, because the government also has FAX and telex machines, as well as access to regular delivery services.

When government officials need to send documents via courier pouch, the tendency is to check around to see who on the embassy staff is scheduled for travel to the place where the documents are to go. Knowing this, they will send the documents off with their own people.

Most governments have their own diplomatic couriers whose job it is to nursemaid diplomatic packets from one place to another. In the case of the United States, these people are State Department employees who enjoy sitting on planes a lot. They work a regular circuit in a very regimented fashion.

The rules of their job dictate that they personally bring the sealed canvas bags of material (papers, samples, machines, etc.) to the airport where they will personally load it into the cargo hold of the plane.

They watch the hold door close and are the last ones on the plane. Upon landing, these diplomatic couriers are the first off the plane so they can again supervise the opening of the cargo hold of the plane.

In many cases, they will have responsibility for ten to twenty or more canvas bags. By U.S.

regulation, they fly only U.S. carriers, and they always fly first class.

The business about flying handcuffed to a briefcase is a myth with no basis in fact.

A State Department diplomatic courier must be very detail-oriented and personally happy with the chore of filling out dozens of detailed forms.

Recruiting for this job is done through the State Department via its normal recruiting procedures that include extensive testing and lengthy interviewing. As a general rule, employment in the State Department is only available to college graduates.

Government officials will trust their established courier system long before they will ever consider using a freelance carrier.

In spite of all the above-noted factors, there is a place for the freelance courier. The only caveat is the business can only be put together by people who are already traveling international routes as part of another business or line of work.

These couriers can be airline pilots, ship captains, cooks, recreation directors and tour guides, stewards, and stewardesses, among others.

Airline and travel personnel often are able to take everything from sales samples, pictures, exposed unprocessed film, medical reports, lab and medical samples, drawings, and small machine parts to pearls (which they wear), gold coins, and gems. At times even small pistols or a few rounds of ammo can be transported.

Sometimes the business grows into something fairly substantial if a person regularly runs the needed route and can make contact with people wishing to make repeat shipments.

American airline pilots regularly take video copies of the latest American movies or cassettes of the hot new groups to Taiwan or Singapore where bootleggers replicate them by the millions for sale back in the United States.

A business acquaintance in Indonesia paid astronomical prices for X-rated videos brought to him by airline stewards.

In many, many places in the world, such as Singapore, Hong Kong, and Islamic countries, *Playboy* and *Penthouse* magazines are well worth surreptitiously hauling in. (The business amounts to petty smuggling. Sometimes it can grow into something fairly substantial, depending on the route and the willingness of the carrier to make contacts and take chances.)

People in the business tell me that the best plan is to let people come to them and make the proposals. Airline and travel people stay in known, predictable places overseas. Nationals know all about these places and where to look if they want something hauled in or out.

The best ongoing example of such transportation of goods that I know of are the airline pilots who haul news photos and exposed color film for international wire services.

A similar experience has been of great value to me when I desperately needed a small packet of seed, some bud cuttings, spray nozzles, or even a sample of ag chemicals sent someplace. The problem is always finding someone in the States who can pick up the correct materials and get them to an airline captain who will put them in his pocket for me.

I have often talked to stewards who are very open about the fact that they are carrying pearls from Hong Kong or emeralds from Bangkok.

Caution is recommended, however. I would, if I were in the business, never, never carry illegal drugs or other materials. Bringing back a few packets of Eradicil, the new miracle clap killer, or some ampicillin, for instance, is one thing. But to haul cocaine or heroin is dangerously foolish.

At one time I worked in northern Thailand among the opium poppy fields. We were on a mountain road almost into Burma when we decided to stop and walk through an especially nice field.

We parked our Toyota LandCruiser out of sight in a little saddle and started off on foot. At the edge of the field, I caught sight of a number of people clad in cammies barreling out of the woods running down into a little draw toward us.

I could plainly see through my 300 mm camera lens that they were all carrying rifles, and, every now and then, one of them would kneel down and sight down the barrel of his rifle. They did not have telescopic sights on their rifles. Obviously, they were trying to see if they could get a clear shot.

Fortunately, no rounds were fired.

We beat a hasty retreat into the woods, down another little scalloped draw, and out of the field guard's sight. As soon as we were hidden, we ran like the devil to the Toyota and drove away.

We were not careful when we retreated through the poppy fields and got covered with the latexy sap from the cut pods. I had the jeans I was wearing washed four times in the hotel laundry. It didn't do much good.

In San Francisco, the customs people asked me where I had been. It does no good to lie. They can see the Thai customs stamp in my passport so I told them that I had been in Thailand.

On hearing that, they brought out a cross-breed fox terrier type of dog who immediately went crazy sniffing my pants.

"Have you been in northern Thailand?" they asked sternly.

"Yes," I cheered, "even in the poppy fields."

There was a long pause. "What were you

doing in the poppy-growing areas?" they asked.

"Growing potatoes," I said. My reply was followed by a long, long, most definitely pregnant pause, accompanied by lots of looking around and smirking.

Finally the ag specialist asked me if I had a business card. I did, of course, but it still took them over an hour to tear my luggage apart.

I could have easily bought a kilo of number 4 heroin for $6,000 in Thailand, but sure as God made green apples I would have been caught trying to bring it into the States.

Virtually any set of government authorities takes a dim view of illegal drugs. There is no sense of humor over even minor amounts.

Frequent travelers who try to engage in a bit of amateur smuggling are easy meat for professional customs people, often watched and not smart enough to avoid detection. That's why I recommend not being a courier for anything more questionable than gemstones, gold, and pornography.

For several years while working in Saudi Arabia, I made a few bucks hauling in X-rated videos and the occasional bottle of scotch.

We made arrangements with the cleaning crew to leave the items in the overhead bins of a certain airline's Dakar to New York SP flight.

I never figured out exactly how the stuff got to my buyers, but it seemed to get there as evidenced by the fact that they paid up promptly.

It was only a hundred or so dollars a flight however, so after a couple of years when the Saudi businessman lost interest, I did not really even care.

If one travels extensively, courier work can be a sideline. If not, there isn't too much reason to consider this line of employment.

How You Can Do It

1. Don't try to compete with regular carriers unless you can offer a unique or different service.
2. Those who travel regularly should think about the possibility of offering a regular service carrying goods. Something will usually come up that the action career person should be alert to.
3. Airline pilots and stewards might consider petty smuggling wherever the opportunity presents itself, provided the risks are low.
4. Start by encouraging contact with people who will pay for a small amount of ho-hum smuggling.
5. Build up the business by offering good prompt honest service.
6. Don't smuggle illegal drugs and don't fool around with the drug traffickers.
7. Try to build a demand on both ends. Pearls from Hong Kong and X-rated videos for Indo-

nesia, for instance.

8. Keep looking around and working at it.

Missionary

My friend, Betty Lou, shot her first leopard when she was fourteen years old. It was prowling around the goat corral, and the natives ran over to get her to see if she could help. She grabbed her 7 x 57 Mauser rifle and blew the leopard out of a high tree with one shot.

Betty Lou never did bag an elephant, although her missionary father figured he got about four hundred in his lifetime. All were turned into elephant burger as a much-needed source of protein for lepers in the leper hospital he managed.

Another close friend, Paul T., was born in Kenya in 1936, son of American missionaries. Through the years, we became inseparable, being both partners and friends. He was just twenty when the Mau Mau went on the rampage.

He told hair-raising stories about the efforts of his small band of missionary kids who organized themselves to do long-distance patrolling in an attempt to keep the lid on things till the British Army showed up.

Paul's outfit was the one that tracked the Mau Mau leaders to their lairs in the deep bush and then, using loyal Kipsigi fighters, drove the insurgents out like white-tailed deer about to be blasted with elephant guns.

Later on, these same missionary kids were instrumental in developing a de-oathing ceremony that aculturally allowed those who had taken the Mau Mau oath to lay down their arms (the episode became one of the cornerstones for Robert Ruark's book, *Something of Value).*

I have traveled all over the world and found that wherever the living is cheap and easy and the climate good, there are missionaries. In the Philippines, missionaries are to be found in Baguio; in Thailand, it's Chiang Mai. Life in the island of Bali, off of Indonesia, would be too obvious, so they open up shop in the Karo Highlands, a place the Dutch have worked for two hundred years that is located seventy-five miles south of Medan on the island of Sumatra.

Most adventurers haven't considered the life of a missionary as constituting a very interesting career. Contrary to popular opinion, however, the life of a missionary can be an extremely hair-raising one, much more so than some more popularly glamorized occupations that may come to mind.

The adventurer who considers a career as a missionary in one of the nicer places in the world had best realize that the good spots are pretty well filled up. Being able to make a living as a missionary in one of these places will necessitate that one have some special skills (such as printing, medical, or mechanical know-how, or, in a pinch, my old standby talent of being an agriculturist). University-educated farmers can definitely make a go of it.

Most missionary jobs don't require the skills of a theologian or Bible scholar. Some of the most interesting specialties do not entail Bible study over and above the obligatory amount expected of one's immediate peer group.

Many missionary groups never openly discuss the matter of religion. Missionaries working in certain societies more nearly become expatriate social workers laboring in a foreign country.

One of the big demands these days in the missionary business is for skilled aircraft mechanics. Often one must cut and paste a bit to get the job done, because funds are scarce for new parts, but the paperwork requirements are minimal.

In other places, missionaries skilled at construction find their skills are needed to build churches, houses, schools, and clinics. At one time, I spent a sinfully enjoyable two weeks installing a sewer system for a set of new missionary houses in Kenya.

The traditional, obvious need for missionaries is for those with medical skills. Depending on the time and place, the required skill level can run from fairly primitive to very sophisticated. Often adventurers with military, medical, or paramedical training can be gainfully employed as medical missionaries.

No matter what else they do, missionaries generally try to help the people around them. One way to help is to teach people how to grow more food. In general, the free world produces far more food than it consumes. However, in some areas of the world there is often room to show the people how to raise more and hardier crops.

During the thirties, a few missionaries did double duty functioning as information clearing-house coordinators in northern China, Burma, and the south Pacific. Today it appears that most missionaries are intent on keeping their houses in order. Little freelance spooking seems to be going on among this group.

Probably the most difficult part of being a missionary is learning a new language. Anyone who intends to maintain his financial backing back home had best learn at least enough of the local dialect to convince one's financial supporters. If it is a common language (such as Spanish or French), it is best to learn it pretty well lest someone at home decides to practice his or her Spanish or French and then discovers that you, the missionary, cannot communicate with the people you are supposed to be helping because you don't know the language.

With such languages as Korean, Indonesian, and Thai, the chances of it becoming known that you can't speak the language are remote. A smattering of conventional ability will generally do the trick in this case.

The kind of people best suited for missionary life are tough farm kids or those who have grown up tough and poor on the streets. Otherwise, the cut-and-paste, make-do philosophy won't necessarily appeal to those of different backgrounds and it is likely that the action-career person will be unhappy with the amenity-less life he must lead.

One wag suggested that good missionaries have a poor sense of smell and a good sense of humor. They must be flexible enough to rig a radio antenna, lay sewer pipe, or operate a small printing press.

Two paths exist to break into the missionary business. Both work, but the first is much more difficult at the outset, while the second provides much more long-term security.

Under plan one, the aspiring missionary will map out a need for his services in great detail. This route should include a location and specific work assignment about which the applicant is familiar. Research on the location, types of people, how to get there, and other pertinent information should be very thorough. Use the *National Geographic, Sunset* magazine, encyclopedias, travel agents, the embassy of the country you wish to go to, and any other appropriate sources in order to get as much information as you can on the area to which you wish to go.

Having this information, the aspiring missionary must use all of his creative skills to conjure up an absolutely essential humanitarian activity in which he can engage in the targeted region. This definitely is the tough part, requiring that one use every bit of his past training and experience, plus lots of salesman hype to put this part of the plan together.

Having put the entire package together, the aspiring missionary must get out and sell it to private companies, wealthy individuals, and organizations. It is essential that one play on the emotions and humanitarian instincts of those likely to give to such causes.

The plan is to ask for X amount of monthly support in perpetuity to be able to perform the wondrous and generous assignment you have outlined in your presentation to potential financial backers.

It is absolutely surprising how many different companies and individuals will go for this type of program, especially if their accountants can be convinced that such an investment is tax deductible. I have met literally scores of people who are living nicely around the world who did little more than sell the correct program to the right people at the right time.

Keep in mind that it does not take much money to live in most parts of the world. A person could live in grand style in Czismir, Turkey; Jalapa, Guatemala; Quito, Ecuador; or the Greek Islands on $1,500 U.S. per month. In most of these places, assuming you learn the language, it is possible for the smart gringo to make another grand a month conducting tours to folks from home or perhaps engaging in import/export activities or land speculation.

It is amazing how many business opportunities will come along to those who have the financial resources to sit and wait for them.

The second method of getting into the missionary field is tougher. It necessitates that one spend at least one semester at a known Bible college or seminary. During that time, it is important that the student identify his area of intended labor (that is to say, the geographical area in which he wants to work and the area of expertise he wants to sell to the home folks).

A missionary candidate need not be a Bible scholar, although a working knowledge of the doctrine related to the selected denomination or sect is useful. Many missionaries simply memorize the line or statement of faith in the local language and make do with this. After a few months in the country, you will, of course, pick up lots of the language.

Again, one can substitute a great deal of technical skill, such as farming, for theological knowledge. It all depends on how well the adventurer has planned his career and how much information has been gathered pertaining to one's intended "station."

The aspiring missionary may want to send away to Audio-Forum in Guilford, Connecticut, for language tapes. Using these tapes, it is possible to painlessly learn almost any language while riding in the car, jogging, or making pasta.

All of this information, as well as language skills, is used when making application to mission boards, organizations that are set up by world religions to raise money for and assist in the performance of missionary duties. These boards are universally old and venerable, with many attending traditions. Many board members are retired missionaries.

Mission boards almost always reflect the doctrinal beliefs of their founders, as well as the current beliefs of the principal supporting order or denomination. Virtually all large denominations and subsets have mission boards. Many times the board will concentrate its efforts on one or two geographic areas in the world (for example, the China Inland Mission, the African Inland Mission, and Missionary Aviation Fellowship).

After deciding on the location the aspiring missionary prefers, he should conduct the necessary research and apply to the appropriate board. In some cases, a board's screening process can be fairly rigorous, while in other cases it is not.

In some cases the screening process is fairly severe. In other situations, board members are happy to have applicants who are warm and mobile. By making the process tough, the more task-oriented mission societies attempt to screen out the insincere and poorly qualified. Smart candidates find out ahead what is selling at that moment and apply to a board whose requirements match their qualifications.

After board sanction or approval, it is then the duty of the candidate to secure financial backing; he is in some cases provided with a list of places in which to hunt for such backing. In the trade, this process is known as deputation work.

On the basis of the candidate's presentation at Sunday evening service or whatever, the local assembly may be persuaded to commit $250 to $750 or more per month in perpetuity for "the work."

Total dollar commitment targets are usually set by the mission society which reckons it knows how much an effective missionary will need in that particular place. The targeted amount is usually fairly generous and might include medical insurance, gasoline for a vehicle, literature, and perhaps the cost of making payments on house and property.

Effective candidates never reach their monetary goal. They keep inventing new needs and keep working the system for more money (i.e., "we need expense money for a new printing press, well, airplane, four-wheel drive vehicle, airline travel, etc."). Under this guise, the sky's the limit depending, of course, on one's skills as a salesman.

Once on station as a missionary, the smart adventurist will keep in mind that it is important to keep the home folks sold on that project (this applies to adventurers using either Plan A or B). The most common device used to accomplish this objective is a newsletter. You will also need to include lots of pictures and collect numerous pieces of native paraphernalia (such as clothing, spears, idols, dolls, and trinkets) related to the indigenous religion.

When I got to Africa, I was somewhat nonplussed to learn that the native dances that the missionaries so carefully recorded on film to be shown to the home folks were simply fertility rites used to work the women into a wild frenzy. When the ladies ran off into the bush, the men followed -- much to their enjoyment. (This part seldom makes the movies, at least not in a form recognizable to the home folks.)

Lots and lots of action can go with being a missionary. I was on a mission station that was flattened by marauding elephants. Another time we were unsuccessfully attacked by Somali raiders, while on another occasion I got to clean up after a successful attack on a Catholic mission located nearby.

Being a missionary requires that a person conduct himself in a circumspect manner whenever possible. One missionary wrote home complaining that life was awfully tough. He often had to sleep on the ground, he said. People at home with their automatic thermostats and warm beds should remember that the poor missionary had nothing between him and the cold hard ground except a poor little Indian girl. Needless to say, he lost most of his funding when that particular tale got around!

How You Can Do It

1. Talk to missionaries and read as much about the career as possible.
2. Decide whether this type of career sounds exciting.
3. Decide where in the world you would like to do missionary work. Survey the world for nice locations.
4. Develop a work plan for the area in which you wish to be employed as a missionary, emphasizing any grossly unmet social need.

5. Research the lifestyle of the people in the area in which you wish to work, as well as their needs and the topography; interface these with your proven skills.
6. Contact the country's embassy and travel agencies; look through pertinent magazines.
7. Research the visa requirements and likelihood of getting into the country as a missionary.
8. Develop a budget on which you know you can live.
9. Take your plan to philanthropic organizations and sell it to them.
10. Attend a Bible college or seminary.
11. Take the same plan developed in items 3 through 5 and take it to a denominational mission board.
12. Become a missionary candidate approved by that board to go out and look for funding to do the work you have proposed.
13. Begin some self-taught language training.
14. Once a station is set up, continue to inundate your supporters with PR.
15. Be alert to any new social and philanthropic opportunities and any new funding sources.
16. Use the time on the mission station to develop local business enterprises that directly relate to your skills, needs, and desires.

Peace Corps Volunteer

The scenario is a familiar one: a paunchy, middle-aged executive decides he has had enough corporate politics and company intrigue. In one, last outburst of mid-life rebellion, he decides he will do something exciting and daring for once and run off to join the Peace Corps.

Elsewhere, a divorced senior secretary in a dead-end job with nothing more exciting to look forward to than being hit on by the marketing department hotshots sees her adult daughter join the Peace Corps and head off to Belize to help with what she is told are desperately needed community projects.

The Peace Corps is something the executive and secretary both feel they need to put some excitement into their almost terminally dull lives.

Americans who are only mildly adventurous tend to think of the Peace Corps as the ultimate expression of their otherwise actionless lives. True adventurers, however, tend to dismiss such ambitions as errant, facetious dreaming on the part of those who have and always will lead dull lives.

In reality, the truth lies somewhere between the scorn of the hardened adventurer and the action-seeking executive going through a mid-life crisis. Peace Corps volunteers do have a pretty good shot at adventure, though there is no guarantee. But, after all, the likelihood of something interesting happening is greater in Ghana than it is in Grangeville or Charlottesville.

A job in the Peace Corps is in itself about as exciting as holding somebody's horse. The incredible aspect of Peace Corps work, however, is that nobody expects you to get anything done.

The situation is tightening up a bit but, in general, Peace Corps volunteers receive a smattering of language and cultural training, a free plane ticket, a handsome in-country per-diem allowance, free dental and medical care, a huge readjustment allowance payable on completion of one's tour, and that's all. Input is measured. Not output.

In return, the volunteer is expected to do virtually nothing, according to some accounts. There are few reports, absent superiors who seldom travel to one's duty station, few contacts with potentially whistle-blowing compatriots, or other points of accountability.

All this gives the innovative adventurist an interesting and secure platform from which to come up with his own schemes and ideas for getting on with life.

The concept is especially intriguing because the entrance requirements for Peace Corps volunteers are extremely relaxed. They are up a bit from the halcyon days when the agency actively sought out "generalists" with no particular skills to fill job slots that had no work description or specifically enumerated duties.

The Peace Corps came into being in 1961, the creation of John F. Kennedy. Its mission was to save the world and to boost American popularity abroad. Recruiters won't tell you this, but the Peace Corps has been thrown out of twenty-one countries, generally for gross incompetence and a general failure to produce any tangible results.

Not to despair, however. There are still sixty-three countries where Peace Corps volunteers are currently assigned. Some of these are pretty nice places with lots of chances for action; Nepal, Thailand, the Philippines, Sri Lanka, Ecuador, Kenya, and Honduras are a few that come to mind.

Application is made by writing to the Peace Corps, P-301, Washington, D.C. 20526. At this writing, the toll-free hot-line number is 1-800-424-8580, extension 93. There are fifteen regional recruiting offices throughout the United States, and you can find out which office is closest to you when you call the hot-line.

After application, the agency does a fairly extensive background and adaptability analysis on the individual in order to determine whether an applicant is likely to pull off the overseas assignment. Field analysts say their biggest chore is to weed out religious zealots.

About 10,000 people apply each year, of which an estimated 3,000 are accepted. Applicants who are passed over the first time can reapply and are often selected on the second pass if there were no deep, overriding reasons for their first failure.

Adventurers with a wide range of skills can be considered by the Peace Corps. As in any organization, requirements for employment cycle dramatically from year to year. Generally, one can be safest going in as some kind of agriculturist; foresters, fisheries specialists, ag engineers, animal health people, and ag economists are also in demand most of the time. Journeyman welders, mechanics, draftsmen, and machinists can also usually find work with the Peace Corps. Other professionals who are in demand include architects, planners, experienced builders, accountants, marketing people, health professionals, and teachers. Those already having a language skill are very much in demand.

At present, the hot language is French, and Africa is the place where most Peace Corps types are going. The Peace Corps does not, of course, demand or even care greatly about previous experience as long as the applicant is technically competent and adept at his skill. Previous foreign experience is appreciated but seldom encountered among volunteer applicants.

College is helpful but not necessary. People with the correct, needed traits can reasonably be expected to make it into the Peace Corps, but college experience and the demonstrated ability to do a specific skill would give one a lock on a job.

Married couples are now accepted if they do not have dependents. If one of the couple receives a nomination for a job, the other will go along as a special assignment volunteer. They both receive the standard per diem and both earn the regular $175-per-month readjustment allowance at the end of the tour.

Although handicapped people are accepted, one's health must otherwise be just about perfect.

Tours last two years. At the end of that time a total of $4,200 will be credited to an account back in the States. Since those working in the Peace Corps are not employees but rather volunteers, the $4,200 is called a readjustment allowance and not a salary. If, after two years, the adventurist decides he likes this sort of business, he can reapply and be given another assignment. Assignments are generally seldom made to the same place twice.

The Peace Corps likes its volunteers to be "mature, experienced" and twenty years of age or older. During the sixties, the average age was twenty-three; today it is about thirty. There is no upper age limit for volunteer applicants. (There are reports that an eighty-two-year-old still serves as a volunteer. He is on his eighth two-year tour, we are told, having started sixteen years ago when he was sixty-six.)

During the time a volunteer is on station, he receives a living allowance of approximately $300 per month and the use of a house and probably a car or truck (many Peace Corps volunteers use motorcycles).

Three hundred dollars per month plus housing, which is usually supplied, will allow one to live rather nicely in most places in the world. Contrary to the popular impression one has of the living conditions endured by the volunteers, Peace Corps volunteers do not live in abject poverty or in grass shacks among the natives. Most have servants and/or house girls, as well as telephones, flush johns, and American-style beds. Volunteers may live in isolation, but definitely not in poverty. (Three hundred dollars a month is more than the average yearly income for most residents of places where Peace Corps volunteers customarily volunteer.)

At present, there are about 4,500 volunteers around the world, and the federal budget cuts have put the kibosh on plans to expand the volunteer pool back up to 10,000. The high for the agency occurred in the early sixties when 16,000 volunteers were scattered around the globe. At that time, there were no job descriptions and no real firm idea as to exactly what the volunteers were supposed to do. Many simply got on the plane to their assigned country. When they got there, they jumped on a bus and wandered around the country till they saw a project they wanted to work on and stayed.

It sounds incredible today, but the first batch of volunteers to leave the States were given tennis racquets when they got on the plane. Peace Corps recruiters tell us that today things are different. Volunteers operate from job descriptions filled at the request of, and approved by, the host country. (The 1982 agency budget was $124 million.)

Efforts to evaluate programs have been downgraded. In that regard, there is little accountability for one's work. For instance, between 1980 and 1983, only seven final reports were issued.

Most volunteers seldom absolutely have to show up for work. An official report issued in Ethiopia during the sixties pointed out that "a sizable number of volunteer teachers make it to school about half the time." Volunteers in Venezuela were assigned only three hours of teaching duty per week! In Honduras, an official report concluded that "the volunteer appears to be someone with nothing to do. His skills are not utilized and the community doesn't know what he has to offer in the way of help."

These reports don't indicate what the volunteers do with the rest of their time. But one would have to conclude that there is plenty of time to do "whatever" in any Peace Corps regimen.

There are two areas of involvement that are absolutely forbidden to Peace Corps people. Any work at religious or espionage activities will result in immediate suspension. (I personally don't know of any volunteers who have either engaged in spying or any religious activities other than individual worship who have been fired.) Ex-Peace Corps workers, as a matter of strict policy, will never be considered as CIA agents.

It is estimated that 20 percent of the volunteers quit before their term is up, usually for personal reasons. (Having a girlfriend tops the list.)

The agency is quite proud of the fact that no volunteer has ever been killed as a result of terrorist or political upheaval. Volunteers are often killed in accidents, but never as a result of hostile activities. The most common fatality comes as the result of canning up one's motorcycle. So many Peace Corps volunteers have gobbled the road that it is now de rigueur to wear a helmet while out cruising on one's bike.

The most successful volunteer I know of is the guy who went to Korea to teach English to the Koreans. He had plenty of spare time, so he started to use the American APO system to air-mail leather garments back to the States. At the end of his two-year term, he had a good business going. It was done at Uncle Sam's expense for air-mail postage, but it supported him for several years while he readjusted.

The Peace Corps image in the United States is one of selfless volunteers giving up golden opportunities at home to spend two years living in abject poverty helping the natives. Professional PR types keep up the hype. They go any length to convince the taxpayers that this is really what these poor, hardworking people are all about. (Stories to the contrary abound. Volunteers in Togo, for instance, started a rabbit-raising scheme even though eating rabbits is a basic taboo among most Togolese tribes!)

Adventurers who aspire to a two-year hitch in

the Peace Corps must obviously develop another agenda if they genuinely want to be adventurously employed.

These additional goals could include a bit of salvage work, hunting, guiding, exploration, gold-panning, gunrunning, private medical work, and, of course, collecting commercial information.

Experience in the Peace Corps is not necessarily the key to a good job back in the United States. Volunteers I have known who have come back to the States have had problems mostly because they have become used to measuring performance in terms of input rather than output or actual production.

The Peace Corps concept has not gained international recognition. The Japanese sponsor a type of Peace Corps to build export markets and to establish business connections. For a time, the Israelis sent out Peace Corps volunteers. (The only one I knew departed the NFD of Kenya in a rush, leaving twelve pregnant girls behind!)

Still, the adventurist who wants a couple of years to collect his thoughts should at least consider the Peace Corps. It ain't where the action is, but it is a place from which to start some action.

How You Can Do It

1. Look at the Peace Corps' mode of operation and decide whether what it offers will fit your action career plan.
2. Involve yourself in acquiring the types of training and skills that the Peace Corps likes.
3. Check with the nearest university placement center, congressional office, or Peace Corps hot line for information, current requirements and an application form.
4. Go through the process of applying and being assigned a foreign post.
5. Go to the foreign post and set up housekeeping at Peace Corps expense.
6. Think up some sort of activity in which to engage while handling the otherwise dull Peace Corps assignment.

Photojournalist

Men who are looking for an action career who are also artistically inclined need not despair. There is a good action job available that takes artistic ability into account -- photo war correspondent. Unfortunately, it is also one of the more risky, dangerously demanding careers.

I have a good friend who was editor of the *Bangkok Post,* a paper renowned for its excellent photographs of the fighting on the Campuchean border and in north Thailand with the drug lords.

"Our photographers have a tradition of getting right out ahead of the forward patrols," he told me. "That's why we get great action shots, but we lose a lot of our people."

"I like to keep two or three new guys coming on the staff at all times," he explained. "We continuously recruit for promising (read brave) talent."

This sort of reasoning may only work in

Thailand where there is an abundance of people who are willing to take on work of this nature. Nevertheless, the same philosophy seems to apply to the Associated Press (AP) and most others who buy photographs. They just aren't as up-front about admitting that their need for action shots creates a feeling that the photographers are expendable.

My last experience with a fledgling photo correspondent was in the United Arab Emirates. We drove on the national highway from Dubai to Abu Dabi. On the outskirts of Abu Dabi we passed a military airport. Just then a Soviet-built Hind helicopter flew over.

"Roy," I said, "a shot of that chopper would make a great background photo for some of the stuff you are trying to sell."

We both cranked down the windows of the car and started shooting. I did two quick shots on 300 mm lens, rolled the window back up and put the camera under the seat of the car.

Roy slowly and painfully started to click off a long, long series of carefully orchestrated shots.

The driver of an Isuzu truck that was behind us started honking and blinking his lights.

He pulled up next to us and hollered something in Arabic. Our driver immediately turned into a parking spot and stopped.

The passenger of the Isuzu jumped out and hustled over to our car.

"Why are you taking pictures?" he asked Roy. "I am UAE CIA," he said. "It is forbidden." He held up a blue and green card that said CIA.

Roy mumbled something about not knowing that there was a problem with our taking pictures. The CIA guy asked who we were and what we were doing in the UAE. Until he saw our business cards, he refused to believe we were in the country to set up a seed potato program.

After he saw our credentials, he seemed to figure that we were nothing more than dumb farmers.

Next time around, we weren't so lucky. Roy and I hired a taxi to take us from Al Ahma Di in Kuwait up to Sabriyah on the Iraqi border. As luck would have it, it was the day the Iranians picked to launch an offensive against Basra.

We could hear the explosive thumps twenty kilometers down the road from the border. At the border, we could occasionally make out low-flying jets on the horizon.

I left my camera in the taxi. Roy, intent on coming up with pictures for his "client," jumped out and started firing away.

Right on cue, we heard a booming loud "Hey!" from behind us. "Not permitted! Not permitted!" the frantic border guard screamed. "No picture. No picture."

"OK, OK," Roy responded. "No more pictures. We are just potato farmers."

This time it didn't work. "Give camera! Give camera!" the guard hollered.

When the guard pulled his pistol out, Roy handed over his brand new Nikon F-3.

The guard swung it vigorously by the strap and bashed the camera against a rock, blowing it to smithereens.

Later, after everyone settled down a bit, I noticed that the rock was not a virgin. Other camera parts lay strewn about.

Even sans his camera, I had enough of Roy. Our next stop was Damascus, Syria.

I went alone.

Making a business of being an action or war photographer requires that one learn early on how to be at the right place at the right time, but to do so with some finesse.

Getting the right pictures is tough. Staying alive to bring them back is often tougher.

Doing pictures that news buyers will pay money for is far more of an art than most macho photographers want to admit.

War photo correspondents make a living in the business by selling photos on a freelance basis to international, national, regional, and local media. It is important to remember that the best technique is to attempt to sell to the widest possible market and then work down the system from there.

Good working photographers seem to have a

common thread leading to their nurturing and development. As a general rule, they start in high school as sports photographers. The experience seems to weed out those who are frustrated by fast-moving events and teaches them how to deal with such highly technical, intricate mechanical devices as cameras. High school sports photographers are also forced by the nature of the events they cover to recognize the vital necessary human element in their photography. Without this human element (pictures of people doing whatever they are doing), photo buyers are seldom interested. People and their relationship to an event are what photo editors feel is newsworthy. Unless one's photos graphically depict people and the emotion they bring to the event, they will seldom be purchased.

Sports photographers learn this all-important rule early on and are further encouraged by having their photos published.

They also learn that they are under intense time pressure to get the news photos. This whole news world turns on the most perishable commodity in existence. What may be in intense demand today may be worthless tomorrow. Pictures of Tip O'Neill voting "no" on President Reagan's 1982 budget are the best example I can think of how fleeting a timely photo can be; no one would buy that picture today.

The average home owner with a 35mm SLR trying to break into the business may never figure out this basic rule until it's too late.

Having published a few sports photos, the aspiring war correspondent will feel confident about carrying a camera while out making his rounds -- always in the hope that a photo opportunity will come along.

Good photojournalists are generally news junkies. They avidly read three or four newspapers per day, as well as all of the news magazines the day they hit the stands. This obsession with what is going on gives them a leg up when out looking for photos.

Luck and skill are not readily separable. If the situation clicks and the photographer gets a really good shot, he is on his way. No one really knows why or how it happens. Perhaps it really is skill. It can't all be fortuitous circumstances.

Local newspapers generally pay from ten to twenty-five dollars for a good news photo. Regionals pay from seventy-five to one hundred dollars per photo. As mentioned previously, the trick is to start with the largest market possible and work your way on down.

Phone the photo editors of the largest regional paper in the area. Tell them the shot is in the camera. Ask if they would like to look. If the answer is, "we will take a look," ask what their deadline is. Process the film and make prints.

If they say "sorry," try progressively smaller papers till you finally get a "yes." Don't bother the larger papers about photos that are definitely local in character, but try to concentrate on taking photos that are regional in nature.

After you have processed the film, make several five-by-seven prints of the best frames. Always take in a selection of three to show to the photo editor. You are far more likely to sell one photograph if you go in with a set of three.

Keep copies of photos sold, along with the date and place of sale. These should go into a permanent portfolio. Building up a portfolio of photos will provide you with an excellent sales tool when approaching national and international media buyers.

If action photography seems to be your forte, there will soon be a photo or two that was originally purchased by the local or regional papers that the wire services have picked up. Major stories, along with especially good photos, are almost always filed with the wire services by the local or regional media.

Good stuff will get picked up by the AP. Ideally they will call and attempt to negotiate a price for national use of your photo.

National media buyers may pay from $150 to $250 for pictures that are unique and tough to get provided the pictures have national appeal. Later on you will find that good war photos generally meet this criterion.

At this time, a published novice must decide whether news photography is the career to pursue or whether fixing lawn mowers is better. The neophyte who wants to continue must then sit down and think about places where news is happening that no one is covering. The Philippines, South Africa, and Lebanon are places that currently have an oversupply of both staff and freelance photographers on station. Competition in these places is fierce.

Instead, pick a place that's off the beaten track where your nose for news suggests stories are or will be developing. Sri Lanka, northern India, Somalia, and Eastern Turkey are places that come to mind, places where little wars are likely to break out that no one anticipates or is otherwise interested in.

Go to the Associated Press office in your city and ask to talk to the photo editor. By now you should know the people and the language and feel comfortable making a proposal.

Show the editor your up-to-date portfolio and tell him you are going to Timbuktoo, or wherever, and that you would like to bring photos in on a "show good" basis. If the editor agrees, ask for the name, address, and telephone number of their nearest office to where you will be working.

Emphasize that you are operating only as a stringer and expect to pay all expenses out of sales and that no retainer is requested. Assuming the portfolio has anything at all, the photo buyer has little to lose by cooperating.

The Associated Press has offices in virtually every major city in the world. In other places, it may be Reuters (an England-based international news agency) which is more difficult to deal with than other news services since it maintains few U.S. offices.

As soon as you are on station, stop in and talk to the wire-service contact.

Wire-service buyers generally want the right to a first-time use only. They may specify to whom the photo cannot be resold, but the issue may never come up. Photographers always retain physical possession of the negatives.

As a rule, once an agreement is reached, payment is made the next day in dollars or, in the case of Reuters, in pounds. Currency of the realm is seldom given unless it is specifically requested.

The freelance stringer must arrange and pay for the passport, visa, plane tickets, hotel accommodations, and other expenses himself. Places where there is action offer many opportunities for sales. The down side is getting a stake together for the trip and expenses to live on until sales are made.

A serious problem often comes up over the perishability of war photos. I got some super pictures of the New People's Army in the Philippines after they pulled a raid on one of my experiment stations. The shots were eminently salable except for one thing: I was on Mindanao, eight hundred kilometers from the AP buyer in Manila. A commercial flight took one hour, not including the two-hour cab ride to and from the airport. Cost of the ticket was eighty-nine dollars. Because of the time element and money considerations, I couldn't afford to go to Manila and make a sale. The Filipino phone system is and was so bad that there was no chance of calling and making other arrangements. As a result, I gave up on the project.

The only method to get around this sort of impasse is to call the photo editor and tell him what you have and ask whether he is interested. In my particular situation, even this option was not available to me since there were no phones.

You also need to know about deadlines. An editor who really wants to see the photo will usually find a way to get the pictures. News copy and photos move around the world by amazing means. Airline pilots and stewardesses carry them in pouches and pockets, special couriers can be used, and the material can be transported in suitcases. In the case of my Mindanao photos, there was absolutely no phone service and no way to contact the AP in

Manila.

Once the photo is in the wire service office, it can be transmitted any place in the world via electronic FAX-type machines. When using this machine, it is even possible for the wire service to sell and deliver a photo to one's hometown paper.

Another problem that a duffer like myself often encounters is with film. Because I usually sell to magazines or use photos for books, I always shoot color transparencies, and some magazine photographers also shoot color. However, virtually all photo editors still demand black-and-white prints.

Color is too tricky to process quickly, they say. The colors are not consistent, and color often does not provide the sharp prints that are standard with black-and-white film.

As a result, almost all war correspondents use Kodak Tri-X film. The professional trick here seems to be to always use the same film. Learning more than one film is an unnecessary chore that can lead to confusion when the action is hot and heavy, the experts say.

War correspondents need the usual complement of hard cases for their gear, and, of course, a huge quantity of film. Although film is available all over the world, problems arise with buying it abroad. Buying it is not nearly as big a chore as keeping it from being spoiled. Most pros use double lead bags and still never,

never run it through airport X-ray machines if they can help it.

The best that one can usually hope for is a fairly stable situation that will permit the photographer to set up a semi-permanent shop, perhaps with a local photographer or photography store, using his chemicals, equipment, and darkroom on a rental basis.

Equipment recommendations actually vary more than amateurs (who were brought up to believe professionals use only Nikons) would ever believe. I don't like needlessly complex cameras so I tend to remember professionals who share my feeling about the use of complex cameras. There really are a lot of them out there.

There is, however, agreement on lenses; it seems that 24, 50, 85, 110, and 150 are standard recommendations. The old aversion to zoom lenses persists.

War correspondents must develop a trick or strategy for getting into a war zone. It helps immensely to have had military training.

As most of my regular readers know, I have always posed as an agricultural expert and gone just about any place I wanted to. Once on the front line, being a farmer-advisor won't work; it is then a matter of who you know and who you can get to know.

This sort of effective cultivation of friends takes time and money. It is best done before the serious action starts so that everyone gets used to seeing your face.

Less-publicized areas where the stringer is first likely to assign himself have fewer news people, are less structured, and generally are easier places in which to work. Photographers who learn some small smattering of the local customs get along infinitely better than the newly arrived staff photographer sent on the spur of the moment from New York or headquarters.

After four to five years of this uncertainty, assuming you have made enough sales to keep the dragon away from the doorstep, it is time to think about a more permanent staff position.

The wire services hire proven, skilled photographers on a staff basis for $1,800 to $2,000 or more per month. These positions are nice because they also provide for daily living expenses and airline tickets.

Sometimes these daily expenses are really enormous. Photographers who learn to live off the economy can fare much better than the guy who has to depend on first-class hotels. The best, when it can be done, is to find a niche and live right with the military unit you are photographing.

A war photo correspondent's career can zoom ahead quickly on the basis of some really timely, unique photos or, alternately, if the photographer has some skill as a writer. Being able to provide a cut line that backgrounds the photo with information regarding the time, place, and name is essential. Being able to crank out a short written news piece to go with the photo is valuable.

When taking photos in to show the buyer, always have all the cut-line info available attached to the photo. A common trick is to take along a contact sheet showing other pictures in which you feel the buyer may have an interest.

Picky editors sometimes want to choose between vertical and horizontal shots to aid in makeup and layout. It's a drag, but that's the way these people are.

Cut lines should be typed if possible. In addition, the maker's name and local and U.S. address must be affixed to every print. Most photographers carry sticky tags for this purpose.

B&W processing using a portable change bag and sealed plastic wash can is often easier in the field than finding a warm meal or hot shower. There are several tabletop processing systems available that make this possible.

By the time a stringer gets to Timbuktoo, he should have this part of the business down as well as he knows how to use a gum-ball machine.

Even in remote places, such as northern

Burma, there are photo studios with cheap Japanese enlargers that one could use. Arrangements should be made before the day the important, critical shot comes in.

Anti-Americanism is often nowadays rampant wherever news is breaking. Stringers who are there first, can learn to speak a bit of the language, and take the time to make some initial friendships will have a much easier time than the guy who recently walked off the plane from New York.

How You Can Do It

1. Start taking pictures in high school and selling them to local papers.
2. Learn fast-moving sports photography and how to do film processing.
3. Learn the significance of the human element in photography and how to deal with time pressures.
4. Have a good collection of photo equipment.
5. Carry a camera with you at all times.
6. Become a news junkie. Read all the papers and news magazines you can get your hands on.
7. Start selling photos to local and regional papers.
8. Put together a portfolio of published photos.
9. Learn to use a desk-top or hotel processing system.
10. Thoroughly learn one film -- preferably Ko-

dak Tri-X.

11. Evaluate obscure places where news might break where news photographers are unlikely to already be on the scene. Locations where little wars are likely to occur are best.

12. Go to a regional photo editor and propose that you go to one of these places and work on a "show good" basis.

13. Go to the selected foreign station. On the way, stop in and see the nearest wire service office to introduce yourself.

14. Make contact with local military people.

15. Learn the local language and customs.

16. Befriend a local photographer so you can use his dark room and enlarger.

17. Developing skills as a writer will help sell photos. Practice writing.

Process Server

Becoming a process server is probably the easiest, most straightforward action career one can choose. One can be a process server virtually anyplace. All it takes is an intense will and desire; no military training, no knowing the right people. You don't even have to know the territory!

Process servers work in every area in which a sheriff has jurisdiction. The only prerequisites are a quick mind, attention to detail, and, at times, absolute fearlessness. An innovative and creative mind will help make the job pay much better. Sometimes it helps to be a strong runner, too.

Probably the largest single users of process servers are collection agencies. The neophyte who wants to take a run at the business could reasonably expect to pick up quite a bit of work by going around to the various collection agencies listed in the phone book and offering to serve deadbeats when the agency finally decides to sue. The neophyte would work on a contingency basis.

Collection agencies are especially good places to learn the trade because a high-priced process server can earn fat fees by finding people who know they are about to be hauled into court and are purposely laying low. At collection agencies, the process server can work with people who are expert "skip tracers," or people finders, to learn that business as well.

Contrary to popular wisdom, a sheriff does not have to serve a summons on people being brought into court. Many people, even county prosecutors, hesitate to use the sheriff's office because the deputies who usually do the work are awfully wooden about how they go about it.

The sheriff gets what are known as sheriff's instructions from the people who have filed suit in court. These instructions list the work and home addresses of the defendant and instruct the sheriff to take the papers out to the guy.

The sheriff is paid a flat fee -- usually about twenty-five dollars plus fifty cents per mile -- for doing the job. Problems arise when the guy isn't where he is supposed to be. Unless it is a major state case and the prosecuting attorney is pressing the sheriff to get the guy served, most sheriffs will make little or no real creative effort to find the culprit.

This is where the private process server comes in. He can peddle his services by being bright and persistent in finding the defendant and getting the papers to him. In many, many cases involving suits for business fraud, divorce and property disputes, this dedication to persistence is very important.

Situations vary a bit from state to state, so it is wise to check a code book in the library, or ask the people at the collection agencies you start working with. A summons is not usually legally binding unless you, the process server, personally hand the summons and complaint to the defendant. In a few states, it is adequate to drop the summons at the guy's feet if you are certain that you have the right guy.

Stories about process servers who have worked weeks to find a particularly bad apple, serve him, and then have their arms broken for the trouble are legion, and probably mostly true. I knew one lady who got all her front teeth knocked out performing a fifty-dollar service.

While I was working my way through college, I served process in particularly tough logging country in northern California. Late one afternoon, I finally found my man sitting home drinking beer and watching TV.

Usually, getting your target alone is safest since he then does not have a macho compulsion to show his friends how tough he is.

I knocked on the door and, when the grizzled critter came lumbering up, said cheerily, "If you are Mr. Smith, I have this envelope for you."

"I am Mr. Smith," he gruffed. "Who are you?" he asked.

I handed him the envelope, but he smelled a rat and dropped it.

"You son-of-a-bitch!" he bellowed.

I then trotted down the street, followed by an ongoing welter of curses. Those old loggers could swear for fifteen minutes straight and not repeat themselves. No matter, my man had been legally served, and I collected twenty dollars plus mileage which, in the above-noted case, was quite a bit.

Process servers who do their jobs well have knives pulled on them, and dogs and charges of bird shot will chase them down the street, but they will make money. Other than filing assault charges against your attacker, there is no special protection under the law for the process server. Process servers will find that the second-best clients are attorneys who, by and large, do not want to sully their lily-white hands with finding the subject of a summons. Attorneys will, of course, often prepare papers and sue someone. In a larger office, there may be as many as three or four suits filed per day.

After you, the budding process server, have learned the ropes from the collection agencies (most of whom work through retained attorneys), you will want to go around to all the larger law offices with a card and brochure listing the services you can provide and your general range of prices.

If the service is easy, attorneys will generally have the sheriff do it, unless you start out by working for less than the sheriff. In many localities, to do so is quite possible. Local budgets are so tight that fees for such services have raisen astronomically.

A sales call on the sheriff can do two things: you can thereby verify his fee structure and also sell the idea of your doing what most sheriffs really don't want to do anyway. You may be very surprised how often the sheriff will refer cases to you.

The one exception occurs when attorneys specify that the service must be made by a uniformed officer at 7 in the morning so as to have the greatest impact on the fellow's neighbors and, of course, his family.

Tough assignments which involve a lot of skip tracing skill usually run around $200, being as high as $350 or more per service. One's overhead for phone, restaurant meals and coffee, and auto expenses, as well as the value of your time just hanging around, can be astronomical when working on the hard-core people. Without exception, the big fees come from attorneys who don't care how much it costs to get the suit started. They simply add

10 percent to their client's bill to make up the amount they are to pay the process server. In that regard, the higher the better. If it's a dicey divorce and you do a particularly showy job, the client doesn't even care about how high the bill is.

Some of the toughest people to serve are businessmen who know what's coming and insulate themselves with four layers of receptionists.

Prosecutors and deputy prosecutors are the flip side of the process-serving business. They work for the city or county and often have very limited budgets. They expect the sheriff to do the job for free and will only occasionally use the services of a professional process server when they are really in a bind.

Unless the process server is very good and has an excellent reputation, he will seldom get work right out of the court system.

Serving is an excellent business for brave women who can run like hell. There is some prejudice against them that is fairly easy to work with, and a team of process servers will often include a woman.

The toughest part of the job is, of course, to find the guy in question. Women can do skip tracing as well as men, of course, and some successful process servers have secretaries who sit around and do nothing but skip tracing.

There is some travel connected with process

serving. Higher fees can sometimes be generated by going to a city after a defendant who has fled the scene. However, the most profitable method may be to contract with another process server in the city where your research indicates the culprit may have fled. Of course, referrals come in to the successful process server at an equal rate.

Other than an answering machine, automobile, phone, pad of forms with which to file a proof of service, a pocket full of business cards, and some photocopied brochures, the process server does not need any special equipment.

Anyone who is interested in a lot of action right around home can play this game.

How You Can Do It

1. Study the job of being a process server and make up your mind to go for it.
2. Work with a local process server on a pro-bono basis if necessary.
3. Have cards printed up.
4. Set up your own business after you know how the system works.
5. Get a telephone-answering machine.
6. Contact the collection agencies in your area to see if they have work.
7. Learn the skip-tracing business from collection agencies and books.
8. Research the state laws regarding process

serving.

9. Get some expensive locating and servicing processes for collection agencies.

10. Contact the sheriffs and prosecuting attorneys in your region, offering to work for them. Find out their fee schedules.

11. Visit all the attorneys in your region, leaving the copies of your card and fee schedule.

12. Do a quick, competent job -- especially on the tough cases.

13. Be very innovative about finding and serving the hard cases.

14. Learn to run like hell.

15. Provide your services over a wide area so that it is possible to make a living.

Private Eye

Demand for private investigators is growing at a rate far above the increase in the general population. No one knows for sure how many PIs work in the United States, but estimates run as high as 400,000 or more.

Some of these positions are on a part-time basis, but the pool is larger than virtually any other single action career. Men who like this sort of work and do reasonably well at it can certainly find employment.

Many regions, especially where the population has not grown, have no PIs at all -- presenting an ideal situation for the action careerist who wants to be in business for himself. In the larger, more populated areas of the United States, there are often several PIs or even PI companies employing a number of investigators. The novice private investigator can often get some training and a start at one of these places.

Many investigators work full-time for banks, credit bureaus, and insurance companies.

If private investigators are characterized by one trait, it is that they are detail people. The successful PI is extremely persistent, intellectually honest, and thorough. Those who prove they can keep their noses to the grindstone and can turn out credible work will make from $175 to $250 or more per day.

If a PI does well under cross-examination in court and is particularly adept in a relevant field or two (such as chemistry or forgery), he will be sought as an expert witness, thereby commanding much larger fees.

In times past, PIs were principally hired to gather evidence for tacky divorce cases. The stories about stakeouts waiting for the milkman, iceman, or studman are probably all true. In the last few years, this situation has changed so dramatically that only a small percentage of the PI's time is spent directly doing divorce-related work. (He may now more likely be locating property held by divorcing spouses rather than keeping tabs on unfaithful spouses.)

Today's PI will find employment by such customers as:

1. Insurance companies. Investigators do background investigation and claims verification, as well as arson and fraud investigation. In addition to the in-house investigators perma-

nently employed by the insurance company, a PI may work as a contractor out of smaller offices where the level of work cannot justify keeping a person on the payroll full-time.

2. Industrial tycoons. These people are businessmen who want to find out whether someone is stealing their secrets and/or selling shipping information. They also desire background checks on potential investors, large customers, and clients. Work for these people involves doing research in the down-and-dirty areas where these businessmen pay $250 per day to keep their hands clean while having lots of dirt gathered on the competition; for them, that makes a good day.

3. Retail stores. A PI provides training for and protection from shoplifting, hold employee bad-check seminars, uncover theft rings and cash-register scams, do background checks for key employees, conduct credit investigations, and may be involved in debt collections.

4. Banks. Banks will hire PIs to do background investigations, credit checks, property checks, vehicle locations and other work verifying information on credit applications.

5. Law firms. PIs do extensive investigations related to civil actions, background checks, property verifications, bank checks, skip tracing, divorce-related investigations, claims investigations, and many other information-gathering activities for attorneys.

Requirements necessary to qualify as a PI vary greatly from state to state. Some states have no requirements, while others want almost everything. Some say a PI must be at least eighteen to twenty-five years old, while others require U.S. or state citizenship and residence, surety bonds running up to $10,000, a complete lack of felony connections, three years' experience, high scores on a written exam, and the completion of a lengthy and detailed written questionnaire.

It is relatively easy to find the local requirements pertaining to PIs as enforced by state codes. Prospective PIs can contact their local sheriff, chief of police, or, better yet, the state attorney general, keeping in mind that many states have no requirements. A novice PI might be in for a pleasant surprise. Official requirements might be as easy as hanging out a shingle!

Regardless of state requirements, working PIs are universal in their agreement that a new investigator cannot hope to do a credible job of learning the ropes enough to be on his own in less than two to three years. It takes that much time as an apprentice to pick up the tricks of the trade and develop a nose for the job.

Apprentice work can be done with a local police department, as an in-house insurance investigator, or, in some cases, as a student of a local junior college.

Television shows notwithstanding, being a PI is often nothing more than painstakingly extensive, smart research. "Booze, guns, and broads" play only a very minor role.

A thorough detail man who finds the truth in the end is the one who makes the best PI. Most of the time, the work has to do with civil rather than criminal proceedings. It is not exciting, unless one really gets excited by doing research and writing lengthy reports.

Private investigators usually specialize to the point where they become expert witnesses in one area, ignoring all others. Conventional wisdom holds that specialization is fine but generalists are better, most especially those living in smaller communities.

PIs must work on the premise that there has been criminal intent and a criminal act has been committed.

Some years ago, a farmer insured a barn on a farm that he purchased for the land. All of the buildings were in good shape, but they were of no value to the farmer in question. Later, when the barn burned under suspicious circumstances, the insurance company tried to demonstrate criminal intent by pointing out that extensive insurance was kept on buildings that had no value to the insured.

A PI investigated the case and found that the fire had been started with diesel oil that had been splashed in a horse stall. He also showed that the farmer was in dire financial straits and that insurance money could have been used to pay long-overdue bills.

It seemed fairly easy, at least superficially, to show criminal intent. Showing criminal acts proved in this case to be another kettle of fish. The PI never did prove that the farmer certainly torched his barn, so the insurance company did what insurance companies are notorious for doing -- it stonewalled the farmer on payment of the claim.

PIs generally find that criminal cases, including the exciting homicides shown in TV programs, are handled by the police. At times, civil and criminal actions mix, but the action careerist should not get his hopes up unduly thinking that the two most definitely intermesh.

At times, PIs do work for attorneys which the attorneys take credit for. (Many times they work directly for lawyers who simply add 25 percent to the bill and pass it along to their clients.)

A small-town merchant who ran a sewing center was appalled when the tavern next door started featuring nude dancers. The owner called her attorney who, in turn, called in a PI. The PI thought about the problem a bit and then trotted up to the courthouse for a copy of the tavern owner's lease. He suspected that the lease had been filed with the county recorder and was a matter of public record. It took a while, but he eventually found the lease filed and recorded about twelve years earlier.

As the PI suspected, the lease specifically prohibited using the premises for immoral purposes. The attorney was credited with closing down the "public nuisance" after only two nights of operation. The out-of-state owner didn't even have to be contacted; he simply gave up. The folks in the community who were opposed to nude dancing thought the attorney was a genius. The PI simply collected his $400 fee for two days' work.

Because PIs do a great amount of research they must be aware of the rules of evidence, which state that evidence, to be admissible, must be relevant, material, and complete. There are numerous classes of evidence, including direct, circumstantial, real, presumptive, and hearsay. Good PIs will study the laws of evidence and may either take a police science course or two or, if they can manage it, attend an evidence class at a state law school.

PIs spend a considerable amount of time looking over public records -- either items of record at the courthouse or court records themselves. They must be comfortable with this process and be able to use it quickly and effortlessly.

Some records are only quasi-public. Permanent employment records are an example of material that is very difficult to acquire. On the other end of the spectrum, a person's file of traffic violations, including driving records and licensing documents, is available only if one knows whom to ask -- and in which office. Many times just having a person's Social Security number is enough to unlock the information drawer, but the combination of Social Security number, date of birth, and full legal name is much harder to acquire.

Developing a pool of informants or information sources at the licensing bureau and at the courthouse is important. This can be a major initial objective for the PI. Having a gregarious, outgoing personality will help in this area immensely.

At times PIs will do theft investigations for businessmen who may not want to undergo the embarrassment and publicity of dealing directly with the police. PIs who want steady employment find they must offer a wide range of services including crucial investigations under these circumstances. In this context, they must be able to work easily and comfortably with the local police. Often this is tough, as the police view the activities of the PI as an encroachment on their turf.

Good PIs conduct investigations that are objective, thorough, relevant, and accurate. Some especially adept individuals can do more at $250 per day than three $100-per-day men. Knowing how to conduct a proper search is extremely important. Either the PI will learn at school or, in the odd circumstance, out of a book. Most PIs think they have street sense -- resourcefulness and the ability to be observant as well as capable of making speedy, valid deductions.

Along with street sense, good PIs have a sense of propriety when it comes to writing reports. Good, thorough, lucid reports keep good clients happy, providing a never-ending cycle of jobs and income for the PI. PIs must learn that the only thing a client will often see is their report. It must be clean, neat, succinct, and very well written, containing all of the relevant information.

A PI should know which private labs do certain specific tests, chemical analyses, forensic ballistics, and other work a client may desire. This is especially true when the case cannot be handled by police or if the matter might involve police error.

Some PIs do fingerprints for clients, while others simply call in the police. In this, as in many other areas, the PIs may not actually do the job. Their role is limited to observing that the police or other professionals do an adequate professional job.

Because a PI's job consists mostly of research, few PIs actually carry a pistol. Many don't even learn to shoot. The only significant exception is when PIs are called in to provide or supervise security at a plant office or facility guard system.

Other skills most PIs find helpful are how to manage an interview, how to conduct effective surveillance, how to investigate possible fraud, and the old standbys -- skip tracing and forgery.

Skip tracing, or locating someone who has disappeared, could consume quite a lot of a PI's time, especially if the PI is particularly good at it and begins to get a reputation as a finder of people. It is as much an art as it is a science. Some people seem to be born to do it, while others never catch on.

In this day and age, a PI must have a good working knowledge of illegal drugs. Employers want investigators who will locate and expose illegal drug use among employees. Drug users, on the other hand, pay good money to keep from getting found out or to be sure the tests they submit to are fair and competently run.

As mentioned earlier, modern divorce laws have put an end to lengthy detailed investigations geared to determine who is sleeping with whom. The questions of opportunity and inclination pertaining to adultery have been replaced by the much more straightforward concept of irreconcilable differences. Today most people who want a divorce can get one without hiring a private investigator.

Besides skip tracing, or possibly as an adjunct to it, locating missing persons is a bread-and-butter item for the PI.

Some people will hire a PI to investigate auto accidents, especially if there is an insurance or licensing problem or if the official investigation goes against their best interests.

Action careerists who have undertaken the appropriate training by going to school or by working for the police, military, or a senior PI will want to strike out on their own. Before doing so, they must keep in mind that unless they train well, they may never be able to keep a client happy, much less build a business before advanced starvation sets in.

Probably the first hurdle a self-employed PI will face is lining up his insurance. Some states require a surety bond which says that you or the bonding company will pay $5,000 to $10,000 if so required.

Expenses for stationery, cards, and envelopes can be minimal at the start. These items can be purchased for no more than $200 in most U.S. cities.

New agents will have to advertise. The most effective advertising in the short run is to visit all the attorneys and insurance companies in the immediate area. Leave a card and a small brochure that has your letterhead. You may not have to do this for very long before jobs start coming in. Even if it seems as though there is no time in the week, take a few minutes to make a sales call or two.

Direct mail is rather costly at the start, but it is very effective (a reasonable cost is fifty cents each for brochures, postage, and labor, to send to potential business clients). Mail directed to this class of client is most effective since it is tough to arrange direct meetings with businessmen. Attorneys gear their business to handle drop-in clients; businessmen consider this class of people to be a real nuisance and will seldom see such clients.

Almost all PIs run an ad in their local yellow pages. These ads cost twenty dollars or more per month, depending on how much space one buys and the circulation (the charges are tacked onto one's monthly phone bill).

Many new investigators can spend a considerable amount of money setting up offices. Usually, but not always, a desk or a home typewriter with a file cabinet will do the job. Clients don't know when they call your number what location they are reaching. They just assume your office is adequate to get the job done. Palatial PR-oriented offices in the better locations can come later after the business starts making money.

Locating an office in one's home is cheaper and easier than renting office space, but it is only a temporary expedient. Walk-in traffic is nil at home, and really good, well-heeled accounts will doubt your ability without a good storefront office.

At the start, a PI can try to do most of his research at home in his office so that he can access the phone himself. Modern answering machines are very inexpensive and could be effective. However, many people really hate to use them. Answering services are slightly more acceptable, but certainly not that much cheaper than an answering machine in the long run. Good businessmen consider the alternatives and do what works best in their area.

Most investigators own a car and a camera. Use of the car constitutes a major expense. Sometimes mileage can be built into one's fees. In cases where driving is costing more than simply going to the courthouse, the agent will have to negotiate transportation charges into the service contract.

Good PIs use a contract, or at least draft a letter of intent, setting out what is desired, how in general the business will be conducted, and what the fee will be. Then they go to work using a diligence and expertise the client does not have in order to come up with the needed information.

How You Can Do It

1. Contact any local PI companies to see whether they are hiring and the specific experience they are looking for.

2. Take courses in police science at a local junior college or from a correspondent school.
3. Sign on with the local police department, the military, or a local investigator to gain experience.
4. Develop a particularly good skill in one or two areas of investigation.
5. Discipline yourself to be able to do good, in-depth research. Learn to write good, clean, concise reports.
6. Develop a list of banks, credit bureaus, insurance companies, attorneys, and businessmen who might be clients in your area.
7. Develop a stable of information -- cooperators at the licensing bureau, courthouse, and credit bureau, for example, who can help with skip tracing and other information, documents, and research.
8. After two or three years, open your own office.
9. Have stationery printed, a private phone line installed, and put out a simple brochure.
10. Market your services in person to people who expect walk-in clients.
11. Do a direct mailing to those who may otherwise be tough to reach.
12. Apply good business practices and procedures to your business. Make investigation your career.

Repo Man

A career as a repo man is a truly interesting, action-filled occupation that does not require a college degree, very much special study, a lot of money to start, or, for that matter, much of anything else. A very nimble mind, an innovative spirit, and balls like Batman's are what's needed.

The first time I attempted to repo anything was with a hyper young attorney. I was managing a law firm/collection agency/credit bureau for a conglomeration of lawyers of which this fellow was part. As is true with all too many newly ordained lawyers, this guy was hungry to do virtually anything to make a buck. As a recently ordained office manager, I was anxious to do whatever the man who signed the checks wanted.

In this case the bank still owned the vehicle so that no legal niceties were involved.

When making a pickup to satisfy a bad debt, for instance, the holder of the debt must sue the debtor, take judgment and then get out a writ of attachment in order to legally pick up a deadbeat's goods. The goods must then be held for auction by the sheriff who will deduct expenses and turn the proceeds over to the creditor.

In the case of bank-financed consumer goods, the bank retains title to the stuff and can have it picked up under terms of the contract after giving proper notice any time payments are not made. Anyone who wants to go into the repo business should check with the holders of the contract on the goods and state law regarding this entire activity before proceeding so as not to be hit with a felony warrant for improper action. As a general rule, various states will have similar laws, but, of course, the serious repo man will check the appropriate code section before going into business.

But let's get back to our pickup truck in the little village in north central California. We located the vehicle, which is very often the real core of a repo-man's job.

Like so many other action occupations, repo men must be excellent skip tracers. They must learn to use court records, past employers, ex-spouses, relatives, and whatever else their fertile imaginations can drum up to find their man and the goods he holds. The rules for effective skip tracing are varied, but always include a huge measure of stick-to-it-iveness.

About nine Saturday morning the two of us boldly marched up onto the guy's porch and beat on his door. When he appeared we told him we had to take the truck in because of non-payment and would he please give us the keys.

In many, many cases the repo man does not sneak in and steal the item back. Instead he will call the person in possession and make arrangements to come by and get the goods. This is universally true with items such as furniture and appliances and usually true with vehicles.

Contrary to popular opinion, repo men do not always limit their work to picking up vehicles. Some go after motorcycles, travel trailers, snowmobiles, furniture, dishwashers, airplanes, tractors, and a host of similar items. They can work for car agencies, banks, finance companies, or any business that may have guaranteed a loan on a big-ticket item for a financing group such as a financial institution.

Repo men must have lots and lots of courage, plus a line of bullshit like a used-camel salesman. The goal is to talk the victim out of his goods without further ado. Sometimes, but not very often, an owner will deliberately take a tough line on a vehicle and purposely try to hide it from the finance company. Then the real professional skill of the repo man comes into play.

However, in one instance after another, the repo man will get an assignment simply because the owner can't or does not know how to find the location of the goods even though the owner may not be hiding.

There is also the situation in which a client does not want to get his hands dirty with such matters. Businessmen turn bills over to collection agencies because they don't like the down-and-dirty aspects of going after deadbeats. Loan officers at banks also don't like the business of going after cars of people who haven't been making their payments. Remuneration or a repo man is usually calculated on a sliding scale pegged back to a targeted amount per hour. Most people in the business try to come in at twenty-five to forty-five dollars per hour, including phone time and charges, pickup vehicle use, helpers, drivers, insurance, and other attending expenses.

Getting a vehicle back will usually run the financing institution from $200 to $400, depending on where the work is performed. Charges in larger cities sometimes are higher, but the competition tends to be more severe so that no one ever gets to ride a gravy train. Picking up a travel trailer, motorcycle, boat, or snowmobile is usually done by the owner. This keeps the amount a repo man can charge down a bit, but $50 to $100 to bid and bring in the goods is common. Repo men make a comfortable thirty-five to fifty grand a year if they hustle.

Repo-ing motorcycles is tough. Many times this becomes a specialized business in and of itself. Most companies don't try to repo bikes, since it just isn't worth the expense.

As in our case, asking for and getting the keys to a vehicle is the usual pattern. People usually want to cooperate, stories to the contrary notwithstanding. Repo men like to brag about the tough deal they put together or about the little chickadee with the Corvette who parked it at her boyfriend's house so no one would find it. As the tales go, the smart repo man found the rig in the dead of night, put the wheels back on, opened the door, pulled the steering column lock, and hot-wired the ignition. He got the rig for the bank, he will say, under almost insurmountable circumstances.

Most good repo stories basically follow this line. But in the real world, one does not usually have to go to all this trouble once the vehicle and current holder are located. This depends a great deal on the place in the country where the repo man is working.

Whenever we had a vehicle to nab where the owner would not surrender the keys, we used a little gin pole outfit on a pickup to set the front wheels on a dolly, which we pulled in to a garage so that we could work on the vehicle at our own leisure. That way we could open the doors by making a key from code without tearing up the ignition lock and scarring the panels and windows.

Owner finance companies want their vehicles brought back in as good a shape as possible. Most repossessed vehicles are in horrible shape from user neglect. They have a low resale value and the general public is conditioned not to pay very much for this type of vehicle. In that regard, the repo process is a no-win situation for both parties.

Repo men are generally fair locksmiths. There is a lot to the locksmith business in and of itself. The occupation alone probably can't be classified as an action career but a good, solid knowledge of locksmithing can open doors (pun intended) for the action-career-oriented man.

A skilled locksmith working with a complete inventory of coded keys and sophisticated smithing tools has a very real advantage working as a repo man. The best way for a novice repo man to learn forced entry and field-expedient ignition-lock mechanics is to get a good book and go to a junkyard to play around with the vehicles in a context where damage is not serious if done.

But back at the repo site that fateful Saturday morning. With pickup keys in hand, we walked back out to the pickup that was parked in front of the guy's house. Fortunately, the rig was parked backward on the street, with the steering wheel on the street side away from the house. It was a good thing that it worked out that way.

Like most professional repo men, we had a photocopy of the vehicle title. I opened the truck door and started to check to make sure the serial number and color matched the title copy we received from the bank.

Our guy apparently went into a quick brood about the injustice of us just driving away with his beloved truck, snatched up a shotgun, and came bellowing out onto the little porch of his house. He was about thirty to forty yards away and slightly above us as we crouched on the street. His bellowing warned us, however, so we ducked down in time to miss the shot he fired.

About half the Number 4 shot whizzed on over the top of the rig, while the other half dippled the passenger side of the rig. My guess is that the noise of the shot in town deterred the guy from firing a second round. It got a bit tense crouched down behind the rig, not knowing whether he would resume shooting. Later in the day, we had the sheriff pick up the shotgun, a Remington Model 1100, which we then turned over to the bank as seized collateral.

Most regional areas and large cities have at

least one or two repo men working the vicinity. Aspiring repo men, as well as curious action careerists, might try contacting those already in the business to see whether they would accept help on a volunteer basis.

Once having spent a little time working the trade, it is easier to see whether you really like this type of work and whether this is the business you eventually want to get into.

A repo man needs a small office (one in the house is fine), a telephone with an answering machine, a stack of business cards, some statement forms, a set of locksmith tools, coded keys, and forced-entry tools. That's about all it takes. Getting started is not expensive.

Once the business is in the black, extras could include a small truck with a winch and gin pole. Some sort of vehicle will be needed to get out to the scene of the repo. The family car, which is what most repo men use when they start, works fine for this purpose.

An assistant to drive you to the vehicle to be picked up is a necessity; this can be a girlfriend, high-school student, friend, or spouse.

Finding work is not all that tough. Almost every branch bank will have about twelve or fifteen vehicles it needs brought in each year; collection agencies often do eight to ten per month unless they are very small or very lazy.

In the case of collection agencies, private

repo men will often be competing with the sheriff's office. Usually, sheriffs don't like to pick up vehicles and will simply call a wrecking company to pull the rig in when they get this business. This is both expensive and destructive. Good repo men have, in that context, a good chance to be competitive.

The freelance repo artist will have to develop rate schedules which include charges for mileage, charges for forced entry, skip tracing, touring, and costs for other elements of the job. Be sure to offer similar rates to the competition or, if not that, at least better service.

Other potential clients are car agencies, leasing companies, trailer-sales outfits, finance companies, and anyone doing big-ticket sales. If you want to go around and pick up furniture and appliances, you might go around and leave cards with people who sell these items. Generally, however, this business is small and pays relatively poorly.

New repo men have to build lists of clients. They do this by visiting the major users of their services throughout the region in which they want to work. Some associate with other repo men in larger cities; they put together a multistate service group that handles a large volume of rigs.

As part of his ability to deliver professional services, the repo man must develop and cultivate a list of friends in various courthouses, auto licensing offices, local sheriff's office, and various police departments.

It is a business that requires a huge measure of professional skill, lots of contacts in the correct agencies and offices, no college, little capital, and no formal training!

How You Can Do It

1. Locate a repo man in your area and go to work for him as a driver.
2. Take a locksmith course or read some good books on the subject.
3. Practice forced entry on some junkyard cars.
4. Decide to set up your own concern.
5. Pick a region in which to work where the competition is not intense.
6. Have cards and letterhead printed up.
7. Put a desk in a spare room in your home, along with a file cabinet and phone. Install an answering machine.
8. Develop a list of contacts in the licensing bureaus, county sheriffs' departments, and at the collection agencies.
9. Develop a standard pricing sheet.
10. Learn how to do effective skip tracing.
11. Map out a marketing program, taking a couple of weeks to visit the various banks, finance companies, auto dealerships, leasing companies, big-ticket item sellers, and others for whom you want to do repo work in the area

of your choosing.

12. Go into business. Offer good, prompt, and courteous service.

River Rafting Guide

Picture-taking out of the way for the moment, our guide motioned us down off a rocky lookout high above the confluence of the Snake and Salmon rivers back to the raft tethered below. Our mission today was to take a few pictures as we let the wild river sweep us along through the nation's deepest gorge.

People talk about the wonder of the Grand Canyon, but that hole in the ground pales in comparison to Hell's Canyon in Idaho. Although only purists realize it, Hell's Canyon is almost a mile deeper than the Grand Canyon.

Guiding dudes on wild rivers can be exhilarating as one fends his way through massive boulder-strewn waterfalls with millions of tons of frothy, wild water cascading over them and the indescribable beauty and tranquility of nature in its primeval state.

Working as a rafting guide for an outfitter or, better yet, as an outfitter contains the elements that many action careerists look for in the perfect life.

The challenges -- both mental and physical -- are very real. Successfully running rivers is much like quarterbacking a football team. One must plan and scheme continually, or the opposition will win. Some very hard work is involved, but one's ego is continually stroked by the very, very appreciative people one is escorting down the river.

Wild rivers have a way of taming otherwise harried, hyper people. High-powered executives used to barking orders at a bevy of secretaries find that they might as well surrender to the river's relentless flow.

As a general rule, they learn to respect and admire the boatmen who guide them and tell them interesting stories about the history and geology of the river. The fifty to eighty-five dollars per day the boatmen earn garners more healthy respect than these men's attorneys who often charge that much per hour!

Major business problems come into sharper focus and are more easily and logically solved over a glass of river-chilled wine and a thick, juicy campfire steak. The boatman's land is one without phones, of course, where the river always sets the pace. In this place, Mother Nature's laws are inviolate.

Every day she puts on a new show. Coyotes howl, beavers splash, bobcats sneak along the bank, otters play in the water, and the living is truly fine. Possibly in part because of its therapeutic value and certainly due to our rising affluence, work on our nation's wild rivers has become big business, a business that is complex and not well understood. The days when an average citizen could walk in and spend $3,500 for a surplus raft and rowing rack (you need two or three surplus rafts, as well as oar sets, rowing racks, and decks) and go into business as a guide/outfitter are gone forever.

The actual use of wild rivers today is tightly controlled by private landowners (where private land is involved) and the appropriate federal agencies such as the Bureau of Land Management (BLM), National Park Service, Forest Service, and the Bureau of Indian Affairs. They control how many private and commercial use permits are issued, how the rafters get in and out of the river, and where users can camp or picnic along the river.

These public agencies are under federal mandate to minimize the impact on the public resource and to maximize the quality of the experience for all citizens. They do this by sharply limiting the number of permits issued during the popular months of July and August on the high-demand, more famous wild rivers. They also issue directives regarding fire building, hauling of waste material, types of temporary shelters that can be erected, and the qualifications of those who haul dudes for pay on the rivers over which they have jurisdiction.

The feds are also charged with the duty of collecting a 3 percent user fee. Accurate books must be kept by the outfitter so that the fees might be assessed on a regular basis.

There are three major routes by which an action-career man can get into the rafting business. All are fairly difficult and, to an extent, uncertain. They absolutely must be viewed in the long term.

The first way is to make a pile of dough someplace else besides on the river. Such activities as gunrunning or bounty hunting, for instance, may provide enough money to buy out an existing outfitter who already has the necessary permits from the landowner/managers. The cost of a buyout will depend on the length of time the business has been operational, number and quality of clients, the permits and permissions to run rivers the operator/outfitter has, the popularity of the rivers and the amount of equipment the outfitter can throw in on the deal. The cost may reflect equipment, office buildings, and homes, and may run from $15,000 to one million dollars or more!

The second, less-costly method is to locate a section of river on which no one is currently operating commercial tours and begin operations there. This method is difficult because it entails building up a clientele and simultaneously publicizing the virtues of that particular river segment (i.e., everyone knows about the virtues of the Colorado River through the Grand Canyon, but who knows about the Murtaugh in Idaho?). This building process is much like starting any service-oriented small business. Considering that there aren't many unclaimed wild rivers or even segments in the continental United States, the distances to Alaska, and the short river-rafting season, the prospects of finding a new river are not all that good.

Nevertheless, the method is a valid one. Adventure careerists who are especially good at publicity and at generating stories in national magazines might give this gambit a try. It will take a small amount of money to buy equipment, but the capital acquisition can be done in small, easy stages as the business builds.

It should even be possible to combine river rafting and guiding with other businesses, such as hunting and fishing guide, process server, pest control, private investigator, and repo man. As with any business, the goal will always be to make the venture self-supporting and self-sustaining, as well as to provide a pleasant way of life.

Colorado, Washington, Oregon, Utah, Idaho, Montana, and Arizona all have at least small segments of rivers that have not been "discovered." Any of these might be open to a new guide/outfitter. The question to consider is whether these small segments or a collection thereof can actually generate enough business to support the outfitters and his hired help.

Discovery, at best, won't be easy. Most commercial operators are continually looking for "other rivers" on which to float customers in order to take up the slack from the big-name rivers that rapidly fill each year.

Having located a river, the new outfitter must go to the appropriate local management entity (public or private) and work out a user arrangement. Sometimes this is easily done; in other cases though, it can be a bureaucratic nightmare.

The third, and most viable, method to break into this trade is to work for an existing outfitter as a boatman, with an eye to eventually buying out the outfit.

Forest Service and BLM rules say that novice rowers must float the river on which they will operate at least three times before they can be certified to take people on that river for pay. Insurance companies have similar rules.

Like many other businessmen in the United States, river operators worry about losing their liability insurance. Insurance for a concession holder is a major item. Most pay $50,000 and up per year for a package which includes vehicle insurance, liability insurance, and workmen's compensation for the boatmen.

This amount is followed closely in magnitude by the expense of buying fuel for the rigs and, of course, groceries. Depending on the size of the operation, these costs can exceed $50,000 per year as well.

Outfitters have a liability waiver they ask people to sign. They cannot get a general umbrella policy without it. All liability insurance must name the appropriate federal and/or state agencies as co-holders of the policy. This is meant to preclude individuals from joining the government and the outfitter in any action. Government agencies closely monitor commercial float operators to ensure compliance with the insurance requirement.

Action careerists who have a better-than-average line of BS and are good with people have the best chance of initially hiring on as boatmen. In addition, they must be physically fit, able to work at hard labor for long hours, and possess knowledge of one or more of the following jobs: camp cook, storyteller, historian, photographer, fishing guide, camp mechanic, and geologist.

Outfitters agree that they won't hire a boatman who is not extremely amicable, an excellent camp cook, and knowledgeable about first aid. Other skills are nice but not absolute prerequisites.

Men who are going to apply for jobs with outfitters can find which outfitters are working which rivers by contacting the appropriate state departments of tourism. These departments are all found in the state capitals. Some also have branches in the chambers of commerce in larger cities. A phone call can do it, or you can write.

Once having received a list or, even better, the brochures of the outfitters, the aspiring boatman can pick the ones that look best and make application. It is definitely helpful to have dinked around with rafts on a river or two before going to the outfitters with the idea of employment. Action-oriented men who have friends with rafts should not miss an opportunity to get in a bit of private experience.

Most outfitters try to do an absolutely outstanding job with the food they serve, explaining why every employee must be an excellent bullcook. Outfitters start out with high-quality groceries. Their desire is to capitalize on the ravenous appetites river rafting can produce, with meals that people remember the remainder of their lives.

In some places, the governing agencies will not allow the outfitter to cook over an open fire. In that case, guides must take charcoal and/or propane stoves along on which to cook. On some wild rivers, campfires can be made, but all the ashes must be removed as part of the pack-it-in, pack-it-out program. Day-to-day handling of these requirements is usually left to the boatmen.

On the popular rivers, the Forest Service or BLM will often sport trash bins and portable potties around as an aid to the floaters.

It will cost you $20 to $150 per day to float wild rivers, depending on the popularity of the river outfitter and the level of amenities he offers.

Professional outfitters will figure a minimum average of six dollars a meal for groceries, including the cheaper breakfast and lunch meals. Day trips which include only lunch are, of course, less expensive for the outfitter to put together.

Outfitters who have several river packages to offer, ranging from numerous one-day events on a variety of rivers to several four- to six-day trips, have a better chance of making it financially. As a practical matter, this might entail buying out two or more existing operators along with their respective concessions. That way, a livable unit that will support the operator can be put together. (Boatmen who are working their way up through the ranks will soon become very aware of these financial restraints.)

In times past, it was common for boatmen and outfitters to be natives of the western states where most of the wild rivers they ran are located. Recently, Easterners with money have seen river-rafting expeditions as ideal means of making a living in the nicest possible context. As a result, both boatmen and outfitters can be found coming from all over the States.

Equipment needed by outfitters for use by guides includes obvious items, such as rafts and raft accessories, plus some not-so-obvious stuff. In some places, for instance, it is permitted to use outboard motors on the rafts to speed them downstream through places where the waters are placid, calm, and often a bit boring. Little 10 hp outboards will run another $1,500 each (and one has already spent $4,500 for a new raft and accessories!).

Camp stoves, grills, fire boxes, and tent flies are not, in the total scheme of things, that expensive. Most outfitters buy several and get by for less than $1,000.

Trucks and trailers used to haul equipment are very expensive items; sometimes a less expensive pickup will work, but many river outfitters find they like larger flatbed trucks better.

Customers must be met at the airport or at the trail's end and delivered in good condition to the river. This requires that one use a van or small bus. Buses can cost up to whatever the outfitter wants to pay. Bus insurance constitutes the major portion of the liability insurance bill in many cases.

Other equipment includes such items as food

coolers, waterproof personal gear carriers, dozens of bright-orange commercial-size life jackets, hundreds of rubber binders, cots, ground cloths, and, of course, sleeping bags. Pots and pans are an expensive item because they get beat up and fire-blackened so quickly.

Most outfitters and guides worry more about rattlesnakes, bees, and scorpions on shore than they do about dangers on the water. Skinned shins and barked ankles from scrambling over wet rocks are a constant hazard. Sunburn seems epidemic on some trips.

Action careerists who are physically fit and have some camp-cooking experience and first-aid skills should contact a guide outfitter about a summer job. If they like the business, they could stay on in the fall until business dies down for the winter. If all goes well, the guide could be on deck again the following spring.

Like many action careers, river rafting must be viewed as a lifelong vocation, not a temporary hobby. The business must be viewed for its long-term potential.

The boatman/guide may find it is best to look around for an outfitter who wants to retire in a few years, and work for him until he knows the ropes and can then buy the outfit.

Having once gained his initial experience, the guide may find he has to look around a bit for an available outfit.

Other means and ideas are fun to consider,

but are really not practical in this day and age. River rafting is so popular that there just ain't many other opportunities except for you to work your way up.

How You Can Do It

1. Brush up on first-aid and camp-cooking skills. If necessary, get some professional instruction.
2. Borrow a raft from a friend and run a few rivers to gain experience.
3. Become knowledgeable in such areas as fishing, game lore, history, or geology so that you can be a more interesting and more employable guide.
4. Contact the state director of tourism in Montana, Oregon, Idaho, California, Washington, Arizona, Utah, Nevada, or Colorado for the names of river outfitters operating in their states.
5. If possible, contact those river outfitters by phone or, better, in person, about hiring on as a boatman.
6. Convince the outfitter to give you a job.
7. Make the obligatory three training trips on your outfitter's river. Do as many different rivers as time will allow.
8. Learn the business end of the job (insurance, grocery shopping, equipment repair, and people and equipment movement).
9. Learn the BLM and Forest Service official

procedures.

10. Move around from outfitter to outfitter until you find one who might sell out in a few years.
11. Begin the process of buying out an outfit.
12. Promote the business well and run it to your customers' satisfaction.

Rodeo Cowboy

In times past, rodeo cowboys spent most of their considerable spare time drinking in bars, womanizing, and, when the time was right, brawling.

Rodeo riders were considered to be a bunch of macho lowlifes who participated in a show rather than a sport. As a general rule, rodeo cowboys came from the farms and ranches of the West. Without such a background, it was virtually impossible to break into the business.

The changes in the sport have, in the last twenty years or so, been so dramatic that rodeoing now presents one of the greatest opportunities ever for the action-oriented individual who is also a very good athlete.

In 1985, there was a total of $15.87 million in prize money awarded to the 6,000 or so cowboys in the business in North America. The thirty or forty top individual winners in the trade were pulling down about $150,000 per year.

In times past, a rodeo cowboy faced a long,

dreary, demanding life on the road as he gypsied from place to place in a pickup truck pulling a horse trailer.

Even this has changed. The 350 full-time professional rodeo cowboys in the United States today are more nearly jet-setters than they are itinerants going down the road wherever fate takes them.

By flying around to major rodeos, modern professionals hit more money-paying events, earn more, and, because of their many continued widespread appearances, become popular, well-known superstars. Earnings and recognition may match those of many basketball, baseball, and hockey players.

Circuit-flying cowboys still use excellent, well-trained horses. The era of dragging the poor beast around from city to city has also passed from the scene. Some events, such as saddle-bronc and bull riding, do not require a horse. For other events, such as calf roping and bulldogging, professional horse suppliers at the rodeo provide for the use of mounts, usually for a percentage of the cowboy's winnings. Like their riders, the professional horses perform better as a result of the decreased stress of travel and the increased opportunities to compete.

Better-trained, more-experienced horses are now right there on the rodeo circuit for any experienced cowboy to use. This situation is especially fortunate for the new guy trying to break in who cannot afford to spend thousands of dollars for a suitable, well-trained horse.

You don't have to grow up on a stock ranch to learn the rodeo trade. Anyone who is an especially good athlete, and is immune to pain, pulled muscles, and broken bones can make it as a rodeo cowboy. The occupation is wide open and, of all action careers, is probably the most potentially profitable. This will be especially true as the purses get larger and larger. (One champion bull rider, Bobby Del Vecchio, started in the Bronx by knowing a rodeo-stock provider there who let him do practice rides whenever he was inclined.) Neophytes can also get some initial practice and experience at riding clubs, summer camps, in stockyards, and even in many big-city police departments.

Opportunities to ride are more numerous today than ever in the United States. Ownership of horses is extremely widespread. Statistically, there are more horses now than during the time when they constituted our major means of transportation. Most of these horses are seldom or poorly ridden; as a result, they become gimpy (just the kind of semi-broken stock on which young, aspiring riders need to start their practice).

Contractors who provide bucking stock for rodeos have increased in number, along with the dramatic increase in rodeos in general.

Because of the trouble and expense involved, bucking stock is no longer hauled from the West for specific events. Local providers are much more numerous than outsiders would ever suppose.

Champions commonly offer numerous seminars and training sessions throughout the States in which virtually anyone with the few dollars it takes to register can participate. Since much of rodeoing is very technical, these seminars can be invaluable to the newcomer. The sessions are widely advertised in the many horse and rodeo magazines available on any newsstand. Such sessions provide extra, off-season income for the pros and instant access to expert training for the new rodeo rider.

Because of the greatly expanded interest in rodeos and horses in the States, many high schools -- even in urban areas -- now have rodeo clubs. These clubs often organize rodeos or at least send teams to scheduled rodeos. Amateur rodeos by the thousands are held throughout the States. Some are strictly youth rodeos, limited to the non-professional sixteen- to eighteen-year-olds; popular "little britches" rodeos cater to even younger kids. Besides the regular bull-riding, saddle-bronc, bareback, calf-roping and team-roping events, the amateurs often include steer riding.

Like many other sports, one can get in the

circuit at virtually any point his drive and talent will allow. If, at the first levels, the adventurer finds that participating really charges his batteries, he can attend some of the pro seminars and, depending on talent and drive, work up to the more-demanding pro-circuit rodeos where the real money is.

Registering as a rodeo rider is deceptively simple. The act is accomplished by taking out a $145 permit with the Professional Rodeo Cowboys Association in Colorado Springs, Colorado, allowing the holder to participate as an apprentice rodeo cowboy. Some of the popular rich rodeos of the 630 held each year in thirty-nine states are not open to apprentice cowboys. Most of the hundreds of other rodeos outside the Professional Rodeo Cowboys Association circuit are more than happy to have as many permit holders as possible compete.

Once a permit holder earns $2,500 in prize money in one year in any type of rodeo, he can pay another $105 in fees and then become a full-fledged member. Full members can compete in any rodeos open to pros but are, of course, barred from the youth and team nonpro events.

Rodeo riding is dangerous. Pulled muscles and broken bones are very common. Pros claim they are happy to be able to ride six months per year during their peak years (nineteen to about thirty-three). The mid-thirties are about the top limit for competition in the rough-stock bull-riding, saddle-bronc, bareback events. Roy Cooper, a champion money winner in 1986, was born in 1955. The registrar at the NRCA (National Rodeo Cowboy Association) said she could only think of two active members in their forties who still rode "rough stock." Calf ropers and team ropers often compete well into their sixties in these less-bruising events. A professional association also exists for women rodeo riders. However, the NRCA sanctions only barrel racing for females.

Mother Nature has endowed Brahma bulls with an especially nasty disposition and, of course, great size (1,800 pounds is common).

Bucking bulls are so large and so hyper that they give off an odor recognizable up to fifty feet away. As soon as they are taken from the holding pen and trapped in the crowd chute, one of the handlers starts sticking an electric stock prod up the bull's bunghole. The bull's eyes then roll round and round, literally turning red. (Humans who have had this happen to them haven't lived through it, the stock prods are so powerful.)

All a rider has to hold onto is a piece of rope wrapped around the bull's middle that is called a bull rope by people in the business. I can't think of a more fitting name. At the whistle, the gate swings open, and all hell breaks loose. There are bulls on this earth that have never been ridden the allocated eight seconds.

At the second whistle or buzzer, the rider is free to bail off and escape any way he can. Once you are on, the only way off is to be bucked off. Bucking bulls don't have an elephantlike memory, but they do seem to remember the electric stock prods, the riders, and, to some extent, the clowns who try to distract them (most try in the most determined sort of way to kill these three classes of people).

My son rode bulls on the amateur circuit for a few years. It always amazed me that anyone, especially my own flesh and blood, would voluntarily drop down on such enraged beasts.

"Why don't you," I often pleaded with my son, "pick some more traditional line of not-so-dangerous work? Maybe something like underwater demolition. Gunrunning. Bill collecting for the Mob, or whatever!"

I found the argument worked best if I presented it just as my son was about to drop onto the enraged bull in the squeeze chute.

Finally, one day as he gimped off the field, he told me, "Dad. You are right. I quit."

He did, too, but it took two months for the pulled muscles to return to normal. Now he chases dope runners in long-range helicopters in the Caribbean.

How You Can Do It

1. Start young to ride whatever stock is available. Seek out opportunities to ride wherever they might be.
2. Strive to make arrangements to ride and train pleasure horses for people who normally ride little.
3. Join high-school rodeo clubs if possible.
4. Practice roping at home in the backyard.
5. Seek out local bucking stock and take every opportunity to ride.
6. Keep physically fit by running and pumping iron.
7. Attend as many rodeo seminars conducted by experts as possible.
8. Save your money to buy saddles and bridles.
9. Rodeo in youth and little-britches rodeos whenever possible.
10. Attend as many rodeos as possible as a spectator.
11. Join the Professional Rodeo Cowboys Association as an apprentice permit holder.
12. Work as a field hand in rodeos when possible.
13. Work your way up to the $2,500-in-prizes category by participating as often as possible.
14. Take out a full membership in the NRCA and go to rodeos.

Secret Service Agent

Captains of British ships of the line during Nelson's time had a reputation for absolute fearlessness. It was their custom as their vessels sailed into hell, to exchange short-range broadsides with the enemy, to walk the quarterdeck in an exposed, unconcerned, and nonchalant fashion.

The Secret Service agent may be one of the few modern equivalents to this old and honorable tradition of staring death in the eye without blinking.

Who can forget the TV footage of agent Dennis McCarthy as he unlimbered his Uzi during John Hinckley's attempt to assassinate President Reagan? With incredible coolness, he inserted the magazine in the weapon, extended the stock and levered back the bolt -- all the while looking for additional bad guys as Hinckley was wrestled to the ground by others.

On November 1, 1950, two Puerto Rican nationalists attempted to shoot their way into

Blair House where President Truman was in temporary residence. They were engaged in a desperate pistol duel by police private William Crawford, who just two months previous had fired 300 bull's-eyes with 300 consecutive shots on the incredibly difficult Secret Service range in Beltsville. He was aided by privates Donald Birdzell, Leslie Coffelt, and Joseph Downs. At least twenty-seven shots were fired in less than three minutes.

Agent Stewart Stout, who was stationed inside the Blair House, could see one of the would-be assassins through the window firing from the Blair House steps. Calmly, Stout walked over to the inside weapons' cabinet and took out a Thompson submachine gun. Carefully and deliberately, he positioned himself in the center of the hall, covering both the door and the inside stairs and elevator.

It was the unanimous opinion of the Board of Inquiry that even in the unlikely event that the pair of assassins had succeeded in shooting their way past the gate guards, they would have been summarily wasted by Agent Stout and his ready Thompson.

The U.S. Secret Service has an intensely proud tradition. It is charged, by a congressional mandate, with protecting the president and vice president and their immediate families. Former presidents and their wives or widows are also protected, in the latter case, until remarriage. The Service is also charged with the security of visiting heads of state and with guarding major vice-presidential and presidential candidates.

Providing security for our leaders is a relatively new duty for the Secret Service. From Day One, the Service was only responsible for enforcement of American counterfeiting laws. During the War Between the States, it was estimated that one-third to one-half of the currency in circulation was counterfeit.

At that time, there were about 1,600 state banks designing and printing their own notes. Each note carried a different design, making it tough to detect one of the 4,000 varieties of counterfeit notes from the 7,000 kinds that were genuine.

Government officials hoped that the problem of counterfeiting would be solved when, in 1863, a national currency was adopted. However, even then, counterfeiters circulated so many bogus notes that it became necessary to take enforcement measures.

Counterfeiting is again rampant in the land -- not only of currency, but also bonds, stamps, U.S. government checks, and computer fraud perpetrated on the direct-deposit system. All these areas are responsibilities of the Secret Service.

In the past, the service has also been called on to investigate the Teapot Dome Oil Scandal, the Ku Klux Klan, and government land frauds, and to perform counterespionage duties during the Spanish American War and World War I.

During World War II, the Service took responsibility for the safekeeping of several precious documents including the Declaration of Independence and the original copy of the U.S. Constitution.

President Abraham Lincoln set up the Secret Service on April 14, 1865, when Secretary of the Treasury Hugh McCullouch told the president that more effective measures were needed to fight counterfeiters. The president asked if McCullouch had any suggestions.

"Yes," McCullouch replied, "I think we should have a regular permanent force whose job it will be to put these counterfeiters out of business."

President Lincoln agreed and said, "I think you have the right idea. Go ahead and work it out your own way."

No mention was made of the possible protective role the Service might eventually play which was unfortunate since that same night John Wilkes Booth shot President Lincoln while he was watching the show at Ford's Theatre.

In subsequent years, the fortunes of the Secret Service rose and fell to a great extent in sync with the willingness of Congress to provide funding. For the next ten years, agents were rewarded with a twenty-five-dollar bonus upon conviction of any counterfeiter clearly traceable to that agent's efforts.

When President McKinley was assassinated in Buffalo, New York, in 1901, he became the third president to fall to an assassin in thirty-six years. Public opinion quickly mobilized in favor of better, more professional guard service for our leaders. The Secret Service, being the nation's only general law-enforcement agency at the time, was a natural for the task.

Congress directed the Service to protect the president and, in 1906, legislation was enacted making presidential protection a permanent Service responsibility.

The duties of the White House police force and the Secret Service were kept separate until May 1930. On May 13, an alleged sightseer walked past the White House guards and Secret Service into the dining room where President Hoover was eating dinner. Upon investigation, it was found that the incident occurred principally because the two groups were under separate command. Satisfactory arrangements between the White House police and the Secret Service had never been worked out relative to admitting guests, both groups said.

By July 1, 1930, the Secret Service had assumed responsibility for what today is called the Secret Service Uniformed Division. This outfit's sole function is to provide protection for residents of the White House. These people are some of the best-trained, most highly motivated uniformed police in the world. They are the ones who successfully duked it out with the Puerto Ricans on November 1, 1950.

The Secret Service today has more than 3,500 employees, including clerks, computer programmers, police officers, and more than 150 field agents.

At present, recruiting for new agents is in a laid-back phase. The Service claims it has more applicants than it can do security clearances for, or even for which to find vacant slots.

The names of those who do clear are currently put into a pending file till a vacancy turns up. Once chosen, the new recruits are sent for training to the Service's specialized center in Glynco, Georgia. Applicants are expected to have a bachelor's degree, be younger than thirty-five but older than twenty-one, and have two years of experience in criminal investigation.

Any field of college study is supposedly acceptable, but preferences seem to be given for electrical engineers, research psychologists, armourer engineers, communications technicians, forensic lab technicians, and experts in the area of printing, inks, paper, and photocopier identification. Computer operators and programmers are also actively sought by the Service.

The Service runs an extremely specialized department that is unique in its ability to identify fingerprints from paper stock. Anyone who has any previous experience in this area could be a serious candidate.

Like so many agencies, special emphasis is now being placed on knowledge of languages; those fluent in Spanish, Italian, or French will all receive especially additional consideration.

Previous military training is a plus, but unless the applicant worked as an MP or in the CID (Criminal Investigation Division), the experience won't count heavily.

Training conducted in Glynco, Georgia, includes a strenuous program which includes instruction in the rules of evidence, surveillance techniques, undercover operations, courtroom demeanor, police procedure, police-community relations, basic criminal law, first aid, and laws of arrest and search and seizure. Firearms and physical fitness training, including physical defense techniques, continue at an intense rate throughout the agent's career.

Firearms training is done at one of the most sophisticated ranges in the world, located in Beltsville, Maryland. This unique range has twenty-four indoor shooters stations where daytime and nighttime conditions can be simulated. The one-hundred-yard outdoor range, used for rifle, submachine gun, and shotgun practice, has twelve firing stations. Agents also train on what the Service calls a vehicular range. This range is actually a facade of buildings equipped with twenty-five movable hit-sensitive targets having audio shoot-back capacity.

Three life-size targets move along a running man track directly in front of the buildings. A total of twenty-eight targets portray people in diverse situations holding a variety of weapons. All are operated by a small computer programmed to make the targets suddenly appear at various windows or doors, hold for a second or two, and then disappear. Some targets simulate return fire if not immediately fired upon.

It doesn't take much imagination to appreciate the fact that agents that get a chance to play around a bit on this range are absolute hell on wheels in a shoot-out.

After completing the course, agents are assigned to the field offices for three years for on-the-job training. All of the agents will live and work in the Washington, D.C., area during part of their careers.

The Secret Service is unique in that it has a liaison office in Paris, France, and that agents seldom stay in their assigned field office for very long. Field agents are continually being pulled from their offices for special, temporary assignments someplace else. These assignments are usually for temporary protective duty of visiting heads of state or traveling American leaders.

Computer records are kept as to which agents are proficient horseback riders, skiers, motorcycle riders, surfers, or possess other such special skills needed at the time. Whenever a foreign dignitary comes to the States, the Secret Service in Washington, D.C., will run its computers to see who is available with the correct skills to watch the VIP without looking obvious. Action-career people who like lots of movement and diversity will find this part of the program to be most enjoyable.

Investigation of counterfeiting during an election year is chopped back to an absolute minimum because so many agents are assigned to protective duty. Given the surge in counterfeiting-related crime brought on by the widespread ownership of high-quality printing equipment, the situation is said to be of a most serious nature. More funding is needed so that more time can be spent dealing with counterfeiters, the Service says.

Other current duties include investigating credit-card fraud, bogus bank paper, and the fraudulent use of some of the 700 million checks the government issues each year -- all crimes that are said to be increasing in number and intensity in the United States, adding to the Secret Service duty burden.

In addition to providing physical presence for the people it is protecting, the Secret Service also does extensive work in the field of protective intelligence. This duty involves the collection, evaluation, coordination, and filing of data regarding people it seeks to protect and those who are likely to want to harm them. Secret Service agents collect files, follow up on tips, and do wiretaps on crazies who are likely to want to do violence to the people they are charged with protecting.

In 1975 the Secret Service had an operating budget of $95 million. Starting pay for field agents is about $22,000; standard government medical, dental, and retirement plans are provided.

The Secret Service is an extremely elite group, of which it is very difficult to become a part. The waiting list is long and the training rigorous. However, the rule of thumb for almost any organization is that it will rotate its people on about a one-to-one basis annually. In other words, a group like the Secret Service having 3,500 employees will, in any given twelve-month period, hire another 3,500 as people retire, quit, or otherwise rotate.

This estimate may be somewhat high but, nevertheless, illustrates the fact that applying is not a complete waste of time for people who fancy this work as their type of action career.

Action-career-oriented people who want the

ultimate in varied, interesting assignments should call the nearest field office for an application form.

The work is about the most varied and exciting one would be able to find working for a regular professional organization that provides a regular paycheck.

How You Can Do It

1. Check with the nearest college recruiting office for current information as to which disciplines the Secret Service is currently looking for.
2. Plan a college major in that field.
3. Work hard enough to finish in the top of your class.
4. Plan your military career to include work as an MP or in the CID.
5. Keep yourself in good physical shape.
6. Learn a foreign language if possible.
7. Keep your act clean so as to pass a security clearance.
8. Make application to the Secret Service.
9. Undergo security checks and wait for an opening to occur.
10. Begin training at Glynco, Georgia.
11. Transfer to Washington, D.C.
12. Go through various field assignments until a permanent station assignment is made.

Skydiving Instructor

Jim Anderson, my favorite used-car salesman, has a wonderful story about parachuting.

"I took twenty-seven plane rides," he says, "before I ever landed in one of the damn things. On my twenty-eighth jump, they scrubbed because of high winds at the DZ [drop zone]. I thought the wheels fell off the Dakota it was so rough on that grass strip when it landed. I am glad to report that I now know firsthand that planes can and do come back to earth."

Jim's story is obviously an odd perspective on the conventional wisdom that only fools jump out of perfectly good airplanes.

Because military jump training has become so widespread, significant numbers of people have found that jumping really is fun.

The origin of the usage of "rush" or "high" is not from the drug culture as many believe. It is instead from what happens mentally when one slips out the door of a plane in flight.

Jumping, or skydiving, has an enthusiastic following, and only an estimated 15 percent of the jumpers have had previous military training. The message that jumping is fun came originally from the military people (who got to try it on an involuntary basis!).

Interest in sport jumping has really billowed since World War II. Up until that time, the equipment was so bad that 1.5 to 3 percent of the jumpers were expected to end up as casualties. Civilians participating for fun don't generally like those kind of odds.

Jumping is still perceived as being very dangerous and is, in fact, quite risky. Because of many radically new equipment designs, however, the risks are seen by many as being acceptable. Statistically, most jumping fatalities today occur as a result of aircraft malfunction on takeoff. Most parachute jump planes are notoriously poorly maintained.

Many such planes have only the most basic instruments and radios. They tend to go long periods with little maintenance, and jump pilots tend to overload their machines badly trying to get as many people up to jump altitude as cheaply as possible.

Risks notwithstanding, enough people of all ages want to try at least one jump so that the demand for jump instructors is actually quite high. Unlike many other action careers, jump instructors find that they do not generally have to root and hog for their existence. In the case of a skydiving instructor, making a reasonable living will not be entirely dependent on how well he sells an offbeat or seldom-needed service, such as explosives handling or even stunting.

As is true with any instructing, the teacher must be able to understand human nature and to appreciate people, their wants, needs, and unspoken desires. On the other hand, no special education is required. A college degree would only help insofar as young, affluent, college males are ideal-paying customers for skydiving instructors (perhaps with a B.S. degree, the instructor could meet more people in this potential market group).

Best estimates indicate that there are about 25,000 active skydivers in the United States today. Out of a population of 225,000,000, such a number does not represent many people, but it is a fairly large pool in which to market a service.

The number of people who have actually gone through jump school, jumped just once, and quit, is much higher. An estimated one million people make their first jumps each year in the States. This class of jumpers is the average instructors' bread and butter and would constitute a major source of income if they could only be kept actively involved in the sport.

In some places where the combination of weather and topography is particularly ideal, up to 30 percent of the young males in the area have made at least one jump. Unfortunately, a large number is satisfied with this one jump. Only about 20 percent of the first-time students come back for a second jump. Good jump instructors try to psyche out their students so they do continue on with the sport, thereby doing a huge amount of recruiting. Starting jumpers with big egos can be programmed to do a bit of bragging to their friends, who might feel they want to give the sport a try.

The ideal combination of factors needed at the location of a jump school includes fairly warm, cloudless days for most of the year; gentle, consistent winds; and a modestly high-incomed, younger generation. It is important to be away from big cities, where there is a lot of air traffic. Running a jump school near a larger metropolitan area can result in nothing but headaches.

Texas, Arizona, and some parts of California and central Florida are areas where jump schools are very popular.

Like many action careers, jumping appeals to the young and daring who have money to spend on rush-inducing frivolities (such as skydiving!). Work as a jump instructor is available to just about anyone who can pass the physical, starve and deprive himself in order to raise the money for the requisite number of jumps, and who likes the sport so much he can't possibly live without it. Like everything else, dedication counts ninety points to start, especially when getting enough jumps to qualify for an instructor's rating. There is no way to tell ahead of time whether a person will be turned on by jumping, but many are in a mighty way. The first step to becoming an instructor is to become a sky diver.

A great deal of elitism exists in some places regarding the number and types of jumps one may have made. Types of jumps include those made into water, at night, in higher winds, with both round and square chutes, and those made close to targets.

The United States Parachute Association (USPA), 1440-P Duke Street, Alexandria, VA 22314, is the official membership organization for U.S. sky divers. It is a division of the National Aeronautic Association, which in turn represents the Federation Aeronautique Internationale of Paris.

Membership in the USPA is open to anyone who applies and pays the $32.50 registration fee. Membership is not an absolute requirement for either the student or the instructor, but due to the elitism involved, most students join the USPA early on.

Taking a first jump will entail going to ground school and complying with the basic requirements set up by that instructor and the local school (these requirements are usually the rules set out by the USPA).

The instructor is the one who, using USPA materials, does the classroom instruction for novice sky divers, while the jump master is the hands-on person who actually accompanies the students on their first jumps. He is the local organizer. Even seasoned jumpers will elect a jump master from their ranks to oversee the details of getting the plane aloft and the people out the door. The instructor and jump master are often the same person.

An instructor must have two hundred jumps, attend a USPA two-day seminar, and pass a written examination. Manuals and course materials are provided by the USPA.

There's a twenty-five-dollar instructors' rating fee, a ten-dollar fee for class materials, and an instructor's fee that is set by negotiation between the student seminar attendees and the teacher.

Some schools are actually clubs or cooperatives. There is little difference between them other than the cost of club memberships and the fact that equipment rental and plane fees may be a bit less at a club.

The first jump costs around $120, depending to a great extent on where it is made and how active a club is operating in the region. The fee will cover ground school (the instructor will get about twenty-five dollars of this sum), equipment rental, and, of course, the plane ride. Instructors for such groups do fairly well financially if the area is large enough to support fifteen to twenty first-time students per week on a regular year-in, year-out basis. The weather must cooperate, of course, and not shut down the operation for very long.

Jumps number two through perhaps six will cost progressively less money. The neophyte will still need an instructor as part of an increasingly smaller and more elite, more trained group. Instructors here will find that they can expect to get fifteen dollars per student or fifteen dollars per hour, whichever the market will bear.

USPA rules state that a jumper can stop using an instructor after he has completed twenty-five free-falls. New jumpers can also be signed off of student status by the instructor whenever he feels the student qualifies.

Equipment rental will cost from fifteen dollars to twenty-five dollars per jump, depending on the region of the United States in which you are jumping. Clubs sometimes have less expensive rentals.

Equipment for sky divers, as compared to many other sports/occupations, is actually quite minimal. It will include a certified parachute and reserve, jumpsuit, helmet, and at least one altimeter. If the club or co-op does not have equipment, the skydiving instructor will have to put enough equipment together to at least make a planeload of jumpers.

By federal law, the pilot of a skydiver's plane must also wear a parachute. Very few pilots have chutes, comprising another expense that the instructor must contend with if there is no club to support him.

There are two parachute designs: round and square. Round chutes are more difficult to manage and are seldom used unless the diver absolutely can't find or afford a square chute or he wants to try the old methods of jumping for nostalgia or for training purposes.

Modern square chutes are easier to control and to use to precisely hit a landing zone (LZ), and can descend much more slowly. They are, however, more dangerous near the ground where mishandling can cause them to stall out in a fashion similar to what happens to the wing of a plane.

Because square chutes descend slower, and one can pick his LZ with much more certainty, jump boots are no longer a critical item of equipment. People can, and often do, jump in nothing more than thongs held on by rubber bands. Expensive jump boots are more of a vanity item used mostly for show.

Buying a completely new square chute with reserve and harness will cost about $3,200. Good round chutes, because of their limited popularity, can now be purchased for from $400 to $600. Used square chutes can often be had for $1,000 to $1,500. Like other sports, vanity enters into the buying deal; jumpers are turned on by the latest, most showy gear.

Socially acceptable jumpsuits cost about $150; altimeters, $80 to $120 depending on type and quality.

The USPA is a self-policing, self-regulating agency. According to its rules, no one under sixteen years of age is permitted to jump, principally because it is impossible for those below the age of sixteen to sign a liability waiver even with parental or guardian consent. There is no upper age limit for jumpers. Many fifty- to sixty-year-olds take their first jumps, probably too late in life to try to qualify as instructors.

Jumpers keep a detailed log, which contains more information than is required of pilots. Dates, number of jumps in progression, type of jumps, and type of equipment all are listed. Each jump must be verified and signed off by the jump master instructor.

At about six to eight jumps, the aspiring instructor can begin to make his jump arrangements on his own. According to USPA requirements, he must be under the supervision of an instructor up until this time. Even after eight jumps, the neophyte will usually work closely with the instructor, adding materially to the instructor's income.

Commercial flight organizations charge about one dollar plus one dollar per thousand feet of altitude the plane climbs to haul jumpers, which works out to about eight dollars per jump. Clubs sometimes own their own planes and charge slightly less for their services. Jumps are made as close to 10,000 feet above ground level as possible. Regions of the country where the airport or drop zone is 5,000 feet or higher above sea level are not popular with jumpers because it takes too long for an expensive plane to get to a proper altitude. To the cost of this service, the jumper must add the cost of equipment that he purchased or rented.

Jumpers and instructors must hold a current FAA (Federal Aviation Administration) medical certificate (either class I, II, or III) and a physician certificate showing that the holder is physically fit to sky dive. A USPA medical statement should also be filled out and kept current by the jumper. An instructor will have to diligently accomplish all these.

The first two medical certificates are provided by doctors in one's home area who have been approved as medical examiners by the FAA. Most communities have one or two rated MDs to service the needs of private and commercial pilots as well as sky divers.

Aspiring instructors must stay on course with

a program to make as many jumps as possible and as quickly as possible. At twenty-five jumps, the sky diver moves from an A-class rating, attaining a B rating once he has done fifty jumps. At one hundred jumps, the sky diver can be rated as either a C-class sky diver or as an instructor; at two hundred jumps, he can take another physical as prescribed by the USPA and a written test to become an instructor/examiner. Prospective instructor examiners also must attend a two-day (weekend) training seminar given by the USPA in addition to the two-day course for the regular one-hundred-jump instructor.

The written tests are structured to verify the taker's knowledge of USPA regulations and are based on a study book issued for that purpose by the USPA.

USPA-rated instructor/examiners give the tests. These people can be found in most medium-sized and large cities in the United States. Jumpers working their way up the ranks will soon determine where the closest instructor/examiner is located who can sign them off. The USPA can also make arrangements for the FAA to administer the instructor/examiner test.

The test is exhaustive. It is designed to test for a working knowledge of the regulations and to wash people with weak knowledge of the sport out of the program. Few people pass the written test the first time. After a waiting period, they take it again and can even take it a third time if necessary. After three failures, it is necessary to reapply and pay the fifty-dollar registration fee again. After the test, the instructor/examiner will verify the score and sign it off for the taker. The testee must send the document, along with the appropriate registration fee, to the USPA in Alexandria which will then issue a certificate.

This test is the last one and is as far as an individual can go with certifications. At this point, the instructor is on his own to sell his services. In the course of collecting two hundred jumps, he will have figured out where he could profitably instruct and if there is a particular club or jump organization for which he would like to work. In many cases, the really ambitious instructor may opt to start his own jump school.

Jump-school owner-operators make most of their money by pushing groups of first-time students through their programs on a weekly basis. In that regard, a shrewd operator will be certain to locate his school where the demographics, weather, and operating terrain are as optimal as possible. (A school in the heart of Miami, for instance, would undoubtedly sell well. There are plenty of young men with money who are potential attendees, but the air traffic in the immediate area is so intense that there would be little chance of getting FAA approval to drop jumpers on a regular basis.)

Jump instructors who are otherwise good businessmen will intuitively know that they must perform a valid, workable marketing plan and pay close attention to details. There are an estimated 2,000 to 4,000 instructors in the United States today, but fewer than 150 instructor/examiners, making the field wide open for instructors/examiners.

Dedicated skydiving instructors who like the sport and who work at it will make from about $30,000 to $100,000 per year, the latter being the top unless the sky diver organizes meets, endorses products, and does demonstrations at an intense level. Some especially adept individuals will put together a combination of benefits and really make a lot of money, though most instructors think $100,000 per annum is a perfectly reasonable goal.

Although the business is self-regulating, the FAA does license parachute packers. Two grades (master and senior packer) exist.

A senior packer rigger must have packed a minimum of twenty parachutes (the three most common being back, chest, and seat) of the specific type for which he is being certified. A written log must be kept for at least two years after the last chute is packed. A fairly tough written exam administered by the FAA must be passed at each grade level.

A master packer is one who has packed at least two hundred parachutes in the previous three-year period and has passed the appropriate FAA exam.

Packers have a lead seal-affixing machine used to seal the parachutes they have packed and use a mark specifically assigned by the FAA. (Most skydiving instructors are also parachute packers.)

If the students will patronize his services, it is not absolutely necessary to be rated by the USPA to be an instructor. However, a packer must be rated and certified by the FAA. In addition, an instructor must have his physical examination documents in order. There are no exceptions to these rules.

My first experience with sky divers was at the county fair back when I just earned my private pilot's certificate. The local fair committee offered two sky divers fifty dollars each to make a jump over the fairgrounds -- hoping, I am sure, to attract a bigger crowd. The ploy worked much better than we would ever have supposed -- thousands came to watch.

Fifty dollars each seemed like all the money in the world back in those days; after all, I got a penny a bale when bucking bales and a dollar per muskrat hide.

I was flying a Piper Tri-Pacer at the time. It infuriated me to find out that if I hauled these guys it took a special FAA approval to take off without the right side door in place. Having secured the necessary approval, I flew them to the fairgrounds about twenty miles away. It was a bit of a chore to locate the fair and then to call in the exact location to center to get permission to drop. Today I would use my dual VORs to triangulate my position but I am sure that old Tri-Pacer never ever packed dual NavComs in its entire life!

Having secured permission, found my DZ, and reached 10,000 feet above sea level, it was time for "bombs away!" Without so much as a word, the two were out the door and gone. It took me a week to get over the horribly odd sensation of having my passengers suddenly disappear out the door in flight!

How You Can Do It

1. Call the nearest airport where private planes are kept and ask how to locate the nearest skydiving or jump school. Expect something of a runaround because pilots don't usually like sky divers. Be polite and persistent.
2. Call the local skydiving instructor to get information on taking his first jump course.
3. Do the ground-school training.
4. Get your flight physical as well as doctor's certificate, and fill out the USPA medical card.
5. Do your first jump.
6. Take additional lessons and make addi-

tional jumps.

7. Carefully keep your flight log.
8. Find a certified parachute packer who can show you how to pack parachutes.
9. Keep a log of your parachute packings.
10. Investigate buying new and used equipment, making purchases as finances permit.
11. Join the USPA.
12. Try to get as many jumps as possible.
13. Take the USPA and FAA tests as you make twenty-five jumps and twenty packings, as well as subsequent tests.
14. At one hundred hours, attend the instructor's weekend seminar and pass the necessary tests.
15. Keep your eye out for an ideal location for a new school and/or location where you would like to teach where there is little competition.
16. At two hundred jumps, take the instructor/examiner seminar and test.
17. Keep buying additional equipment.
18. At two hundred jumps, when you get your last rating, start a jump school.
19. Run as many first jumpers as possible through your school.
20. Do sports endorsements insofar as possible.

Soldier of Fortune

In times past, a soldier of fortune was considered to be a fellow who was happy to take life a bit at a time, always attempting to be where the action was. The term was often used in a negative sense because such a man was considered to be erratic, hard to predict, and a ne'er-do-well.

During the last few years, we have narrowed the definition to mean a person who goes to an exotic land to fight a war for somebody else, usually for pay. Because virtually all wars today are fomented by the communists, an American soldier of fortune will usually find himself fighting those under the domination of the hammer and sickle.

Americans seem to operate more out of a sense of justice and adventure than out of a personal debt they want to settle. Americans reading this book who become soldiers of fortune will most likely do so due to a desire for adventure rather than any deep-seated personal hatred of communists or their own political beliefs.

In this regard, opportunities for men who simply want to go and fight are endless. On the other hand, there are relatively few places on earth where one can go to sign up to actually be paid to fight as a front-line soldier (Rhodesia was the best example of such a place).

During the war in Vietnam, a surprising number of Canadians, French, Germans, and Swiss who wanted adventure mixed the chance to shoot communists with the opportunity to earn U.S. citizenship by enlisting in the U.S. Army.

Today there seems to be relatively few such opportunities throughout the world in spite of the fact that a number of fairly hot wars are raging in a score of places. Wherever this fighting goes on, it is being undertaken by Third World soldiers making a dollar or two a week. Conditions are such that Americans could not survive very long. The Afghans, for instance, are generally pleased to have Americans join them in their crusade against the Big Bear. The problem is that everyone in Afghanistan is there on a volunteer basis. No central authority exists to meet payrolls or even provide medical help.

Surprising as it may seem, some Americans do occasionally go to places like Afghanistan and serve. One can see them in the Philippines, Laos, northern Thailand, and central Africa. The basic problem is that most Americans cannot endure the low pay, poor food, and desperate living conditions demanded by these kinds of jobs.

There also exists the very grave problem of learning how to survive in a total military situation. An American GI might, at a maximum, spend perhaps ninety minutes in actual combat during his entire military career. This, experts agree, is not enough time to really learn to stay alive.

As a rule, Third World soldiers, such as Koreans, Ethiopians, and Turks, have an incredible ability to stay alive in combat. Koreans and Turks, for instance, are expected to live permanently in their foxholes and trenches. Men on the other side of the firing line have a similar lifestyle, along with a comparable will to live. Americans who do not know beyond a reasonable shadow of doubt that they have the requisite skills and determination to do this sort of thing had best not fool around with this business.

Fortunately, there is a place where Americans who want to fight can fit in around the world. Rather than sign up as grunts, their best shot at the business is to hire out as training officers.

As a group, Americans generally tend not to

be the tough disciplinarians the French, Israelis, or even the British have a reputation of being. This leaves them, as a group, out of contention for jobs as drill sergeants training elite palace guards or inclusion in commando outfits or tough front-line groups that are being raised for particularly difficult assignments.

Occasionally, mixed groups of foreign nationals are raised to pull off some particularly onerous front-line assignment. I encountered one of these outfits in the late sixties working for government officials in the Central African Republic. The group was a mixed bag of French, South Africans, Belgians, Canadians, Germans, and British, but no Americans. Taken together, they were one of the most motley, disgusting groups I have ever run into.

The one assignment I saw them carry out involved turning a .50 caliber onto a large group of Africans herding cattle. The blood and gore from the cattle added dramatically to the total impact of the carnage they created.

These guys were physically dirty beyond human belief as a result of going weeks at a time sleeping along the road, in trucks, or in the back of Landrovers without bathing, shaving, or any sort of cleanup. Most had open body ulcers. All were scarred and gnarled from being beat around so much.

They ate food and drank water that would have killed me in three days. After twenty-six years of international work, I am mostly immune to the bugs Americans generally have to worry about, but I would have had no chance living the way these men did.

These guys -- there were about 110 of them, but they seldom operated as a unit -- were getting about six hundred U.S. dollars per month from the central government officials. Their job was to do the officials' dirty work, when and how they were told.

They spent their money for rotgut and on bush native whores who would line up behind the petrol stations to collect the few cents these guys could afford. Most of them had bad cases of internal parasites, as well as a wide assortment of probably incurable diseases. Medical supplies, along with trained personnel to use them, were non-existent. At the time I was using veterinary medical supplies to get by.

There may have been more to it, but as far as I could tell, the basic duty of this outfit was to carry out punitive raids against suspected rebel groups in the old style of the British and French empires.

Outwardly, the communists weren't involved, although most of the government people who paid the crew were fire-breathing Marxists. The opposition was usually poorly armed and virtually unorganized. This certainly isn't always the case for soldiers of fortune, but in the above instance it certainly was. The fact that the people they were after often couldn't shoot back was not necessarily a ticket to a life of ease in combat. The group operated under the South African concept that the only effective way to deal with black dissidents was to whomp them very hard. There was a tremendous emphasis on high body counts.

Probably no similar outfit still exists in the world today.

Rather than situations like the above, the place where Americans can, as a practical matter, find employment as warriors is as high-tech trainers and organizers.

One often hears of the need for helicopter-pilot instruction in South Africa, Israel, Brunei, Argentina, and Nigeria. Mechanic instructors, motor-pool operators, radio repair and maintenance men, fire controllers, and jump trainers can often find work on the international market.

There are several caveats, however. Because of U.S. laws, it is tough to find out about these jobs. One must be very, very good at his job, and the pay is not usually particularly attractive. Short-term assignments as tank-commander trainers and armourers come up in places like Thailand and Pakistan, but these are usually handled by our military on a contract basis. Private companies who may be supplying equipment may put out the word, but, of course, they have to be very, very discreet. Any contracting for services done outside these normal channels is usually so covert that it is tough to find out what is going on.

American GIs who have recently left the service certainly remember how often rumors circulated that somebody was looking for people with a particular set of skills, usually on a TDY-type of assignment basis. My experience has been that there is almost always a basis in fact for these rumors if one really is willing to track it down and wants to go to some god-awful place to work on contract. In reality, the work is a challenge, but exciting it isn't. The problem is that only those in the military hear about these deals. Usually, it is only those in a very specific part of the military. Men who want to get involved but are civilians must keep close contact with their military friends and be prepared to spend a huge amount of time and money running down rumors, some of which may lead nowhere.

At times, it is possible to get some leads from the stories in certain magazines. My experience has been that the material is so dated by the time it appears in print that it is impossible to follow up on the information. In that regard, *Soldier of Fortune, Gung Ho,* and *Eagle* have become mostly history books.

It helps to a great extent to live on the edge of the world's trouble spots. A person skilled in the repair of night-vision devices could easily find employment now in Syria; fighters in Beirut are generally employed on a day-to-day basis, and helicopter mechanics can go to work in an instant in Turkey.

A soldier of fortune willing to go Bangkok or Chiang Mai, Thailand, and wait will, for instance, eventually run into something interesting. The trouble with this plan is that it is so uncertain. An American warrior may never make enough money to buy his plane ticket home. All over the world, I have seen desperate people who have run out of luck and money and who live in some terrible, dirty, buggy hotel eating food that is so bad that they spend one-third of their waking hours in the bathroom. Not much of an action career in my opinion.

Probably the most direct route for those with the necessary military experience, but no contacts, is to go into the gunrunning business. Other than that, one would have to go to France to join the Foreign Legion. People who look at this route closely generally don't take it. The fact that they will be drilled and trained in French and have a six-year enlistment discourages many. Volunteers will probably end up going to the deserts of Libya or Chad before seeing any action -- another discouragement for many.

The Thais run a mercenary army, and my

prediction is that the South Africans will start one before long. Other than these options, the Foreign Legion is it.

It has been my experience that people who make deals to supply arms can often move into training work, teaching buyers how to use their new supplies. As a general rule, I recommend that gunrunners never take up arms in favor of a client. If that's what it takes to get into that business and it's the business you want to be in, you might give the gunrunning business a try.

Neophyte soldiers of fortune who are looking for leads might try their local merchant of death. Helicopter brokers, armoured-vehicle salesmen, and people selling exotic electronic military hardware all have numerous opportunities to put people to work who have been trained in maintenance by the U.S. military. If one can get through to the original supplier or manufacturer, there is an excellent opportunity for job leads.

Lately, a number of schools have sprung up that reportedly will teach the aspiring mercenary how to be a soldier of fortune. These schools aren't much of a deal, though. They don't have a job-referral system and, without question, the schools cannot match the training given by the U.S. Army.

Private schools do not have the manpower, facilities, and money for munitions, rockets, electronics, and other equipment that is the cornerstone of modern armies.

Robert K. Brown, publisher and founder of *Soldier of Fortune* magazine, stated his feelings about these mercenary training schools on national television. He said that none of them could be recommended. Instead, one should plan to go to the schools at Benning; Bragg; Dix; Knox; and Fort Leonard Wood, Missouri; he said.

Brown also pointed out that anyone aspiring to this trade had better gobble up every specialized jungle-training, Ranger, jump, and heavy-weapons school the well-financed U.S. government offers that he can possibly arrange to attend, rather than go to some hokey, shoestring survival operation. An effective long-lived soldier of fortune, he pointed out, has got to have a huge amount of very, very expensive training. He absolutely must have a great dollop of good, solid, combat work that will allow that merc to gain enough experience to stay alive.

Schools that are run by the government are an important element of the merc's training. Contacts within the industry are vital when looking for a job. At best, the process is slow and tough. The situation will probably change very quickly. When it does, a number of Americans will be ready to take part. Most important, one must be close to the action in order to take part in it.

How You Can Do It

1. Go through basic training in a program that is run by one of the world's major powers.
2. Be sure to get as much advanced military training as possible.
3. Participate in as much military action as humanly possible. Learn how to stay alive.
4. Stay in excellent physical shape.
5. Be alert for any TDY assignments or opportunities in foreign countries around the world.
6. Keep in contact with military suppliers and consider working as a civilian for them.
7. Cultivate people in the business of supplying helicopters, electronics, or armour to foreign buyers to see if they know of some work.
8. Be a news junkie; keep track of the world's trouble spots and technology. Be ready to jump in at a moment's notice.
9. Consider starting as a gunrunner or weapons peddler.

Spy

During the late sixties, a friend decided he was going to be a spy. He had been a mechanic in an army motorized outfit and had seen service in Vietnam, Germany, and the United States.

The guy took his discharge in Germany, but after a few months, the little fraulein he was going to marry found someone else. Daddy put the new fellow in his business and, in the process, put my friend out on the street.

My friend, who still had acquaintances at his old base of discharge, rounded up some official-looking documents relating to fueling procedures for tanks and trucks as well as some papers on points of origin for replacement parts. He had a rubber classified stamp made with which to authenticate his papers.

The rest of the story is horribly ridiculous but, at the time, my friend had a genuine plan -- a plan born out of desperation but, nevertheless, a plan.

The guy took his packet of papers, slipped it, believe it or not, inside a raincoat, and went to the Soviet consul in Frankfurt.

Once inside, he announced to the receptionist that he would like to talk to a Soviet official. He said he sat there for quite a long time until a little, stocky, balding man appeared wearing a well-fitting, expensive, dark blue suit.

My friend told the fellow who he was and that he had some classified documents from the U.S. Army he was willing to sell. The Russian asked to see the documents and snatched them out of the guy's hand as soon as he had them out of his coat. Without saying a word, the Russian wheeled around and marched back through a set of solid wood doors, disappearing for about twenty minutes. My friend tried to wait patiently.

When the official returned, he appeared to be red-faced mad.

"What do you take me for, idiot!" he hollered. "Here, take your junk," he screamed, and threw the whole thing into the trash basket.

"Get out! Get out, fool!" he screamed. My friend left. Obviously, there was no sale, and no money. In his haste and frustration, he left the documents in the Russians' circular file. The information may not have been worth anything but the Soviets didn't end up paying anything for it, either.

Maybe there is more than one moral to this

story. The one that comes immediately to mind is that the Soviets are so plagued by phony walk-ins providing information that they are very suspicious of anyone. One must also assume they know the real thing from the not-so-real thing.

Of course, the second moral is that information-providing spies are recruited and do not usually volunteer. Being recruited requires that one be in a position where one has information and/or paper of actual value to sell whether one is employed in the business world or in government service. Action careerists who want to work for the other team had best keep this reality in mind.

The chances of being recruited by either side are best if the action careerist is living overseas, preferably in a sensitive area. There are, of course, spies -- those who are serving an employer other than the immediate one who is providing the weekly paycheck. And then there are agents. CIA employees are agents. As agents, they may recruit spies to help them with information or, more commonly, they may be analysts and statisticians who study publicly available information.

Becoming a CIA agent is not particularly mysterious. One can do so coming out of college when establishing a career path. CIA recruiters generally like to talk to liberal arts majors with strong analytical and writing skills.

Proficiency in another language is a big plus. At times, specialty skills such as electrical engineering, geography, cartography, computer science, chemistry, or statistics are in demand but, as a rule, college students with high grades and what is said to be a good attitude are the first picks.

A good attitude is one which includes "honesty and a work ethic," along with a big dose of patriotism. CIA recruiters say the "my country, my flag" feeling they look for is more prevalent in the West and parts of the South; therefore, potential agents going to college might consider going to school in the West or the South. By so doing, they will more likely catch the eye of a recruiter. However, they must not only be willing, they must also be anxious to move to Washington, D.C., for a few years. Overseas assignments come only after two or three years in D.C. Like the military, CIA people are transferred arbitrarily. CIA recruiters like not only patriotic people who can pass rigorous security clearance procedures, but they absolutely insist on men in the top of their class.

Previous military experience can be of help during the consideration process. CIA recruiters feel that ex-GIs have more street sense and more maturity. Without a military background, it may be tough to prove you have these qualities.

Potential employees undergo a security

clearance that may, in some cases, take from three to six months. Drug users, convicted felons, and those with financial problems are immediately weeded out at this point. Sons and daughters of first-generation immigrants are especially closely screened and will probably not be accepted.

The official attitude of the CIA is that it wants people who have been through the mud but have kept their feet clean. Invariably, there is the security check that must be made that will establish this trait on an individual basis. This characteristic applies to men with known drug pushers in their family, those whose parents may have been convicted, and other similar associations.

Specific needs of the Agency change rapidly. Some years, it looks for accountants and finance people; other years, math and physics people are needed. People with special skills, such as helicopter pilots or military training officers, are often recruited depending on the needs and political vagaries of the times. They are recruited in military circles by a separate office of the CIA at Langley Field. The process is formally informal. Because of the high pay vis-a-vis military salaries, the CIA does not seem to have trouble getting enough qualified, military-type people. (Note also that the CIA is an equal-opportunity employer.)

CIA caseworkers have what are considered

to be the most glamorous jobs within the Agency. These people are in charge of finding resources (people) in various countries who can provide needed information. Caseworkers have expense accounts with which to buy dinner or pay people's expenses, and to simply give them cash.

Caseworker trainees go through the most rigorous of internal training programs in the CIA. They are expected to spend a minimum of one year at Langley, Virginia, and one year in language training. The CIA runs its own language training program, but it will gladly consider people from the D-lab school in Monterey, California. All this training takes time and is tough, and the less-than-resolute should consider another line of work.

For those who don't want to, or can't, go to college, an alternate career path can be followed into the CIA that does not include a college degree. In such a case, a person desiring an action career as a spy who has good foreign-language abilities should ask to take the Army or Air Force defense lab language test. A high score will qualify that person for the one-year language school in Monterey. Those who choose to study the more demanding and exotic Middle Eastern languages will be seriously considered by the CIA at the completion of the course.

Americans who have learned one of the

currently desired languages at home or while in residence abroad should also check with the CIA recruiter, provided they have not reached their thirty-fifth birthday.

The easiest way to find a recruiter is to call the placement and career office of the nearest state university.

Outside, in the real world, there are actually two kinds of spies -- political/military and industrial -- both of which should be of interest to the action careerist.

Being an industrial spy probably pays more than CIA employment, but it is almost completely dependent on the fortunes of time and place. The CIA starts its people at $22,000 per year, with $85,000 per annum about the top of the pay scale. In contrast, properly placed industrial spies can make $150,000 part-time, depending on the circumstances.

If you work your way up to an expert classification in some area of especially lucrative, modern, whiz-bang technology and are not well known in that field, it is possible to go to a competitor and negotiate a fee in exchange for proprietary information you may possess. Obviously, those who do not possess such information cannot make a living selling it. Industrial spies must be absolute experts in their fields.

My grandfather never worked a lick after he came to the States from Germany in the early

1920s. He lived nicely on the money he made selling American textile manufacturers formulas for dyes. The old duffer brought them out of the old country in his head, and they became his life estate. He was a spy of the type referred to above.

At times, it is possible to strike a deal with a competing business to provide shipping schedules, sources of supply, customer lists, price lists, ingredients, and formulas from the company for whom you are currently employed. One must be enormously creative and mercenary when dealing with a current employer and potential buyers to make this type of business work.

Some smart engineers do hire out on a general basis to do industrial spying for business people, but problems related to matching who wants to buy and who wants to sell often preclude this from being much more than a one-shot deal. Finding an engineer with the correct set of skills and morals is usually so tough most companies don't even consider it to be an option.

About all the adventurer can do is to be alert to possible opportunities and then be prepared to move on them very quickly. He must also know enough about the process to know what it is worth to a competitor.

A clear-cut situation occurs when competitive bids are being prepared. Getting good bid information may require a full-blown and very expensive black-bag operation, including bugs, wiretaps, and surveillance. Businessmen generally know about this kind of operation.

There appear to be quite a lot of business executives who would like to arrange spying projects, but one does not pick up a trade journal to find the telephone number of industrial spies or otherwise acquire their names by personal reference. Printing letterhead and renting an office won't get one into this business.

People who make a living doing this sort of thing are unusually highly adventurist business executives who have otherwise come into the company by conventional means. When the need arises, these people teach themselves to use the electronic gear that their own judgment indicates would be best suited for the situation.

One fellow responded to his supervisor when the fellow wondered out loud, "I wish we could find out where XYZ Company gets its chassis parts made. We could call up its supplier and see how much they would charge us to do the same thing."

The guy put on an old uniform (a green shirt and trousers) and walked into the computer assembly plant one Tuesday night for a look. He not only found out the needed sources of supply, but the destination for a car of finished goods, the night foreman's salary, and the number of people working second shift.

Later, when he reported back, the bosses were so happy that they started wondering all kinds of things out loud. The fellow wondered, in return, if that information would be worth a two-hundred-dollar raise and, sure enough, it was! He even managed to get a budget with which to buy electronic gear and was even able to slip several questionable personal items through on his expense account.

Industrial spies must realize that not only is recruiting and the work by definition very difficult, but it is also sometimes very difficult for company executives to pay for services on a project-by-project basis. Use of company funds is closely monitored by the controller's office, and any deviation from normal will raise immediate red flags.

Industrial spies must also contend with the fact that often it is easier and better for management to hire away a key man who has all the secrets than it is to find someone to go in and steal them from a competitor. Industrial spies become known in their business very quickly. When that happens, they are no longer effective information-gatherers. They are never, never trusted and revered employees, ever again.

On an operational level, industrial spying is generally a matter of absolute brashness. One simply walks in with the cleaning crew and takes a look at whatever is needed. Elementary desk-lock picking skills are often all that one needs.

As mentioned previously, most desirable chemical, electrical, and fabrication processes are complex. It takes an expert in that field to know what is going on.

Usually, the manufacturer/owner of a process feels the wrinkle he has is so obscure that no one will appreciate its significance. A food processor, for instance, put pre-dryers in his line to upgrade the quality of the vegetables going through, but was found out by an obscure junior engineer working for a rival concern when the fellow took a regularly scheduled visitors' tour through the competitor's plant.

In such a case, the situation is more one of expert industrial evaluation rather than of spying.

People who are experts in any field, especially an intensely competitive, fast-charging one, are logical candidates to give industrial spying a whirl.

Electronic gear needed for a real black-bag operation is becoming more available in the United States (there are ads appearing in such publications as *Shotgun News* and *Soldier of Fortune* magazine). The best common, easy, off-the-shelf sources of supply are the airport shops in Frankfurt, Germany, or in the New

World Center in Hong Kong. One can buy miniature long-range transmitters, phone tapping devices, and a host of other electronics gear as easily as a box of Wheaties in these places.

There is some skill needed to run this type of gear, but generally not much more than is needed to assemble stereo components or to operate a VCR. In times past when little surveillance gear was available "off-the-shelf," skilled wiretappers built their reputations by knowing how to build the gear they needed, not so much by knowing how to use it.

Today, the industrial spy who has the money to buy the necessary equipment need have little more than lots of guts and bravado when installing the device. A good imagination also helps immensely.

Just keep in mind that if you are caught, you are very definitely on your own and that the FBI is becoming more concerned about this type of white-collar crime.

Political espionage constitutes another lucrative area of spying that is almost always ignored except for the select few who make some money from such activities. At this writing, the field is wide open in the United States.

It isn't tough in state and local races to tap the campaign manager's phone or to wire a recorder in to the rival candidate's headquarters, though national campaign staffs sometimes watch for this sort of thing. With obscure city council races now costing from $100,000 to $150,000, campaign managers are more receptive to suggestions as to how expenses might be cut by using spies.

Adventurists can break into this business by sorting through the campaign-office trash every night. In the process, they can glean lists of contributors to the campaign. By using old, used, contribution envelopes, and examining telephone-message slips and lists of area and regional campaign coordinators, they can piece together an entire campaign strategy. At times, there will even be lists of campaign expenses that will surface in the trash.

All this information can be compiled into summary form and taken to the rival campaign office of the candidate's best-funded opponent. This works incredibly well during city and state elections, but expensive national campaigns are better organized. These staffs know about the importance of document shredders.

Getting good money for really good information from rival candidates is sometimes a lot tougher than it sounds, even if the stuff you have is very, very good. Most campaigns have to file lists of expenditures with a state or federal monitoring agency, but the bigger, more pervasive problem is that most campaigns are right on the ragged edge financially.

Practitioners of information sales scams may find they have to go onto the payroll of a cooperating industrial sugar daddy or use a similar device to get the money they want.

If a working relationship is established and there does appear to be some money for black-bag services from the campaign treasury, the next step is to suggest that wiretaps and call-monitoring are also possible, compliments of "yours truly."

Pay for this sort of thing is perhaps $1,500 to $2,000 per week, with a small amount thrown in for expenses. Terms of employment are often brief. It is, however, the start of what could become an interesting and exciting career.

In a more conventional sense, action careerists who decide on the more traditional career path through the CIA should expect several years of almost terminal boredom doing analytical work at Langley Field. During this time the neophyte spy will read tons of published data about either the countries or subjects they are assigned to and write unbiased analytical reports.

Overseas assignments generally come to more senior staffers who have proven they can analyze information and can produce good, clear, unbiased reports. In this regard, working for the CIA hardly qualifies as an action career. CIA recruiters usually look for published academic types rather than macho, action-oriented individuals.

How You Can Do It

1. Contact the regional CIA recruiter to find out what college majors the Agency presently prefers to hire.
2. Major in the appropriate subjects while in college and apply to the Agency upon graduation.
3. Be sure to finish in the top of your college class.
4. If going to college is impossible, consider a tour in the military -- preferably assigned to an intelligence outfit where language training is possible.
5. Evaluate your foreign-language abilities and be ready to make application if they are good.
6. Specialists in the military should be alert to any recruitment efforts by the CIA. Helicopter pilots, electronics wizards, and similar types are often asked to serve.
7. Knowing foreign languages can often lead to foreign commercial assignments. Those accepting them who have access to information can and will often be recruited to provide that information to others. Most action careerists will find working for the other team to be objectionable.
8. Attendance at an Army language school

plus a two-year assignment in the Washington, D.C., area can lead to overseas duty for the CIA.

9. Industrial spies can earn good money by becoming experts in a proprietary field and then either selling the info or going to work finding out what the competition is doing. Always be alert to these possibilities.

10. Business executives can often work their way into doing black-bag work on competitors by delivering information to their present employers. Doing this requires that one realistically look at present circumstances to see whether there are any possibilities.

11. Be aware that industrial spies usually have a limited useful life and that this type of life may be rather short.

12. Political spying in the smaller local campaigns is actually quite easy. Often the demand is there, but candidates are seldom able to pay very much for information about their rivals.

13. Industrial and/or political spies should start to accumulate long-playing tape recorders, telephone-tapping devices, and other electronic paraphernalia.

Stunt Man

Without a doubt, the longest-running, money-making movie series in world history -- the James Bond movies -- owes much of its popular appeal to the spectacular application of outlandish and breathtaking stunts.

Who can forget 007 as he skis down the mountain pursued by submachine-gun-firing bad guys, only to be trapped and forced to continue skiing right off a precipice? We see him fall several thousand feet before a Union Jack miraculously appears and then pops a life-saving steerable parachute from his pack.

This stunt and the many more like it that have made James Bond a world-renowned figure were so difficult that just getting them on film was an immense undertaking. People in the industry have suggested that for such filmings it would be desirable for the camera men to also be stunt men.

Stunting is and is not an occupation available to rugged, muscular, and athletic men who want what many people consider to be the ultimate in an action career. Unlike so many other careers, the stunt man can review his handiwork over and over again. In that regard, there is a lot of satisfaction to the job.

Some really action-oriented occupations are very self-limiting. After all, there is only so much room in any given economy for bounty hunters, process servers, trappers, bodyguards, or explosives experts. People who enter these fields will find they must work very hard, or the going will be pretty rough.

Because of the popularity of stunts and their widespread use in virtually every movie and TV film, there are many stunt men around. The best estimate is that about 5,000 people claim to be stunt men, although only 1,200 to 1,500 may actually make an acceptable full-time living stunting.

The problem is not that there are very few stunt men hired and working at any given time, but that breaking into this line of work can be virtually impossible without having established contacts in the industry.

Stunt men come from a variety of backgrounds. Anything that projects physical coordination and timing can be a springboard for a stunt man; many stunt men have a background in ballet, race driving, weight lifting, gymnastics, and acrobatics. A number of ex-rodeo riders, football players, and other athletes now work in Hollywood as stunt men. Military training is said to be helpful, but apparently few stunt men are ex-military men.

Stunt men spend quite a lot of their time just waiting. Coping with a hurry-up-and-wait society may be the principal advantage of military experience.

Despite their reputation for womanizing, heavy drinking, and doping, most stunt men are steady, reliable, intelligent people. A few are definitely wild-assed renegades who don't care about much, trusting everything they do to fate. However, most sit down quietly and simply with calculator, pad, and pencil to safely work out the timing and correct system needed to pull off a requested gig.

Schools and short courses offered in Hollywood teach analytical skills needed to do the mathematical calculations necessary to pull off certain stunts. These schools are not particularly commonplace and do not necessarily guarantee the graduate a job, the possible exceptions being a few well-known, high-speed driving schools and a short stunting course offered occasionally by one of the better-known stunting-fraternity gurus. Neither is held in particularly high regard, however, and do not guarantee employment.

Most stunt men are hired by a movie stunt coordinator whose job it is to put together all of the stunts in a given movie. The coordinator will invariably hire people he knows (in most cases, they will be people who have done him a favor in the past).

In the case of a relatively stunt-free movie, the director may handle the film without a stunt coordinator or he may take the easy way out and call in one of the many stunt troops to handle the whole thing. Directors only take this route if they are very familiar with the abilities of the group with which they will be working and the need for stunts is fairly minimal.

A troop is a loose business association of stunt men who have a general mix of skills and can professionally handle virtually any stunt situation, ranging from driving a car into a pool, to falling off a horse, to getting karate-chopped. Novice stunt men sometimes join with friends in an established troop to get work.

The way an individual or group can get called to work is to know someone in the business and to have excellent credits in the industry for past stunts.

Apprentice stunt men start with simple stunts that may not even earn extra money (called bumps), but such stunts will get them on the lot.

Stunt men sell their services by keeping a portfolio containing pictures of past stunts. The book is used to demonstrate to doubting stunt coordinators that the stuff has actually been done. Being the recipient of a roundhouse punch is an example of a simple, not-for-pay, "bump" stunt. In this case, the stunt man is acting in the capacity of an extra -- not a particularly glamorous role, but nevertheless a start. Every stunt man basically makes his debut in this manner. He checks in at the studio with the casting director and registers to take work as an extra. By checking in every day, he will learn when extras will be hired and perhaps be among those selected to work.

The pay scale for an extra as set by the Screen Actors' Guild is $365 per day. In this case, the aspiring stunt man is acting in the capacity of an extra. Initially, he seldom works for more than an hour or two per day, or even per week. Work as an extra pays well because it is often a long time between assignments.

Sometimes persnickety directors will, for whatever reason, hold up shooting involving hundreds of extras. Such a situation can lead to exasperated name-calling on the part of the movie financial people.

Working as an extra is not bad if one can get an assignment or two per week. However, stunt men usually avoid this kind of work if they can help it because they do not want to be stereotyped as an extra if they take too many extra jobs. A most undesirable situation, they claim.

One can start as an extra and move into stunting as fast as one's abilities will allow.

Stunt men basically work for the $365-per-day flat rate. As the stunts get hairier, a stunt man will negotiate what is referred to as a bump over and above the standard day rate, or daily.

Negotiations for a bump are done with the stunt coordinator or director, both of whom have a pretty good idea what the act should go for or has gone for in the past. Most stunts are not unique; they have been done over and over again for years and years. In virtually all cases, the stunt can be performed by a number of different stunt men. No one has a lock on a given gig.

As a backstop, the director or stunt coordinator usually has a definite friend in mind who will do the gig for a certain rate. A complete package will sometimes be negotiated by a stunting team or troop. The proceeds will be split up among the participants based on the agreed-upon formula when the bid is made.

Movie companies are notorious for waiting till the very last minute before accepting bids and then wanting shooting to start in sixty minutes.

Stunt assignments are usually not made on the basis of any particular skill or ability. The assumption is usually that the stunt man has done, and can do, the called-for stunt in a satisfactory manner. Use of a portfolio and the fact that most stunts are pretty routine supports this way of thinking in the industry.

Past favors and the possibility that you could

do someone a favor in the future (and having a very good-looking, available girlfriend) are more important factors when breaking into the stunt business than anything else.

Bumps will run from $350 to roll a car, $500 to roll a pickup truck (trucks are more difficult to roll), to perhaps $5,000 to jump out of an eighteenth-floor window. Three- or four-story falls are considered normal and do not generally warrant a bump.

The top bump occurs when the chance of survival is fifty-fifty. There are the James-Bond-type bumps that have never been done before and in which there is absolutely no chance of surviving a miscalculation. The bumps for these range up to about $50,000.

As a result of these bumps, the ten best Hollywood stunt men make about $250,000 per year. It is estimated that the next one hundred make around $100,000. The average Joe Blow stunt man will pull down a measly $40,000 to $50,000 per year.

Some stunt men, most of whom are the sons of established stunt men, start their careers as early as age eighteen, while there are working stunt men who are sixty years of age or older.

Stunts involving racing cars, near misses, hairy crashes, rollovers and other assorted vehicle disasters are de rigeur in Hollywood today. Being shot off a horse is no longer in much demand in the City of Glitz.

Stunt men are expected to bring along their own personal equipment, including shin and kidney pads, spine protectors, burning suits, and special boots. Purchased new, a set of pads and boots will run about $300!

Larger, more costly equipment needed for specific stunts is rented for the shot by the stunt coordinator. This includes air bags, safety nets, special pulleys and rigging, ramps, and breathing equipment.

Virtually every stunt is handled in a very thorough, thoughtful, and calculating manner. If the stunt is difficult, the stunt man will spend quite a long time talking with the stunt coordinator or director to be sure he understands just how the gig is supposed to look. He may spec some special equipment, harness, or safety nets for the shot as well as how equipment (such as cars) will be set up. (In the case of cars, how the automatic transmission, roll bar, and tires should be.) All of these negotiations are done verbally; written contracts for specific stunts are seldom done.

Directors sometimes may not like the way a stunt is performed. Unless it was a one-case contract, the stunt man will be expected to do a retake; in reality, this does not present an insurmountable problem. If, for example, the director doesn't like the way a car rolls over, the stunt man simply asks, "you got another car?" The cost of another vehicle keeps the director from becoming abusive.

In spite of increasingly breathtaking stunts, the business is said to be getting safer. Safety equipment is much better, and the means of putting stunts together (including necessary calculations) is much more sophisticated. Stunt men who are still alive and well after ten or fifteen years of working at this trade are pretty damn good practical physicists and mathematicians. They need this mathematical ability to calculate rates of fall, vehicle speeds, effects of weight or impact, and angles of departure for jumps, among other stunts.

Stunt men are covered by the movie production company's medical insurance policy while working. They have workmen's compensation and are further protected against disability by the movie company's basic insurance policy.

Suits for injuries are very, very rare. Producers are generally not held liable for a stunt that was fully explained to the stunt man. In some very rare cases, people are badly hurt but, even then, suits against the movie company are uncommon. As a rule, stunt men are adequately provided for.

If a stunt man does sue, he can be sure he will never work as a stunt man in Hollywood again. No production company in this tight-knit small community will ever hire him.

The role of a stunt man is complex and in many ways limited. A stunt man does not, for instance, set up and orchestrate the use of explosives in a war movie; special-effects experts are hired to handle this aspect of the movie. Scenes in which planes are flown are handled by special movie pilots. Stunt men may be shown being thrown around the plane and out the door if that's what the script calls for, but not flying the machine.

Contrary to widespread tales, especially macho actors do not ever do their own stunts. Movie production companies are always covered by insurance should any of the principal actors get hurt and be unable to continue with the shooting schedule.

The director is considered to be negligent under the terms of most insurance policies if one of his famous actors is hurt doing his own stunts. As a result, the insurance company may not pay for the delays in production while everyone waits for the actor to recover. Virtually no director will take these kinds of risks, guaranteeing that expendable stunt men will always be used and always be in demand.

California laws dealing with the mistreatment of animals are very strict. In fact, they are so strict that some movies have to be made in foreign countries. Stunt men who fall off horses do not use their own horses from which to fall. All stock in Hollywood is supplied by professional horse and cattle handlers. Use is strictly controlled by law.

Producers who schedule movies in a foreign country face some huge problems regarding any stunts they wish to film. Tales circulate in the industry that doing a movie in Canada, Mexico, or Spain is cheaper because stunt men work for as little as twenty dollars per day. As a practical matter, this is not true. Foreign stunt men generally do not offer complete professional packages of skills.

Such items as safety nets, air bags to catch stunt men, and air rams (needed to throw people, say when a bomb hits) are not readily available. All this equipment must be purchased and shipped to the foreign location. As a result, the total cost of doing a stunt abroad is generally the same as doing the stunt in the United States where the equipment can be rented.

If the movie must be shot in a foreign location, American stunt men can pack up their equipment and go with the director to train and supervise local stunting talent. This process always whoops the cost up to just about Hollywood standards.

After a stunt man has done the prerequisite ten to fifteen movies and is making at least $50,000 per year, he can apply to either the Stunt Men's Association or Stunts Unlimited for membership. Membership is finalized by vote of the current membership, and it confirms the lifetime right to work as a stunt man. Membership in either organization is helpful but not essential. Many stunt men work all their lives as independents. The Stunt Men's Association has about 600 members. Stunts Unlimited, considered to be a more elite group, has about 150 in its ranks.

It isn't uncommon for writers and producers to dream up a stunt that is not doable. After looking at the script, the stunt coordinator will check around a bit within the industry to see if anyone has a handle on how it could be done. If he is met with general skepticism, he may go back to the director and suggest a means of modifying the action so it can be performed.

At times, the script will call for a stunt for which there will not be sufficient money in the budget to pull it off. Again, it's back to the director for consultation. Stunts that are written in as an integral part of the script are seldom completely dropped. They are modified or more money is put in the budget for them.

Other than hanging around the film lots and movie company sets or working through central casting on a job or as an extra, suggestions regarding how to break in without a friend or relative already in the business are pretty thin.

Aspiring stunt men can try to hang out with other stunt men, or they can frequent the appropriate Hollywood bars, always trying to meet the right people. A common trick is to go to places frequented by directors and producers and try to meet them there. The only problem is that no one knows precisely where these places are located as they change with maddening frequency.

Another suggestion for those who look, or who are built, like a famous star is to call that person's agent, suggesting that you are a stunt man who looks like "Mr. Star" and that if Mr. Star does not have a stunting double, you would like to be considered. Occasionally that ploy will work.

Stunt men who are so small they can double for children are in constant demand. Almost every stunting troop has two or three men who are no taller than 4'6." In times past, smaller men did stunts for women. Now all women's stand-in work is done by women. By Hollywood labor agreement, men are no longer allowed to double for women.

Breaking into stunting other than through contacts cannot easily and assuredly be reduced to a formula as with many other action careers, but there are openings, no matter how tough or difficult they are to find.

How You Can Do It

1. Develop an interest in the business as a result of watching movies and TV.
2. Hone your physical skills well, developing strength and coordination.
3. Learn to ride, climb, fall, and tumble.

4. Go to Hollywood, check in with central casting and work temporarily as an extra.
5. Watch other stunts, practice them, and push to move in the direction of performing stunts.
6. Meet people in the business; try to develop contacts.
7. Attach yourself to a stunting group.
8. Keep a portfolio of any stunts you have performed.
9. Use every possible opportunity to show your portfolio to directors and stunt coordinators.
10. Establish a reputation in Hollywood by circulating and being known.
11. Develop necessary math skills needed to make the calculations to stay alive when doing stunts.
12. Go to any stunting schools you can.
13. Keep working till you are making $50,000 per year and join one of the professional stunting organizations.

Test Pilot

Pilots tend to live in a world all of their own. They live, breathe, and think about little else other than flying.

Test pilots are a unique, thrill-seeking lot. They go several steps beyond what others may do to discover by dangerous trial and error which aeronautic equipment works and which does not. Even in this day of controller- and computer-verified everything, their occupation is especially dicey. They continually test the theory that knowing (not guessing) what one can get away with constitutes the difference between retiring in one's field and plowing the farm early.

An especially macho navy fighter pilot once asked me, "How would you like to be the first guy to take up a new, off-the-assembly-line F16 and fly it for the very first time?"

I guess I wouldn't, but to hear him tell, it was a real surprise. On the average, one in four navy fighter pilots augers his plane in during a normal twenty-year career spanning the time from flight commission to retirement.

For the most part, modern test pilots are no longer experimenting with dozens of new prototypes as they were during the heady days after World War II when our military converted from prop to jet planes. The glory that Chuck Yeager was accorded when, on October 14, 1947, his ground-crew members became the first people on earth to hear a sonic boom, will probably never be repeated.

Any prototype aircraft, big or small, fast or slow, is -- after all -- nothing more than an imperfect machine waiting to bust the pilot's ass. The job of discovering the plane's flaws will continue to be an important one for the foreseeable future whether the plane is new and just off the assembly line or a new design.

Opportunities exist for test pilots in the space program but very valid questions persist regarding the skill level needed in these programs. Cool, calm people with excellent typing skills needed to handle computers seem to be in more demand than the super-keen athlete with an incredibly well-honed ability to understand and personally fly aircraft. Patience necessary to sit out the delays and postponements is also a must for people in the space program.

Aspiring to such a difficult and challenging career as test pilot is definitely an attainable goal for the very intelligent, very ambitious action careerist who is also a nut about flying. At most there are but five hundred test pilots working in the United States today. The field is opening because many of the pilots are old and about to retire.

Boeing hires about one hundred test pilots, but also uses them to form the pilot-training division of the company. An upsurge in plane sales could hype the demand for people in this group. Northrup, Bell, and Rockwell also have large central testing groups where test pilots can seek employment.

Perhaps because of the rugged individual mystique that has built up around test pilots, people often think there are only one or two in the entire United States!

In the years to come, industry experts predict that the United States will certainly get its space program back on track, providing additional opportunities for test pilots. New, commercial aircraft with new, improved designs will be built, and more technically trained test pilots will help with the initial design phase of these planes. There will be thousands of 767s, 747s, 737s, F111s, F16s, and other planes built that must be taken up for that hairy first ride.

Test pilots will continue to determine not only whether a green plane will fly but also, in the case of new designs, how that particular plane will fly and if it is capable of meeting design specifications. These include stall speed, spin characteristics, best rate of climb, best glide configuration, best climb speed, the red line, green line, and such prosaic information as "can that plane can be landed with a full load of fuel, on its belly."

The life of a test pilot is an exciting ride on a roller coaster that many people feel would exactly suit them, yet there is a career path that one can follow knowing with certainty that someday he will become a member of this elite action-career group. It is one of the few careers that can be approached via a formula.

This does not mean that anybody can become a test pilot; it merely means that if one wants to be a test pilot, there is a definite proven route to follow. Few have got the right stuff it will take to get there from here, but that is an individual matter.

An aspiring test pilot must experience a powerful attraction to planes and flying early on. He will spend hours at the local airport being a salavating idiot about planes and pilots. He will wash planes and work in the hangar in an attempt to earn money for lessons. At night, he will attend ground school, go to flying-club meetings, or hangar fly with older pilots. Cleanup work for mechanics will give an early sense of what goes wrong with planes and why.

On his eighteenth birthday, the aspiring test

pilot will solo; by the age of 18.3, he will have a private ticket.

Although many early test pilots did not get a college degree, such days are gone forever; a successful career path for a test pilot would certainly include at least a B.S. degree (most probably in either mechanical, electrical, or aeronautical engineering).

During college, an adventurist would keep the adrenaline flowing by flying every chance possible. By age 19.5, or midway into his sophomore year in college, the aspiring test pilot would probably earn an instrument rating.

During this time, the student should continue to fly a minimum of ten hours per week. It will become a serious goal for the aspiring test pilot to check out on every different machine on the field, including some work on multi-engine planes.

Since funds are limited, chance and a good line of BS will be important to convince plane owners and corporate pilots to allow the student to fly cross-country in the second seat in as many planes as possible. (Sometimes young women have the best chance at this!)

At the start of the student's senior year, selecting the appropriate military service will be important. If helicopters are the student's forte, the first choice will be the Army.

Both the U.S. Navy and Air Force fly jet aircraft. Even the Coast Guard has Falcon jets. If the adventurist desperately wants to fly, there is some branch of service that can and will accommodate him. It is important to remember this concept later when the only choice may be C-130s or 707s when what the adventurist wanted was fighter jets. Future test pilots may feel that flying fighters is best, but the concept is to fly as many different aircraft as many hours as possible.

The program for the person on track to a career as a test pilot still has to be eating, thinking, dreaming, talking, reading, and studying flying every waking minute. In the military, this should include a heavy dose of tinkering with airplanes.

Good test pilots who stay alive and retire at a ripe old age get their hands dirty working on planes. They learn the systems right out on the line with the mechanics who are looking after their birds. Pilots in fighter wings may have an advantage at this point. Fighter wings usually have a number of designated test pilots who do first flights of newly arrived planes and of aircraft that have undergone major repairs.

Getting into one of these groups can materially boost the career of the pilot who is still on course toward Edwards Air Force Base in California, Boeing in Seattle or the Navy test facility at Pautuxent, Massachusetts.

The military also runs an exclusive two-part, six-months-per-part, test-pilot school, teaching abnormal flight characteristics and control as well as the precision procedures necessary to evaluate an aircraft. Mathematics constitute a major portion of this school program, again suggesting that the fledgling test pilot will not make it without a strong college background. Attendance at such a school is imperative for the career test pilot unless he wants to quit now and try to go into private industry.

Most flight testing of new designs consists of taking a plane through a designated, predesigned flight program in an extremely precise maneuver. Competent test pilots are said to be those who can produce a precision stair-step graph on the flight instrument recorders. Some of the design of these flight programs is done by flight engineers. However, in many cases, this design also becomes the duty of the test pilot who also will fly the program.

Test pilots at Edwards check new manufacturers' prototypes to be certain they meet the design specs the military has prescribed in its design contracts. This is primarily a very technical procedure, for which you need a lot of math.

Gung-ho pilots who come this far report a gruesome and macabre weeding-out process as those with less skill and experience or those who are just plain unlucky thin their own ranks by "buying the farm." Lost friends and acquaintances are depressingly common.

One famous test pilot said the secret to his success was simple. "I just always lived to fly again."

After test-pilot school, it's a matter of flying as many hours as possible in as many different planes as possible. Fighter and carrier pilots have an edge over long-haul captains.

Total flying hours are not nearly as important as what kind of hours. Boeing requires a minimum of 2,000 hours before you can get into their test-pilot program. If most of the flying is long haul, they may not even accept 3,000 hours. Fighter jocks who do their own thing without autopilots, flight programmers, and copilots get better experience, most people say.

After eight to ten years of this kind of schedule, assuming the adventurer still has the desire, the next step is to retire from the military and get a job working for Lockheed, North American, Boeing, Douglas, Cessna, or Piper.

Civilian test piloting is not as exciting as that done in the military. By the age of thirty-two or thirty-five, however, the adventurer is probably ready to make some money as well as establish a bit more of a routine. The salary of a civilian test pilot starts at about $35,000 per year. In times past, some of the real hot-shot pilots living right on the ragged edge made more than that. Nowdays, the risks and pay are less.

Often modern test pilots are expected to support the sales staff and assist with sales calls, especially in foreign countries.

The occupation of test pilot is undeniably the most demanding of the action careers, open only to the most fiercely determined who want to map out their careers early, have that incredible tenacity to stick with it, and genuinely believe flying is the greatest hype one can ever experience.

How You Can Do It

1. Become a nut about flying at an early age.
2. Get a pilot's license when you're young, if possible.
3. Build an above-average number of hours flying early on.
4. Do as much general maintenance on planes as possible.
5. Be mathematically inclined and take as many math courses as possible.
6. Go to college and get at least a B.S. degree in aeronautical, electrical, or mechanical engineering.
7. Continue to fly at least weekly in as many different planes as possible while in college.
8. Get an instrument rating very quickly.
9. Enlist in the military and go into some kind of flight program.
10. Continue to fly as many different planes as possible.

11. Develop skills as a precision pilot.
12. Attend military test-pilot school.
13. Make every attempt to get to Edwards Air Force base or Pautuxent Naval Station.
14. Look around to decide if it is more feasible to get into one of the military test centers or to go to work for private industry.
15. Retire from the military; go to work for a private company.

Wildlife Management Trapper

Americans don't commonly accept the fact that the job of trapping is still around. It is, but the position is hardly ever publicized.

Social pressures are such that people in the trapping and animal-control business are usually relegated to little-noticed, obscure positions specifically designed to draw scant attention or notoriety.

In many cases, this is a good thing. The job can be one of the most difficult and disgusting of the action careers. It is also one of the more demanding; either a person knows the business or he has no chance of making a go of it. No colleges for trappers exist of which I am aware.

During the fifties, I helped a government trapper who worked for the state of Indiana. He was called in to control a pack of domestic dogs that had gone wild and was ravaging local sheep herds.

The balancing act this guy had to perform between irate farmers, dog lovers, and concerned county commissioners who had to pay damage compensation out of scarce tax funds was unbelievable.

To make matters even worse, the dogs were incredibly difficult to nab. They were intelligent, semi-wild creatures used to being around people. They knew how to avoid people and could detect when humans were likely to harm them.

Government trappers are still called in to get rid of unwanted animals, ranging from rats in cities to burrowing muskrats in a guy's fish pond dam, to owls in people's attics.

One trapping story regarding government trappers immediately comes to mind. A neighbor who raised sheep complained to the Fish and Game Department because "some sort of varmint" was getting his lambing ewes.

I looked at the situation and concluded that it was either some resident coyotes or perhaps bobcats who were responsible. Neither critter is particularly difficult to trap in the spring sans frozen ground, snow, and rain, when bait animals are abundant.

However, I didn't want the job even though the guy offered to pay me handsomely -- more than the damn wormy old sheep were worth, I pointed out.

"The pelts are worthless," I said, "and there is

too great a chance of getting a female suckling or carrying young." If the offending animal were, in fact, a bobcat, I could easily destroy hundreds of dollars worth of valuable fur. Even killing a common animal such as a coyote in spring is self-destructive. There are just that many fewer in fall when they are both fun to hunt and valuable. I suggested letting the predators eat the sheep and then trap the critters in the fall for their pelts. You will make more money in the long run, I pointed out.

The Fish and Game people have clamped down on bobcat trapping, so my neighbor, who feared he would never be rid of the predators, turned me down. He wanted to do something now. Fall was too uncertain, he said.

Yet the sheep farmer complained so often and so well that the Fish and Game Department did send around its "control trapper," who set out a bunch of poison stations. Within four days, he poisoned a mama bobcat and three month-old kittens.

The animal control people are encouraged to use devices and chemicals not commonly available to the average person. All that is required is results, in as quiet and unobtrusive a manner as possible. For this reason, and others, control trappers have really got to know their business.

They must be dead cool with small bore shotguns and not shoot out people's windows when controlling barn pigeons in big cities, for instance.

Mixing and handling effective poison bait for rats is also a required skill. In many places, this kind of poison bait will be the only means of managing overgrown colonies of ground squirrels or gophers for golf courses or estate owners.

Control people even have to handle larger animals, such as deer in cabbage patches, bears in dumps, or coons in cornfields. Removing misplaced skunks from basements is another common task.

Some California people who live in a rural subdivision have even had problems with wild coyotes that crept into town and took off with their tabby cats. There was quite an outcry before all that settled down.

A trapper may be called in to plan and also implement the demise of millions of starlings. Another common problem of the last few years has been controlling hordes of jackrabbits in the West. The course of action then taken by the trapper is to organize huge drives, heading the hares into pens.

The real problem encountered by the trapper is knowing how to handle the bleeding heart animal lovers (hyped by the media) and save-the-animal groups who use the occasion to attract bigger and better membership contributions.

Adding it all up, outdoorsmen who have their acts together as hunters, trappers, and game controllers who want lots of action might consider work as a government trapper. As previously mentioned, it helps to have a good knowledge of chemicals, poisons, and unconventional traps, as well as being very adept at handling situations that require a touch of PR.

In most states, the Park Service, the Forest Service, and Bureau of Land Management rely to a great extent on having their own people handle the chores of animal control. The position is not defined on most rosters, yet there are still a few places where the specific job of Government Trapper shows up on an official position roster. Before assuming there are no government trappers any longer, those aspiring to the job might do a bit of checking around.

Control work is considered by many to be a nuisance that is beneath the dignity of some park employees, and, if this is so, perhaps an area supervisor might consider creating a position and title for an especially well-qualified applicant.

Larger cities almost always have an animal control unit to take care of stray cats and dogs. Control of rats or similar vermin, when it is undertaken, is usually left to the contract pest-control people. The in-between chores, made up of the owls in attics, coons in garages, and skunks in cellars, is the area that no one usually wants to handle.

What, for instance, do the municipal police do with a complaint regarding stray, wild animals in town? That's an area where the freelance trapper can often find employment. He can work either for the municipality on a case-by-case basis, or the police can simply refer their callers to him. In this latter case, the trapper can run skunks out of people's basements on a per-skunk basis. Smaller and modest-sized municipalities may, after they gain confidence that you are reliable, be willing to contract out the whole business: dogs, cats, rats, squirrels, and everything.

I have kept a nice business going by being willing to take care of wild animals for every police department within reasonable driving distance. It isn't a big money proposition, but I haven't let it grow as large as it could, either. I occasionally get calls asking if I could handle a major problem such as an epidemic of rabid skunks, removing a prairie dog town, or wiping out millions of blackbirds. People with effective techniques could make a living off this big stuff.

The challenge would be keeping alive and paying the bills until things got rolling. I have never taken a big control project. I have found that the bleeding-heart animal lovers are so out of touch with reality that I find I can't deal with them. I don't want the hassles that go with big, highly visible events, and I am a lousy PR person.

Yet a trapper who worked a large area could live on the little stuff, especially in some of the more heavily populated regions east of the Mississippi.

Getting started should be kept relatively simple. Print up a batch of business cards and buy a telephone-answering machine. Control people can easily operate out of their homes since there is no need to rent an office or incur other expenses.

A car or small truck is a necessity. Hop in it and pay a visit to all of the police departments within reasonable driving distance. If the chief isn't there, get his name and plan another marketing swing later on to pick up the strays whom you missed.

Always leave your card and, if possible, a single folder listing your fees.

Other people to see are the local fire chiefs, the Forest Service district chief, and the local Bureau of Land Management director if there is one in your region. Another trick is to go to the various established pest-control people. Often they don't mind gassing rats, but they may refer a coon or squirrel case rather than fool around with animals they don't understand.

Other possible customers are the animal shelters and the humane societies. Control trappers will find that, if they do the job well, some work will come in -- perhaps even an offer to become a state or county employee on a full-time basis.

Like many other jobs of this type, the trapper should, as much as possible, pay sales calls on his potential and actual customers. Wherever you go, leave a card. Take time to tell a few war stories and, above all, do a good, efficient, sensitive job whenever called out. Part of the job will involve being a good politician. Government trappers must be on guard at all cost so as not to become a liability to their elected employers.

How You Can Do It

1. Think up a new and unique method of controlling a pest or two in your region.
2. Learn animal habits and trapping and hunting in general.
3. Study available poisoning techniques.
4. Put together a library of trapping and control information.
5. Gather a collection of box traps and pen traps.
6. Develop skills talking to those home owners who may consider it to be close to murder to kill a squirrel.
7. Print up cards and hook up an answering machine. Develop a simple brochure or letter listing your services.
8. Visit all of the police and fire departments in

your service area. See the regular commercial pest control people about handling their unwanted wild animal calls.

9. Keep up a schedule of contacts. Do a good job and build the business.

10. If the opportunity comes up, go into the mass blackbird/jackrabbit extermination business. Be alert for any new possibilities.

Conclusion

And so there it is: twenty-four exciting action-career suggestions, ranging from the most difficult in terms of pre-planning, calculations, and aptitude (test pilot) to the most laid-back and pleasant (hunting and fishing guide).

Certainly there is some occupation covered herein that virtually anyone who is disgusted with a sedentary, stick-in-the-mud life can undertake. There are even suggestions for the middle-aged executive who looks down his career path with alarm and decides to do something different and exciting. Now!

These executives are too old to be employed by the FBI and the Secret Service, and certainly are not prime candidates to be rodeo riders. However, they can become fishing guides, missionaries, or Peace Corps volunteers and, if they are smart enough to put the pieces together, they can even work as spies.

For some, the answer may be to do these things for a few years after retirement. People who hire fishing guides think the old men have been doing this all their lives.

Anyone can become a process server or bounty hunter. Those who really want the intense hype can become explosives handlers. No college degree is needed for these three jobs.

Action careers are available to those who are 100 percent adventurers and those who want a bit less than constant action, so I included careers of both kinds.

The careers I covered are legal. I obviously stayed away from those occupations that are just another branch or area of military service. Yet many careers can and should start from a good, solid military background. People who find themselves in the military should take advantage of every training opportunity possible. Certainly there are a great many careers I could have included but did not do so.

One that comes to mind is that of pirate, which was not included here because the best one could do in covering such a topic would be to relate how the modern pirates in the Gulf of Siam and those out of Zamboanga City in the Philippines operate. Perhaps a valid, true career path Americans can follow to become pirates does not exist.

Another occupation not covered here is that

of professional bullfighter. It would have been fun to explore the eroticism supposedly attached to that occupation to find out whether it applied only to Latin ladies or if it was, in fact, an occupational syndrome!

Having actually lived in the midst of action all my life, my recommendation is to go for it. Every few years I break down and take a conventional job and usually stick with it for about three to four months. The money is steady but so is the boredom and bitching. It's like having sex with a skunk (after a bit, one enjoys all of that one can stand.)

Not long after getting back to a conventional job, I am ready to go back to the uncertainty, hard work, loneliness, and grief associated with an action career. Living on an adrenaline high is habit-forming. Anything else is definitely second best.

Bibliography

Allen, Harry. The FBI in Our Open Society. New York: W.W. Norton & Co. Inc., 1969.

Amber. Gun Digest. Arroyo Grande, CA: Gun Digest (Digest Books), 1963.

Barron, John. The KBG Today: The Hidden Hand. Chicago: Coronet, The Multimedia Co., 1974.

Barron, John. MIG Pilot. New York: Avon Books, 1980.

Benson, Ragnar. Gunrunning for Fun and Profit. Boulder, CO: Paladin Press, 1986.

Bolles. What Color Is Your Parachute? Berkeley, CA: Ten Speed Press, 1985.

Burton, Bob. The Bounty Hunter. Boulder, CO: Paladin Press, 1985.

Churchill, Winston S. Memoirs of the Second World War. New York: Bonanza Pub. Co., div. of Crown Pub. Inc., 1968.

Clark, Leonard. The Rivers Ran East. New York: Funk & Wagnalls Inc.,1953.

Cook, Fred. The FBI Nobody Knew. New York: Macmillan Inc., 1964.

Crowley. The New KBG. New York: William Morrow & Co. Inc., 1985.

Daily. Traplines and Trails. Outdoorsman Pub. Co., 1945.

Elhanan, Paul. Keep 'Em Alive. Boulder, CO: Paladin Press, 1984.

Ferrara, J.M. Aviation Electronics. Glendale, CA: El-Jac Pub. Co., dist. by Aviation Book Co.

Finn, M.C. The Complete Book of Smuggling. Boulder, CO: Paladin Press, 1984.

Fox and Schnitzer. Doing Business in Washington. New York: Free Press (Macmillan Inc.), 1981.

Geraghty. This Is the SAS. New York: Arms & Armour Press, dist. by Sterling Pub. Co. Inc.

Gibbs, Rafe. Beckoning the Bold. Moscow, Idaho: University of Idaho Press, 1976.

Great Outdoor Adventures. New York: Outdoor Life Books (Times Mirror Magazines Inc.), 1961.

Hatley, George. Horse Camping. New York: Dial Press, 1981.

Helmericks. Hunting in North America. Harrisburg, PA: Stackpole Books, 1959.

Janos. Yeager. New York: Bantam Books Inc., 1985.

Johnson, R.W. Shootdown. New York: Viking Penguin Inc., 1986.

Kreps. Camp and Trail Methods. Columbus, OH: A.R. Harding Pub. Co., 1944.

Lansdale, E.G. In the Midst of Wars. New York: Harper & Row Pubs. Inc., 1972.

Manchester, William. The Arms of Krupp. New York: Bantam Books Inc.,1978.

Michael. Working on the System. New York: Basic Books Inc., 1974.

Montgomery of Alamein. History of Warfare. Cleveland, OH: World Pub. Co., 1968.

Naisbett. Megatrends. New York: Warner Books Inc., 1984.

People's Republic of China Government Pub. China North Industries Corp. Catalog. San Francisco: China Books & Periodicals Inc., distributors, 1984.

Phillips, David Atlee. Careers in Secret Operations. Bethesda, MD: University Publications of America, 1984.

Powers, Thomas. The Man Who Kept the Secrets. New York: Pocket Books (Simon & Schuster Inc.) 1979.

Rikoff. The Book of Hunting. J. Lowell Pratt & Co., 1964.

Russell, John III. Involuntary Repossession: Or, In the Steal of the Night. Boulder, CO: Paladin Press, 1984.

Ryley, Courtney. Ten Thousand Public Enemies. Boston: Little, Brown & Co. Inc., 1935.

Schott, Joseph. No Left Turns. New York: Praeger Pubs., 1975.

Stephenson. Skip Tracing. Stephenson Press.

Thompson, Leroy. Dead Clients Don't Pay. Boulder, CO: Paladin Press, 1984.

U.S. Arms Control and Disarmament Agency. World Expenditures and Arms Transfers. Washington, D.C.: U.S. Government Printing Office, 1985.

Zoglio. Tracing Missing Persons. Tower Hill Press.

Appendix A
Application Forms

CENTRAL INTELLIGENCE AGENCY

It is the responsibility of the Central Intelligence Agency to collect, research, and analyze the foreign intelligence information which senior officials of our Government must have in order to make the informed decisions necessary to maintain our national security.

CAREER OPPORTUNITIES

CHEMISTRY ENGINEERING PHYSICAL SCIENCES	Analysis and evaluation of the performance capabilities of foreign devices, equipment and systems. Research, design, and development of technical devices, equipment and systems in support of intelligence activities.
MATHEMATICS COMPUTER SCIENCES	Development and maintenance of applications computer programs for business, management information, and scientific systems. Maintenance of interactive, on-line, and batch information processing systems.
PHOTOGRAPHIC INTERPRETATION	Analysis and interpretation of photography and other imagery to identify developments of intelligence value.
ECONOMICS	Research and analysis of the economics of foreign countries, international trade and monetary developments, and international commodity markets. Research and analysis of foreign military developments including strategic capabilities.
FOREIGN AREA STUDIES INTERNATIONAL RELATIONS	Collection, research, analysis, and evaluation of political developments in foreign countries. (Graduate degree preferred.)
FOREIGN LANGUAGES	Translation and transcribing of the Russian, Eastern European, Middle Eastern, and Oriental languages. Technical expertise with language skill is preferred.
COMMUNICATIONS ELECTRONICS	General telecommunication duties including operation of manual radio (Morse Code), landline, and teletype circuits. Technical support of world-wide communications network.
STENOGRAPHER TYPIST	Responsible positions for stenographers (80 WPM) and typists (40 WPM) are available in the Washington, D.C. metropolitan area. Overseas assignments are available to those who are at least 21 years old and who have served in the Washington, D.C. area for a period of time.

This list is by no means all-inclusive. As personnel requirements are filled or modified, recruitment emphasis will vary.

Positions are located in the Washington, D.C. area; some offer opportunities for foreign assignment. U.S. citizenship is required.

Because of the nature of its responsibilities, the Central Intelligence Agency must make a very thorough investigation of the character and qualifications of each applicant who is tentatively selected for employment. You are therefore urged to apply well ahead of the date when you would like to enter on duty with the Agency.

CIA Job Application Form

PERSONAL RÉSUMÉ	*INSTRUCTIONS: Type or print carefully--USE BLACK TYPEWRITER RIBBON OR BLACK INK. Answer questions completely or check appropriate box. If question is NOT APPLICABLE, write "NA." If you have insufficient space, continue on an attached sheet and refer to SECTION and ITEM number for each item continued.*

NOTE

Pursuant to 28 U.S.C. 535 and Executive Order, the Agency is required to report to the Department of Justice possible violations of Federal Criminal Law, by any officer or employee of the United States Government; pursuant to Executive Order, the Agency is also required to report to the Department of Justice possible violations of Federal law by any person as specified by the Attorney General.

SECTION A — GENERAL

1. NAME *(Last-First-Middle)* ☐ *Mr.* ☐ *Miss* ☐ *Mrs.* ☐ *Ms.*
2. DATE OF BIRTH
3. PLACE OF BIRTH
4. MAILING ADDRESS *(Number, Street, City, State, Zip Code)*
5. TELEPHONE NUMBERS *(Incl. area code)* HOME: OFFICE:
6. DATE AND PLACE U.S. CITIZENSHIP ACQUIRED *(If not by birth)*
7. MARITAL STATUS *(If married and spouse is not U.S. citizen, please indicate citizenship)*
8. NUMBER OF DEPENDENTS
9. RELATIVES BY BLOOD, MARRIAGE, OR ADOPTION WHO ARE NOT U.S. CITIZENS *(Indicate only relationship, citizenship)*

Note Special Instructions — *If answer to either Question 10a or 10b is Yes, state form(s) of drugs taken, how administered, dates and places, to what extent, and under what circumstances. Provide the information requested for each question on a separate, signed sheet and attach the sheet to this form.*

10A. DO YOU USE OR HAVE YOU EVER USED NARCOTICS, SUCH AS HEROIN? ☐ YES ☐ NO

10B. DO YOU USE OR HAVE YOU EVER USED SUCH ITEMS AS MARIJUANA, HASHISH, LSD, AMPHETAMINES, OR DRUGS OF A SIMILAR NATURE? ☐ YES ☐ NO

ARE THERE ANY INCIDENTS IN YOUR LIFE *(not mentioned previously)* WHICH YOU DESIRE TO EXPLAIN? IF SO, DESCRIBE INCIDENT(S) AND PROVIDE DATE(S) OF OCCURRENCE(S) ON SEPARATE SHEET IN ACCORDANCE WITH SPECIAL INSTRUCTIONS ABOVE. ☐ YES ☐ NO

SECTION B — EDUCATION AND SUPPLEMENTARY QUALIFICATIONS

1. HIGH SCHOOL, COLLEGE, OR UNIVERSITY, TECHNICAL, COMMERCIAL AND MILITARY SCHOOLS

NAME AND LOCATION	RECEIVED: DEGREE OR H.S. DIPLOMA	RECEIVED: YEAR	MAJOR SUBJECT OR SPECIALIZATION *(Including thesis topics)*	GRADE OR POINT AVERAGE

2. FOREIGN LANGUAGE SKILLS *(Specify language & fluency (read, speak, write) using scale from 1 (slight)-2-3-4-to 5 (native)*
3. APPROXIMATE NUMBER OF WORDS PER MINUTE — TYPING → SHORTHAND →
4. RADIO OPERATOR PROFICIENCY — C/W SENDING → C/W RECEIVING →
5. LIST LICENSES OR TRADE CERTIFICATIONS WHICH YOU HAVE ACQUIRED

SECTION C — MILITARY DATA

1. BRANCH OF SERVICE
2. RANK, GRADE, OR RATE
3. MILITARY OCCUPATIONAL SPECIALITY *(MOS or Designator)* AND TITLE
4. DATES OF SERVICE *(From-to-, by mo. and yr.)*

SECTION D — POSITION DATA

1. INDICATE WILLINGNESS TO ACCEPT ASSIGNMENT IN EACH LOCATION NOTED *(Check X items applicable)*

	WASHINGTON, D.C.		ANYWHERE IN U.S.	CERTAIN LOCATIONS ONLY *(Specify)*
	OUTSIDE CONTINENTAL U.S.			

2. TYPE OF POSITION OR WORK FOR WHICH YOU ARE APPLYING — ☐ PART TIME ☐ FULL TIME
3. ACCEPTABLE SALARY RANGE
4. DATE AVAILABLE

FORM 10-79 444a USE PREVIOUS EDITIONS — (OVER) — (4)

SECTION E		EMPLOYMENT INFORMATION		
LIST PRESENT POSITION FIRST. *When completing "Brief Description of Duties," consider your experience carefully and provide meaningful, objective statements.*				
DATES EMPLOYED *(From-to-)*	NAME OF FIRM *(Incl. location)*	POSITION TITLE	BRIEF DESCRIPTION OF DUTIES *(INCLUDE REASON FOR LEAVING)*	SALARY
WHO REFERRED YOU?		DATE	SIGNATURE OF APPLICANT	

Application for Employment Federal Bureau of Investigation

INSTRUCTIONAL INFORMATION SHEET

This sheet has been prepared for your aid in executing the application for FBI employment. If there are questions which are not applicable to you, please indicate this fact by the notation "N/A" in the appropriate space.

If additional space is needed for any section or question on the application, or if you wish to furnish additional information, attach sheets of the same size as this application, and number answers to correspond to the questions.

The application must be clear and legible. We prefer a typewritten application but will accept a legible printed application using black ink.

COMMON AREAS OF OMISSION

We found that some applicants have excluded middle names of all relatives (see Part XII). If a relative does not have a middle name, indicate (NMN), meaning no middle name. If you are unable to furnish complete information concerning your parents or relatives, give sufficient explanation.

If you have ever served in the Armed Forces, indicate in Part II by each address if you lived on or off base, including overseas tours. If you have a relative currently in the military, indicate complete address, including Military Serial Number, and whether or not his/her residence is on or off base.

TRANSCRIPTS

Transcripts of all college courses are necessary if:

1. Applying for Special Agent under any option of the Science Program.
2. You are applying for a Laboratory Aid or Technician position.

Transcripts should be attached to the completed application so that determination may be made as to your academic qualifications for the position.

CERTIFICATIONS

If you are applying as a Special Agent under our Accounting Program, certification as to your academic qualifications may be necessary. See your local FBI office for further information.

NOTICE—Incomplete information will result in delay in the processing of your application.

DETACH THIS INSTRUCTIONAL SHEET PRIOR TO SUBMITTING YOUR APPLICATION

Application for Employment for the FBI

GENERAL

This information is provided pursuant to Public Law 93-579 (Privacy Act of 1974), December 31, 1974, for individuals completing FBI employment application forms.

AUTHORITY

Title 28, Code of Federal Regulations, Section 0.137, authorizes the Director of the FBI to exercise power and authority vested in the Attorney General by law to take final action in matters pertaining to the employment, direction and general administration of personnel in the FBI.

PURPOSE AND USE

The principal purpose of employment application forms is to collect information needed to determine qualifications, suitability, and availability of applicants for FBI employment and of current FBI employees for reassignment, reinstatement, transfer, or promotion. Your completed application may be used to examine, rate, and/or assess your qualifications; to determine if you are entitled under certain laws and regulations such as Veterans' Preference, and restrictions based on citizenship, members of family already employed, and residence requirements; and to contact you concerning availability and/or interview. All or part of your completed FBI employment application form may be disclosed outside the FBI to:

1. Federal agencies upon request for a list of eligibles to consider for appointment, reassignment, reinstatement, transfer, or promotion.
2. State and local Government agencies under the Intergovernmental Personnel Act terms if you have expressed an interest in and availability for such employment consideration.
3. State and local Government agencies under the President's Executive Exchange Program terms if you have expressed an interest in and availability for such employment consideration.
4. Federal agency investigators to determine your suitability for Federal employment.
5. Federal, State, or local agencies to create other personnel records after you have been appointed.
6. Appropriate Federal, State, or local law enforcement agencies charged with the responsibility of investigating a violation or potential violation of the law.
7. Appropriate Federal, State, or local agencies maintaining records on you to obtain information relevant to an agency decision about you.
8. A requesting Federal, State, or local agency to the extent the information is relevant to the requesting agency's decision.
9. Federal agency selecting officials involved with internal personnel management functions.

EFFECTS OF NONDISCLOSURE

Because the employment application forms request both optional (other skills, training, social security number, etc.) and mandatory (qualifications and biographical, etc.) data, it is in your best interest to answer all questions. Omission of an item means you might not receive full consideration for a position in which this information is needed. A false answer to a question in the employment application may be grounds for not employing you, or for dismissing you after you begin work, and may be punishable by fine or imprisonment (U.S. Code, Title 18, Section 1001). All statements are subject to investigation, including a check of your fingerprints, police records, and former employers. All information you give will be considered in reviewing your statement. In addition to the penalties described above, a false answer to questions relating to membership in the Communist Party, U.S.A., could deprive you of your right to an annuity when you reach retirement age.

FD-140 (Rev. 4-26-85)

APPLICATION FOR EMPLOYMENT
FEDERAL BUREAU OF INVESTIGATION
WASHINGTON, D. C. 20535

Date ____________

☐ **Clerk**
☐ **Typist**
☐ **Stenographer**
☐ **Special Agent**
☐ **Language Specialist**
☐ **Laboratory Aid/Technician**
☐ **Computer Programmer**
☐ **Electronics Technician**
☐ **Accounting Technician**
☐ **Systems Analyst**
☐ **Computer Scientist**
☐ **Nurse**
☐ **Other** ____________

I. PERSONAL HISTORY

1. Name in Full (Last, First, Middle)

2. List all other names you have used including nicknames; if female, furnish maiden name. If you have ever used any surnames other than your true name, during what period and under what circumstances were these names used? If you have ever legally changed your name, give date, place, and court.

3. Birth Date (Month, Date, Year)

4. Place of Birth

5. Age

6. Sex ☐ Male ☐ Female

7. Social Security Number (See Privacy Act Notice on Cover Page)

8. Marital Status: a. ☐ Single ☐ Separated Number of Children ______ ☐ Married ☐ Widowed ☐ Divorced

b. Date and place of marriage

c. State **date, place,** and **reason** for all **separations, divorces** or **annulments.**

____

____

____

9. Citizenship
a. Present citizenship (Country) ____________
b. Citizenship acquired by: ☐ Birth ☐ Marriage ☐ Naturalization
c. Date and place naturalized ____________ d. Naturalization Certificate Number ______

II. RESIDENCES

a. Current Address

____________ Home Phone ____________
Street Address Apt. No. Area Code Number

____________ Work Phone ____________
City State Zip Code Area Code Number

In the event this information becomes invalid, indicate the name and phone number of a relative through whom you may be reached or who could furnish your current address and phone number. ____________
Name Relationship Phone Number

ACTUAL PLACES OF RESIDENCE FOR PAST 10 YEARS

(Any applicant who has been out of high school for more than 10 years must list all residences since high school.) Include address while at school and in military, as well as family-owned vacation homes. For college on-campus residences, give dorm name, city and state. If residences in military service cannot be shown as street address, indicate complete military unit designation and location by city, state, and country. If post office box, give location of post office.

From Month/Yr.	Dates To Month/Yr.	Apt. No.	Street Address	City	State

The Federal Bureau of Investigation is an equal opportunity employer.

Field Office

SEARCHED	INDEXED
SERIALIZED	FILED
FBI-	

Headquarters

67-	
SEARCHED	NUMBERED

THREE

III. EDUCATION

1. High School

Name of High School/Issuer of GED	Address (City, State)	Years Attended	Graduate ☐ Yes ☐ No

2. College or University

Name and location of College or University	Subject: Major	Subject: Minor	Years attended From - To	Degree Received	GPA
a.					
b.					
c.					

3. Specialized Schools

Name and Address of School	Study or Specialization	From	To
a.			
b.			

4. Were you ever dismissed from a school, or was any disciplinary action ever taken against you during your scholastic career? ☐ Yes ☐ No

School ______ Date ______ Action ______

IV. EMPLOYMENT HISTORY

NOTE: LIST LAST POSITION FIRST. Include chronological history of employment starting with current or most recent position. Account for all periods including casual employment and all periods of unemployment. Be sure to include military experience, if applicable.

1. Name and Address of Employer's Organization	Dates Employed: From Month/Yr.	Dates Employed: To Month/Yr.	Salary/Earnings	Average No. of Hrs. Per Week	Place of Employment
			Starting $_____ per____ Ending $_____ per____	☐ Full Time _____ ☐ Part Time	City: State: Phone #:

Exact Title of Your Position	Name of Immediate Supervisor	Reason For Leaving
	______ Area Code ______ Number	

Description of work. (Describe your specific duties, being sure to include any supervisory, managerial, or scientific professional experience, if applicable.)

2. Name and Address of Employer's Organization	Dates Employed: From Month/Yr.	Dates Employed: To Month/Yr.	Salary/Earnings	Average No. of Hrs. Per Week	Place of Employment
			Starting $_____ per____ Ending $_____ per____	☐ Full Time _____ ☐ Part Time	City: State: Phone #:

Exact Title of Your Position	Name of Immediate Supervisor	Reason For Leaving
	______ Area Code ______ Number	

Description of work. (Describe your specific duties, being sure to include any supervisory, managerial, or scientific professional experience, if applicable.)

3. Name and Address of Employer's Organization	Dates Employed: From Month/Yr.	Dates Employed: To Month/Yr.	Salary/Earnings	Average No. of Hrs. Per Week	Place of Employment
			Starting $_____ per____ Ending $_____ per____	☐ Full Time _____ ☐ Part Time	City: State: Phone #:

Exact Title of Your Position	Name of Immediate Supervisor	Reason For Leaving
	______ Area Code ______ Number	

Description of work. (Describe your specific duties, being sure to include any supervisory, managerial, or scientific professional experience, if applicable.)

If additional space is needed, attach additional sheets to the application in the same format.

4. Have you ever been dismissed or asked to resign from any employment or position you have held? ☐ Yes ☐ No If your answer is "Yes.", set forth your explanations on an attached sheet indicating the name of the company, your dates of employment and the reason(s) for your dismissal/resignation.

V. MILITARY RECORD

1. Are You registered for Selective Service? ☐ Yes ☐ No
   Location: City and State ______

2. Have you ever served on active duty in the Armed Forces of the United States? ☐ Yes ☐ No
3. Branch of military service

Type of Discharge Basis:

4. Dates of active duty (month, day, year)
   From: ______ To: ______

5. Serial Number:

6. Member of Reserve? ☐ Yes ☐ No ☐ Ready ☐ Standby ☐ Branch of Service:

7. Was any type of disciplinary action taken against you in the service? Be sure to include nonjudicial punishment(s), if applicable. ☐ Yes ☐ No
   Details:

8. National Guard: ☐ Present ☐ Former ☐ None. If you attend drills, meetings, or camps give name of unit and location:

   Summer Camp Attendance: From: ______ To: ______ Location: ______

9. Do you claim veterans' preference? ☐ Yes ☐ No (If answer is Yes, attach copy of DD-214.) Basis: ☐ Active duty between 12/7/41 and 7/1/55.
   ☐ Entered on active duty between 1/31/55 and 10/14/76 in excess of 180 consecutive days. ☐ Service connected disability
   ☐ Wife ☐ Widow ☐ Mother

VI. REFERENCES AND SOCIAL ACQUAINTANCES

Give three references (not relatives, former or present employers, fellow employees, or school teachers) who are responsible adults of reputable standing in their communities, such as property owners, business or professional men or women including your physician, if you have one, who have known you well for at least five years, preferably those who have known you during the past five years. If retired, give former occupation.

Complete Name ______ (Last, First, Middle)	Home Address ______ Home Phone: Area Code (____) Number ______
Yrs. Acq. | Occupation	Business Address ______ Business Phone: Area Code (____) Number ______
Complete Name ______ (Last, First, Middle)	Home Address ______ Home Phone: Area Code (____) Number ______
Yrs. Acq. | Occupation	Business Address ______ Business Phone: Area Code (____) Number ______
Complete Name ______ (Last, First, Middle)	Home Address ______ Home Phone: Area Code (____) Number ______
Yrs. Acq. | Occupation	Business Address ______ Business Phone: Area Code (____) Number ______

SOCIAL ACQUAINTANCES

Give three social acquaintances in your own age group (including both sexes) who have known you well for at least five years, preferably those who have known you during the past five years.

Complete Name ______ (Last, First, Middle)	Home Address ______ Home Phone: Area Code (____) Number ______
Yrs. Acq. | Occupation	Business Address ______ Business Phone: Area Code (____) Number ______
Complete Name ______ (Last, First, Middle)	Home Address ______ Home Phone: Area Code (____) Number ______
Yrs. Acq. | Occupation	Business Address ______ Business Phone: Area Code (____) Number ______
Complete Name ______ (Last, First, Middle)	Home Address ______ Home Phone: Area Code (____) Number ______
Yrs. Acq. | Occupation	Business Address ______ Business Phone: Area Code (____) Number ______

VII. FOREIGN TRAVEL - (MILITARY SERVICE, RESIDENCE, VISIT)

1. Have you ever visited or resided in any foreign country (including travel in the Armed Forces of the U.S.)? ☐ Yes ☐ No

Passport Number ______ Date and Place Issued ______

Countries Visited	Dates		Reasons for Travel
	From Month/Yr.	To Month/Yr.	

2. Have you ever served in the Armed Forces of a foreign country? ☐ Yes ☐ No (Specify countries; dates)

3. Do you or any member of your immediate family, including in-laws, have any relatives now residing outside the United States (except those in the Armed Forces of the United States or those employed by the United States Government living abroad)? ☐ Yes ☐ No If so, list below and furnish degree of association and contact you and members of your immediate family have with these relatives.

Name	Relation	Age	City	Country	Citizen of What Country

4. Have you or any members of your immediate family, including in-laws, ever had any contact with foreign diplomatic establishments or their representatives in the U.S. or abroad (includes commercial, consular, news media, and trade or travel organizations)? ☐ Yes ☐ No If so, attach a separate page explaining circumstances.

5. Have you or any members of your immediate family, including in-laws, ever been employed by or been a representative or agent of any foreign government or official entity thereof? ☐ Yes ☐ No If so, attach a separate page explaining circumstances.

6. Do you or any members of your immediate family, including in-laws, maintain any contacts with friends, associates, or other individuals residing outside the U.S.? ☐ Yes ☐ No If so, identify by name and country, indicating bases or reasons for contacts, on separate page.

VIII. ORGANIZATION MEMBERSHIP

1. Are you now, or have you ever been a member of any club, society or organization? ☐ Yes ☐ No If Yes, list below; do not abbreviate.

Name	City and State	Former	Present	If Present, List Position and Extent of Activity

IX. COURT RECORD

1. Have you ever been arrested or charged with any violation including traffic, but excluding parking tickets? ☐ Yes ☐ No To your knowledge, has any member of your immediate family ever been arrested for other than traffic violations? ☐ Yes ☐ No If so, list all such matters even if not formally charged or no court appearance, or found not guilty, or matter settled by payment of fine or forfeiture of collateral.

Date	Place and Department	Charge	Court and Place	Disposition	Details

Relatives' Names	Place and Department	Date and Charge	Court and Place	Disposition	Details

2. Have you ever been a plaintiff or defendant in a court action? ☐ Yes ☐ No If so, give date, place, court, names of parties involved, nature of action, and final disposition.

X. FINANCIAL STATUS

1. Do you have any sources of income other than your salary or that of your spouse? ☐ Yes ☐ No
   Specify each with amount ____________

2. Are you indebted to anyone? ☐ Yes ☐ No List any debt over $100. Be sure to include student loans and charge accounts. Also, list any debt regardless of the amount where payment is past due.

Creditor	Address	Amount	Loan or Account Number

3. Have you ever been in or petitioned for bankruptcy? ☐ Yes ☐ No
4. If your answer is Yes to the above, give particulars, including court and date.

XI. SPECIAL QUALIFICATIONS AND SKILLS

1. Do you have foreign language ability? ☐ Yes ☐ No If Yes, indicate your proficiency in each phase of each foreign language, listed as "slight", "good", or "fluent."

Name of Language	Speak	Understand	Read	Write

2. Are you a member of the bar? ☐ Yes ☐ No Date ________ State(s) ____________
3. Are you a CPA? ☐ Yes ☐ No Date ________ State(s) ____________
4. Are you a licensed automobile driver? ☐ Yes ☐ No State(s) ____________ License Number ____________

XII. RELATIVES

All applicants must give complete information concerning their relatives. If you have been married more than once, give the requested information concerning each former husband or wife. Furnish similar information, including date and place of action, for any members of your immediate family who have been divorced. Even though a relative is deceased, give all the information requested, and indicate last residence and year of death. Include stepbrothers and sisters, half brothers and sisters. If you or your spouse have stepparents, legal guardians, or others who have reared you instead of your parents, the requested information should be furnished concerning them, as well as your real parents. If you are engaged to be married or contemplating marriage in the near future, complete information must be included under section 3 and 21 through 26 regarding your future husband or wife and future in-laws, and clearly show that such relationship is a future one.

1. FATHER	2. MOTHER
(Last, First, Middle)	(Last, First, Middle) (Maiden)
Address	Address
Occupation	Occupation
Name of Firm Where Employed	Name of Firm Where Employed
Address of Firm Where Employed	Address of Firm Where Employed
Birth Date Place of Birth	Birth Date Place of Birth

Continued on Next Page

XII. RELATIVES (con't.)

3. **SPOUSE**	4. **FORMER SPOUSE**
(Last, First, Middle) (Maiden)	(Last, First, Middle) (Maiden)
Address	Address
Occupation	Occupation
Name of Firm Where Employed	Name of Firm Where Employed
Address of Firm Where Employed	Address of Firm Where Employed
Birth Date Place of Birth	Birth Date Place of Birth
5. **CHILD**	6. **SPOUSE OF CHILD**
(Last, First, Middle) (Maiden)	(Last, First, Middle) (Maiden)
Address	Address
Occupation	Occupation
Name of Firm Where Employed	Name of Firm Where Employed
Address of Firm Where Employed	Address of Firm Where Employed
Birth Date Place of Birth	Birth Date Place of Birth
7. **CHILD**	8. **SPOUSE OF CHILD**
(Last, First, Middle) (Maiden)	(Last, First, Middle) (Maiden)
Address	Address
Occupation	Occupation
Name of Firm Where Employed	Name of Firm Where Employed
Address of Firm Where Employed	Address of Firm Where Employed
Birth Date Place of Birth	Birth Date Place of Birth
9. **BROTHER**	10. **SPOUSE OF BROTHER**
(Last, First, Middle)	(Last, First, Middle) (Maiden)
Address	Address
Occupation	Occupation
Name of Firm Where Employed	Name of Firm Where Employed
Address of Firm Where Employed	Address of Firm Where Employed
Birth Date Place of Birth	Birth Date Place of Birth

Continued on Next Page

XII. RELATIVES (con't.)

11. **BROTHER**	12. **SPOUSE OF BROTHER**
(Last, First, Middle)	(Last, First, Middle) (Maiden)
Address	Address
Occupation	Occupation
Name of Firm Where Employed	Name of Firm Where Employed
Address of Firm Where Employed	Address of Firm Where Employed
Birth Date Place of Birth	Birth Date Place of Birth
13. **BROTHER**	14. **SPOUSE OF BROTHER**
(Last, First, Middle)	(Last, First, Middle) (Maiden)
Address	Address
Occupation	Occupation
Name of Firm Where Employed	Name of Firm Where Employed
Address of Firm Where Employed	Address of Firm Where Employed
Birth Date Place of Birth	Birth Date Place of Birth
15. **SISTER**	16. **SPOUSE OF SISTER**
(Last, First, Middle) (Maiden)	(Last, First, Middle)
Address	Address
Occupation	Occupation
Name of Firm Where Employed	Name of Firm Where Employed
Address of Firm Where Employed	Address of Firm Where Employed
Birth Date Place of Birth	Birth Date Place of Birth
17. **SISTER**	18. **SPOUSE OF SISTER**
(Last, First, Middle) (Maiden)	(Last, First, Middle)
Address	Address
Occupation	Occupation
Name of Firm Where Employed	Name of Firm Where Employed
Address of Firm Where Employed	Address of Firm Where Employed
Birth Date Place of Birth	Birth Date Place of Birth

Continued on Next Page.

XII. RELATIVES (con't.)

19. **SISTER**	20. **SPOUSE OF SISTER**
(Last, First, Middle) (Maiden)	(Last, First, Middle)
Address	Address
Occupation	Occupation
Name of Firm Where Employed	Name of Firm Where Employed
Address of Firm Where Employed	Address of Firm Where Employed
Birth Date Place of Birth	Birth Date Place of Birth
21. **FATHER-IN-LAW**	22. **MOTHER-IN-LAW**
(Last, First, Middle)	(Last, First, Middle) (Maiden)
Address	Address
Occupation	Occupation
Name of Firm Where Employed	Name of Firm Where Employed
Address of Firm Where Employed	Address of Firm Where Employed
Birth Date Place of Birth	Birth Date Place of Birth
23. **BROTHER OF YOUR SPOUSE**	24. **BROTHER OF YOUR SPOUSE**
(Last, First, Middle)	(Last, First, Middle)
Address	Address
Occupation	Occupation
Name of Firm Where Employed	Name of Firm Where Employed
Address of Firm Where Employed	Address of Firm Where Employed
Birth Date Place of Birth	Birth Date Place of Birth
25. **SISTER OF YOUR SPOUSE**	26. **SISTER OF YOUR SPOUSE**
(Last, First, Middle) (Maiden)	(Last, First, Middle) (Maiden)
Address	Address
Occupation	Occupation
Name of Firm Where Employed	Name of Firm Where Employed
Address of Firm Where Employed	Address of Firm Where Employed
Birth Date Place of Birth	Birth Date Place of Birth

Continued on Next Page.

XII. RELATIVES (con't.)

27. **OTHER INDIVIDUALS WITH WHOM YOU HAVE RESIDED OVER A PERIOD OF 30 DAYS OR MORE. Indicate relationship. Include college roommates.**	28. **OTHER INDIVIDUALS WITH WHOM YOU HAVE RESIDED OVER A PERIOD OF 30 DAYS OR MORE. Indicate relationship. Include college roommates.**
(Last, First, Middle) (Maiden)	(Last, First, Middle) (Maiden)
Address	Address
Occupation	Occupation
Name of Firm Where Employed	Name of Firm Where Employed
Address of Firm Where Employed	Address of Firm Where Employed
Birth Date Place of Birth	Birth Date Place of Birth

29. Of the individuals listed in items 1 through 28, are any naturalized or non-U.S. citizens? ☐ Yes ☐ No If Yes, give full details.

Full Name	Naturalization #, Date, and Place of Naturalization	Alien Registration Number

XIII. RELATIVES EMPLOYED BY THE GOVERNMENT

List the complete names of any of your close relatives (including in-laws) who are employed by the Federal Government.

Complete Name	Relation	Agency by Which Employed	Location

XIV. FRIENDS OR ACQUAINTANCES EMPLOYED BY THE FBI

Complete Name	Location	Length of Acquaintance

XV. PHYSICAL DATA

1. Height Without Shoes
2. Weight Without Clothes
3. Do you now have or have you ever had any of the following: nervous, mental, or emotional disorder of any sort; hypertension; tuberculosis; epilepsy, fainting spells or severe headaches; diabetes; ulcers; rheumatic fever or heart disease; or asthma? ☐ Yes ☐ No If Yes, describe, giving date(s) of illness(es), attending physician, and hospital or institution where treated (if applicable).
4. Do you now have or have you ever had any chronic or serious illnesses; or have you ever had any serious operations or injuries? ☐ Yes ☐ No If Yes, describe, giving date(s) of illness(es), or operation(s), attending physician, and hospital or institution where treated (if applicable).

5. Dates From Month/Yr.	To Month/Yr.	Hospital	Location	Reason

Continued on Next Page.

XV. PHYSICAL DATA (con't.)

6. Describe any past or present physical handicap, or disability, not previously covered, but including extent of defective vision, if any, with and without glasses (Snellen) and deficiencies in color vision and hearing. Have you ever undergone radial keratotomy? ☐ Yes ☐ No If yes, give date(s), attending physician(s), and locations(s) where procedure was performed.

RIGHT EYE	Corrected	20/	LEFT EYE	Corrected	20/
	Uncorrected	20/		Uncorrected	20/

7. Have you ever received, is there pending, have you applied for, or do you intend to apply for pension or compensation for any disability? ☐ Yes ☐ No If Yes, specify what kind, granted by whom, and what amount, when, why. If applicable, include Veterans' Administration claim number.

8. Special Agent Applicants Only: Do you have any physical defect such as, but not limited to, a bone, joint; or other deformity or loss of finger, which would preclude unrestricted, regular participation in all phases of the FBI's firearms training, physical training and defensive tactics? ☐ Yes ☐ No If Yes, describe.

XVI. PERSONAL DECLARATIONS

1. Do you use or have you ever used intoxicants? ☐ Yes ☐ No
2. If so, to what extent?
3. Do you use or have you ever used such items as marijuana, hashish, cocaine, LSD, amphetamines, heroin, or drugs of a similar nature? ☐ Yes ☐ No
4. If answer to Question 3 above is Yes, complete the following items for **each** drug used:

   a. Drug ____________ b. How taken ____________

   c. Circumstances ____________

   d. How many times used ____________ e. First time used ____________ f. Last time used ____________
5. List the names of Federal, state, or local departments, agencies or offices (including law enforcement) to which you have applied for employment.
6. If to your knowledge any of the above have conducted an investigation of you, indicate the name of the agency and the approximate date of the investigation.
7. Are you now or have you ever been a member of the Communist Party, U.S.A., or any communist or fascist organization? ☐ Yes ☐ No
8. Are you now or have you ever been a member of any foreign or domestic organization, association, movement, group, or combination of persons which is totalitarian, fascist, communist, or subversive, or which has adopted, or shows a policy of advocating or approving the commission of acts of force or violence to deny other persons their rights under the Constitution of the United States, or which seeks to alter the form of Government of the U.S. by unconstitutional means? ☐ Yes ☐ No (If answer to any of these is Yes, explain fully.)
9. Have you ever been a member of, or supported, or had any connection with a foreign intelligence organization or its activities? ☐ Yes ☐ No If answer is Yes, give complete details.
10. An investigation will be conducted of all information listed on this application. Because of this, are you aware of any information about yourself or any person with whom you are or have been closely associated (including relatives and roommates) which might tend to reflect unfavorably on your reputation, morals, character, ability or loyalty to the United States? ☐ Yes ☐ No If Yes, please attach a separate piece of paper, appropriately numbered, giving your version of this/these incident(s).

Do you understand all prospective FBI employees will be required to submit to an urinalysis for drugs of abuse prior to employment? Yes ☐ No ☐

XVII. AVAILABILITY OF APPLICANT

1. Have you previously submitted an application for employment with the FBI? ☐ Yes ☐ No

   Date ____________ Place ____________________

4. If appointed as a Special Agent or Electronics Technician, are you willing and prepared to accept assignment or transfer to any part of the U.S. or Puerto Rico for either temporary or permanent durations? ☐ Yes ☐ No

2. Are you willing to relocate to Washington, D.C., or other duty station, at your own expense? ☐ Yes ☐ No

5. If appointed as a Special Agent, I agree to serve a minimum period of three years and completely understand that I must be available for assignment wherever my services are needed. ☐ Yes ☐ No

3. If appointed to a support position, I am willing to serve a minimum period of one year. ☐ Yes ☐ No

6. Earliest date available for employment?

7. How much notice to report do you need?

8. I understand that appointment to a support position does not assure me of being offered a Special Agent appointment in the future even if I meet the basic requirements for this position. I realize I will be evaluated as a prospective Special Agent after I attain basic prerequisites for consideration. ☐ Yes ☐ No

ALL APPLICANTS — Attach an unmounted full-face photograph of yourself, not larger than 2¾ x 2½ inches. Print your name plainly on the back of the photograph. The photograph must have been taken not more than 3 months prior to the date of this application.

ATTENTION — THIS STATEMENT MUST BE SIGNED

I understand that I may be requested to submit to a polygraph examination during the processing of my application, and if hired, subsequent to employment, to assist in determining my suitability for employment or to resolve issues directly related to my employment.

I understand that all appointments are probationary for a period of one year during which I must demonstrate my fitness for continued employment by the Federal Bureau of Investigation. I also understand that, in many parts of the Bureau, it has been necessary to establish regular night and midnight shifts in view of which I must be completely available for such assignments as the needs might arise. I further understand that any appointment tendered me will be contingent upon the results of a complete character and fitness investigation, and I am aware that wilfully withholding information or making false statements on this application will be the basis for dismissal from the Federal Bureau of Investigation, and constitutes a violation of Section 1001, Title 18, U.S. Code. I agree to these conditions and I hereby certify that all statements made by me on this application are true and complete, to the best of my knowledge.

____
Signature of Applicant as usually written.
Do not use nickname.

FD-646 (Rev. 9-9-86)

FEDERAL BUREAU OF INVESTIGATION

Preliminary Application For
Special Agent Position
(Please Type or Print in Ink)

Date: ______________

FIELD OFFICE USE ONLY

Right Thumb Print

Div.: Program:

I. PERSONAL HISTORY

Name in Full: (Last, First, Middle, Maiden)

☐ Mr. ☐ Miss ☐ Ms. ☐ Mrs.

List College Degree(s) Already Received or Pursuing, Major, School, and Month/Year:

Birth Date: (Month, Date, Year)

Birth Place:

Social Security Number: (Optional)

Do you understand FBI employment requires availability for assignment anywhere in the U.S.? ☐ Yes ☐ No

Current Address:

Street ______ Apt. No ______ Home Phone ______ Area Code ______ Number ______

City ______ State ______ Zip Code ______ Work Phone ______ Area Code ______ Number ______

Are you: CPA ☐ Yes ☐ No Licensed Driver ☐ Yes ☐ No U.S. Citizen ☐ Yes ☐ No

Have you served on active duty in the U. S. Military? ☐ Yes ☐ No If yes, indicate branch of service and dates (month/year) of active duty. Include military school attendance (month/year):

How did you learn about or become interested in FBI employment as a Special Agent?

Have you previously applied for FBI employment? ☐ Yes ☐ No If yes, location and date:

Identify **ALL** foreign language backgrounds and your proficiency in each language on the reverse.

Have you ever been arrested or charged with any violation including traffic, but excluding parking tickets? ☐ Yes ☐ No If so list all such matters even if not formally charged or no court appearance, or found not guilty, or matter settled by payment of fine or forfeiture of collateral.

Date	Place and Department	Charge	Disposition	Details

II. EMPLOYMENT HISTORY

Identify your most recent three years FULL-TIME work experience, after high school (excluding summer, part-time and temporary employment).

From Month/Year	To Month/Year	Description of Work	# of hrs. per week	Name/Location of Employer

III. PHYSICAL DATA

Describe any past or present physical handicap, illness, or disability, including asthma (age of last attack), hypertension (past or present medication), epilepsy, diabetes and deficiencies in color vision and hearing. (Use reverse side if necessary.)

Do you wear corrective lenses? ☐ Yes ☐ No / Height ______ Weight ______

Right eye (Snellen) Uncorrected 20/ ____ Corrected 20/ ____ Left eye (Snellen) Uncorrected 20/ ____ Corrected 20/ ____

Have you undergone corrective eye surgery? ☐ Yes ☐ No If yes, what is the name of the surgery?

Do you have any physical defects or other deformity including loss of finger, which would preclude unrestricted regular participation in all phases of the FBI's firearms training, physical training and defensive tactics? ☐ Yes ☐ No If Yes, describe on reverse side.

Do you understand all prospective FBI employees will be required to submit to an urinalysis for drugs of abuse prior to employment? ☐ Yes ☐ No

I am aware that willfully withholding information or making false statements on this application constitutes a violation of Section 1001, Title 18, U.S. Code and if appointed, will be the basis for dismissal from the Federal Bureau of Investigation. I agree to these conditions and I hereby certify that all statements made by me on this application are true and complete, to the best of my knowledge.

____

Signature of Applicant as usually written. **(Do Not Use Nickname)**

The Federal Bureau of Investigation is an equal opportunity employer.

FBI Preliminary Application Form for Special Agent Position

GENERAL

This information is provided pursuant to Public Law 93-579 (Privacy Act of 1974), December 31, 1974, for individuals completing FBI employment application forms.

AUTHORITY

Title 28, Code of Federal Regulations, Section 0.137, authorizes the Director of the FBI to exercise power and authority vested in the Attorney General by law to take final action in matters pertaining to the employment, direction and general administration of personnel in the FBI.

PURPOSE AND USE

The principal purpose of employment application forms is to collect information needed to determine qualifications, suitability, and availability of applicants for FBI employment and of current FBI employees for reassignment, reinstatement, transfer, or promotion. Your completed application may be used to examine, rate and/or assess your qualifications; to determine if you are entitled under certain laws and regulations such as Veterans' Preference, and restrictions based on citizenship, members of family already employed, and residence requirements; and to contact you concerning availability and/or interview. All or part of your completed FBI employment application form may be disclosed outside the FBI to:

1. Federal agencies upon request for a list of eligibles to consider for appointment, reassignment, reinstatement, transfer, or promotion.
2. State and local Government agencies under the Intergovernmental Personnel Act terms if you have expressed an interest in and availability for such employment consideration.
3. State and local Government agencies under the President's Executive Exchange Program terms if you have expressed an interest in and availability for such employment consideration.
4. Federal agency investigators to determine your suitability for Federal employment.
5. Federal, State, or local agencies to create other personnel records after you have been appointed.
6. Appropriate Federal, State, or local law enforcement agencies charged with the responsibility of investigating a violation or potential violation of the law.
7. Appropriate Federal, State, or local agencies maintaining records on you to obtain information relevant to an agency decision about you.
8. A requesting Federal, State, or local agency to the extent the information is relevant to the requesting agency's decision.
9. Federal agency selecting officials involved with internal personnel management functions.

EFFECTS OF NONDISCLOSURE

Because the employment application forms request both optional (other skills, training, etc.) and mandatory (qualifications and biographical, etc.) data, it is in your best interest to answer all questions. Omission of an item means you might not receive full consideration for a position in which this information is needed. A false answer to a question in the employment application may be grounds for not employing you, or for dismissing you after you begin work, and may be punishable by fine or imprisonment (U.S. Code, Title 18, Section 1001). All statements are subject to investigation, including a check of your fingerprints, police records, and former employers. All information you give will be considered in reviewing your statement. In addition to the penalties described above, a false answer to questions relating to membership in the Communist Party, U.S.A., could deprive you of your right to an annuity when you reach retirement age.

Standard Form 171

Application for Federal Employment

(Formerly **Personal Qualifications Statement)**

Read the Following Instructions Carefully Before You Complete This Application

- **DO NOT SUBMIT A RESUME INSTEAD OF THIS APPLICATION.**
- TYPE OR PRINT CLEARLY IN DARK INK. If you need more space for an answer, continue in item **47** on page 4 or use a sheet of paper the same size as this page. On **each** sheet write your name, Social Security Number, and the announcement number or job title. Attach all sheets to this application at the top of page 3.
- If you do not answer **all** questions fully and correctly, you may delay our review of your application and lose job opportunities.
- Unless we ask for additional material in the announcement or qualification information, **do not attach** any materials, such as: official position descriptions, performance evaluations, letters of recommendation, certificates of training, publications, etc. Any materials you attach which we did not ask for may be removed from your application and will **not** be returned to you.
- We suggest that you **keep a copy** of this application for your use. If you plan to make copies of your application, we suggest you leave items **1, 2, 48** and **49** blank. Complete these blank items each time you apply. **YOU MUST SIGN AND DATE, IN INK, EACH COPY YOU SUBMIT.**
- **If you are applying for a specific Federal civil service examination** (whether or not a written test is required):
  - Read the announcement and other material provided. Make sure that your work experience and/or education meet the qualifications described.
  - Make sure that you are allowed to apply at this time. Civil service examinations may be closed to receipt of new applications for specific types of jobs, grade levels, and/or geographic locations. Follow any directions on "How to Apply".
  - If a written test is required, follow the instructions on your admission card (for example: "Bring a completed SF171 to the test").
  - If a written test is **not** required, mail this application to the address in the announcement.
  - Include all forms required by the announcement.
- **If you are applying for a specific vacancy in a Federal agency:**
  - Study the vacancy announcement to make sure that you meet the qualifications for the job **and** are allowed to apply. Some jobs are limited to people who work for the Federal Government, have worked for the Federal Government in the past, or have an application on file with the Office of Personnel Management.
  - Mail this application to the address in the vacancy announcement.
  - Include all forms that are required by the announcement.
- If you change your address, notify all offices that have your application. Always include your Social Security Number.

Work Experience (Item 24)

- Carefully complete each experience block you need to describe your work experience. Unless you qualify based on education alone, **your rating will depend on your description of previous jobs. Do not leave out any jobs you held during the last ten years.**
- Under **Description of Work,** write a **clear** and **brief**, but **complete** description of your **major** duties and responsibilities for each job. Include any supervisory duties, special assignments, and your accomplishments in the job. We may verify your description with your former employers.
- If you had a major change of duties or responsibilities while you worked for the same employer, describe each major change as a separate job.
- Write in each experience block your name at that time, **if** it is different from the name you currently use. Show your former name in parentheses on the first line under **Description of Work**.

Veteran Preference (Item 22)

- DO NOT LEAVE **22** blank. If you do **not** claim veteran preference, place an "X" in box number **1**, "NO PREFERENCE".
- You **cannot** receive veteran preference if you are retired, or plan to retire, at or above the rank of major or lieutenant commander, **unless** you have a service-connected disability (see "10-POINT PREFERENCE" below).
- Some Vietnam Era and disabled veterans qualify for special hiring programs. More information is available from any Federal Job Information Center.
- **5-POINT PREFERENCE**. If you claim 5-point preference you must have:
  - Received an honorable or general discharge *(a clemency discharge does **not** meet the requirements of the Veteran Preference Act)*; **and**
  - Served on active duty anytime between December 7, 1941, and July 1, 1955; **or**
  - Served more than 180 consecutive days of active duty, any part of which was after January 31, 1955, and before October 15, 1976 *(do **not** count active duty for training under the "6-month" Reserve or National Guard programs)*; **or**
  - Served in a military action for which you received or were entitled to receive a Campaign Badge or Expeditionary Medal. Write the names of your Campaign Badges and Expeditionary Medals in **47**.

  If you claim 5-point preference place an "X" in box number **2**, "5-POINT PREFERENCE".
- **10-POINT PREFERENCE.** If you claim 10-point preference you must meet the requirements for **one** of the groups below, as described in the Standard Form 15, Application for 10-Point Veteran Preference (SF-15). The SF-15 is available by mail from any Federal Job Information Center.
  - Non-Compensably Disabled or Purple Heart Recipient;
  - Compensably Disabled (less than 30%);
  - Compensably Disabled (30% or more);
  - Spouse, Widow(er), or Mother of a deceased or disabled veteran.

  If you claim 10-point preference, place an "X" in the box that applies to you (**3** or **4** or **5** or **6**). ATTACH A COMPLETED SF-15 TO THIS APPLICATION, TOGETHER WITH THE PROOF REQUESTED IN THE SF-15

Privacy Act Statement

The Office of Personnel Management is authorized to rate applicants for Federal jobs under sections 1302, 3301, and 3304 of title 5 of the U.S. Code. Section 1104 of title 5 allows the Office of Personnel Management to authorize other Federal agencies to rate applicants for Federal jobs. We need the information you put on this form and associated application forms to see how well your education and work skills qualify you for a Federal job. We also need information on matters such as citizenship and military service to see whether you are affected by laws we must follow in deciding who may be employed by the Federal Government.

We must have your Social Security Number (SSN) to keep your records straight because other people may have the same name and birthdate. The SSN has been used to keep records since 1943, when Executive Order 9397 asked agencies to do so. The Office of Personnel Management may also use your SSN to make requests for information about you from employers, schools, banks, and others who know you, but only as allowed by law or Presidential directive. The information we collect by using your SSN will be used for employment purposes and also for studies and statistics that will not identify you.

Information we have about you may also be given to Federal, State and local agencies for checking on law violations or for other lawful purposes. We may send your name and address to State and local Government agencies, Congressional and other public offices, and public international organizations, if they request names of people to consider for employment. We may also notify your school placement office if you are selected for a Federal job.

Giving us your SSN or any of the other information is voluntary. However, we cannot process your application, which is the first step toward getting a job, if you do not give us the information we request.

DETACH THIS PAGE • NOTE ADDITIONAL WORK EXPERIENCE BLOCKS ON BACK

Application for Federal Employment—SF 171

Form Approved: OMB No. 3206-0012

Read the instructions before you complete this application. *Type or print clearly in dark ink.*

GENERAL INFORMATION

1 What kind of job are you applying for? *Give title and announcement number (if any)*

2 If the announcement lists several job titles, which jobs are you applying for?

3 Social Security Number

4 Birth date *(Month, Day, Year)*

5 Name *(Last, First, Middle)*

Street address or RFD number *(include apartment number, if any)*

City | State | ZIP Code

6 Other names ever used

7 Sex *(for statistical use)* ☐ Male ☐ Female

8 Home Phone — Area Code | Number

9 Work Phone — Area Code | Number | Ext

10 Were you ever employed as a civilian by the Federal Government? If **"NO"**, go to **11**. If **"YES"**, mark each type of job you held with an **"X"**.
☐ Temporary ☐ Career-Conditional ☐ Career ☐ Excepted
What is your highest grade, classification series and job title?

Dates at highest grade: FROM TO

11 Do you have any applications for Federal employment on file with the U.S. Office of Personnel Management? If **"NO"**, mark here ☐ and go to **12**. If **"YES"**, write below and continue in **47** the information for each application: (a) the name of the office that has your application; (b) the title of the job; (c) the date of your Notice of Results; and (d) your rating.

FOR USE OF EXAMINING OFFICE ONLY

Material ☐ Submitted ☐ Returned

Entered register:

Notations:

Form reviewed:

Form approved:

Option	Grade	Earned Rating	Preference	Aug Rating
			☐ 5 Points (Tent.)	
			☐ 10 Pts (30%) Or More Comp. Dis.	
			☐ 10 Pts Less Than 30% Comp. Dis.	
			☐ Other 10 Points	
			☐ Disallowed	

Initials and Date ☐ Being Investigated

ANNOUNCEMENT NO.

APPLICATION NO.

FOR USE OF APPOINTING OFFICER ONLY

Preference has been verified through proof that the separation was under honorable conditions, and other proof as required.

☐ 5-Point ☐ 10 Point—30% or More Compensable Disability ☐ 10-Point—Less Than 30% Compensable Disability ☐ 10 Point - Other

Signature and Title

Agency | Date

AVAILABILITY

12 When can you start work? *(Month and Year)*

13 What is the **lowest** pay you will accept? Pay $______ per ______ **OR** Grade ______

14 Are you willing to work:	YES	NO
A. In the Washington, D.C. metropolitan area?		
B. Outside the 50 United States?		
C. Any place in the United States?		
D. Only in *(list the location[s])*		

		YES	NO
15 Are you willing to work:	A. 40 hours per week (full-time)?		
	B. 25-32 hours per week (part-time)?		
	C. 17-24 hours per week (part-time)?		
	D. 16 or fewer hours per week (part-time)?		
	E. In an intermittent job (on-call/seasonal)?		
	F. Weekends, shifts, or rotating shifts?		
16 Are you willing to take a temporary job lasting:	A. 5 to 12 months (sometimes longer)?		
	B. 1 to 4 months?		
	C. Less than 1 month?		
17 Are you willing to travel away from home for:	A. 1 to 5 nights each month?		
	B. 6 to 10 nights each month?		
	C. 11 or more nights each month?		

MILITARY SERVICE AND VETERAN PREFERENCE

	YES	NO
18 Have you served on active duty in the United States Military Service? *If your only active duty was training in the Reserves or National Guard, answer "NO".* If **"NO"**, go to **22**		
19 Were you honorably discharged from the military service? *If your discharge was changed to "honorable" or "general" by a Discharge Review Board, answer "YES". If you received a clemency discharge, answer "NO".* If **"NO"**, explain in **47**		
20 Did you or will you retire at or above the rank of major or lieutenant commander?		

21 List the dates, branch, and serial number for all active duty service.

FROM	TO	BRANCH OF SERVICE	SERIAL NUMBER

22 Place an **"X"** in the box next to your Veteran Preference claim. Mark only **one** box. *See the instructions for eligibility information.*

1 NO PREFERENCE

2 5-POINT PREFERENCE—You must show proof when you are hired.

10-POINT PREFERENCE—**If you claim 10-point preference, you must complete a Standard Form 15, which is available at any Federal Job Information Center. ATTACH THE COMPLETED SF 15 TO THIS APPLICATION, TOGETHER WITH THE PROOF REQUESTED IN THE SF 15.**

3 Non-compensably disabled or Purple Heart recipient.

4 Compensably disabled (less than 30%).

5 Spouse, widow(er), or mother.

6 Compensably disabled (30% or more).

THE FEDERAL GOVERNMENT IS AN EQUAL OPPORTUNITY EMPLOYER

Page 1 PREVIOUS EDITION USABLE NSN 7540-00-935-7150 171-108

Standard Form 171 (Rev. 2/84) Office of Personnel Management FPM Chapter 295

WORK EXPERIENCE *If you have no work experience, write "NONE" in A below and go to 25 on page 3*

23 May we ask your present employer about your character, qualifications and work record? *A "NO" will not affect our review of your qualifications. If you answer "NO" and we need to contact your present employer before we can offer you a job, we will contact you first* | YES | NO |

24 READ **WORK EXPERIENCE** ON THE INSTRUCTION PAGE BEFORE YOU BEGIN

- Describe your current or most recent job in Block **A** and work backwards, describing each job you held **during the past 10 years**
- You may sum up in one block work that you did **more than 10 years ago**. But, if that work **is related** to the type of job you are applying for, describe each related job in a separate block
- If you were **unemployed** for longer than **3 months**, list the dates and your address(es) at that time in **47**. Do **not** list unemployment that was more than 10 years ago
- INCLUDE VOLUNTEER WORK *(non-paid work)*—**If the work** *(or a part of the work)* **is like the job you are applying for**, complete **all** parts of the experience block just as you would for a paying job. You may receive credit for work experience with religious, community, welfare, service, and other organizations
- INCLUDE MILITARY SERVICE—You should complete **all** parts of the experience block just as you would for a non-military job, including all supervisory experience. Describe each major change of duties or responsibilities in a separate experience block
- IF YOU NEED MORE EXPERIENCE BLOCKS OR MORE SPACE TO DESCRIBE A JOB—**For more blocks**, use the SF 171-A or sheets of paper the same size as this page (be sure to include **all** information we ask for in **A** or **B** below). On **each** sheet show your name, Social Security Number, and the announcement number or job title. **For more space** continue in **47** or on a sheet of paper as described above
- IF YOU NEED TO UPDATE (ADD MORE RECENT JOBS), use the SF 172 or a sheet of paper as described above

A

Name and address of employer's organization *(include ZIP Code, if known)*

Dates employed *(give month and year)*
From: To:

Average number of hours per week

Salary or earnings
Starting $ per
Ending $ per

Place of employment
City
State

Exact title of your job

Your immediate supervisor
Name | Area Code | Telephone Number

Number and job titles of any employees you supervise(d)

Kind of business or organization *(manufacturing, accounting, social service, etc.)*

If Federal employment *(civilian or military)* list series, grade or rank, and the date of your last promotion

Your reason for wanting to leave

Description of work: Describe your specific duties, responsibilities and accomplishments in this job. *If you describe more than one type of work (for example, carpentry and painting, or personnel and budget), write the approximate percentage of time you spent doing each*

For Agency Use (skill codes, etc.)

B

Name and address of employer's organization *(include ZIP Code, if known)*

Dates employed *(give month and year)*
From To

Average number of hours per week

Salary or earnings
Starting $ per
Ending $ per

Place of employment
City
State

Exact title of your job

Your immediate supervisor
Name | Area Code | Telephone Number

Number and job titles of any employees you supervised

Kind of business or organization *(manufacturing, accounting, social service, etc.)*

If Federal employment *(civilian or military)* list series, grade or rank, and the date of your last promotion

Your reason for leaving

Description of work: Describe your specific duties, responsibilities and accomplishments in this job. *If you describe more than one type of work (for example, carpentry and painting, or personnel and budget), write the approximate percentage of time you spent doing each*

For Agency Use (skill codes, etc.)

Page **2**

FOR MORE EXPERIENCE BLOCKS SEE SF 171-A ON BACK OF INSTRUCTION PAGE

ATTACH ANY ADDITIONAL FORMS AND SHEETS HERE

ATTACH ANY ADDITIONAL FORMS AND SHEETS HERE

EDUCATION

25 Did you graduate from high school? *If you have a GED high school equivalency or will graduate within the next nine months, answer* "YES".

YES ▶ If "YES" give month and year of graduation ______

NO ▶ If "NO" give the highest grade you completed ______

26 Write the name and location *(city and state)* of the last high school you attended

27 Have you ever attended college or graduate school? **YES** ▶ If "YES", continue with **28** **NO** ▶ If "NO", go to **31**

28 NAME AND LOCATION *(city, state and ZIP code)* OF COLLEGE OR UNIVERSITY *If you expect to graduate within nine months, give the* **month** *and* **year** *you expect to receive your degree.*	MONTH AND YEAR ATTENDED		NO. OF CREDITS COMPLETED		TYPE OF DEGREE *(e.g. B.A., M.A.)*	YEAR OF DEGREE
	From	To	Semester Hours	OR Quarter Hours		
1)						
2)						
3)						

29 CHIEF UNDERGRADUATE SUBJECTS *Show major on the first line*	NO. OF CREDITS COMPLETED	
	Semester Hours	OR Quarter Hours
1)		
2)		
3)		

30 CHIEF GRADUATE SUBJECTS *Show major on the first line*	NO. OF CREDITS COMPLETED	
	Semester Hours	OR Quarter Hours
1)		
2)		
3)		

31 Have you completed any other courses or training **related to the kind of jobs you are applying for** *(for example, trade, vocational, Armed Forces, or business)*? **YES** ▶ If "YES", give the information requested below. *(More courses?—Use a sheet of paper)* **NO** ▶ If "NO", go to **32**

MONTH AND YEAR TRAINING COMPLETED	TOTAL CLASSROOM HOURS	SUBJECT(S)	NAME AND LOCATION OF SCHOOL *(City, state and ZIP code, if known)*	CERTIFICATE, DIPLOMA, etc. *(if any)*
1)				
2)				
3)				

SPECIAL SKILLS, ACCOMPLISHMENTS AND AWARDS

32 List your special qualifications, skills or accomplishments that may help you get a job. *Some examples are: skills with machines, most important publications (do not submit copies), public speaking and writing experience, membership in professional or scientific societies, patents or inventions, etc.*

33 How many words per minute can you:

TYPE?	TAKE DICTATION?

Agencies may test your skills before hiring you.

34 List **job-related** licenses or certificates that you have, such as: *registered nurse, lawyer, radio operator, driver's, pilot's, etc.*

LICENSE OR CERTIFICATE	DATE OF LATEST LICENSE OR CERTIFICATE	STATE OR OTHER LICENSING AGENCY
1)		
2)		

35 Do you speak or read a language other than English *(include sign language)*? ***Applicants for jobs that require a language other than English may be given an interview conducted solely in that language.*** **YES** ▶ If "YES", list each language and place an "X" in each column that applies to you. **NO** ▶ If "NO", go to **36**.

LANGUAGE(S)	CAN PREPARE AND GIVE LECTURES		CAN SPEAK AND UNDERSTAND		CAN TRANSLATE ARTICLES		CAN READ ARTICLES FOR OWN USE	
	Fluently	With Difficulty	Fluently	Passably	Into English	From English	Easily	With Difficulty
1)								
2)								

36 List any honors, awards, or fellowships you have received. For each, give the year it was received.

REFERENCES

37 List three people who are **not** related to you and who know your qualifications and fitness for the kind of job(s) for which you are applying. **Do not** list supervisors you listed under **24**.

FULL NAME OF REFERENCE	PRESENT BUSINESS OR HOME ADDRESS *(Number, street, city, state and ZIP code)*	TELEPHONE NUMBER(S) *(Include area code)*	BUSINESS OR OCCUPATION
1)			
2)			
3)			

Page **3**

BACKGROUND INFORMATION—*You must answer each question in this section before we can process your application*

Place an "X" in the proper column for each question below | YES | NO

38 Are you a citizen of the United States? If "NO" write the country or countries you are a citizen of

Important note about questions 39 through 44: We will consider the date, facts, and circumstances of each event you list. In most cases you can still be considered for Federal jobs. However, if you fail to tell the truth or fail to list all relevant events, this failure may be grounds for not hiring you, for firing you after you begin work, or for criminal prosecution [18 USC 1001]

39 During the last **10 years**, were you **fired from any job** for any reason, did you **quit after being told that you would be fired**, or did you leave by mutual agreement because of specific problems? **If "YES"**, use **47** to write for each job. *a) the name of the employer, b) the approximate date you left the job, and c) the reason(s) why you left*

When answering questions 40 through 44 you may omit: 1) traffic fines of $100.00 or less; 2) any violation of law committed before your 18th birthday, if finally decided in juvenile court or under a youth offender law, 3) any conviction set aside under the Federal Youth Corrections Act or similar State law, 4) any conviction whose record was expunged under Federal or State law

40 Have you **ever** been convicted of or forfeited collateral for **any felony**?
A felony is defined as any violation of law punishable by imprisonment of longer than one year except for violations called misdemeanors under State law which are punishable by imprisonment of two years or less

41 Have you **ever** been convicted of or forfeited collateral for any **firearms** or **explosives** violation?

42 During the last **10 years** have you forfeited collateral, been convicted, been imprisoned, been on probation, or been on parole? Do **not** include violations reported in **40** or **41** above

43 Are you **now** under charges for **any** violation of law?

44 Have you **ever** been convicted by a **court-martial**? If no military service, answer "NO"

IF YOU ANSWERED "YES" TO 40, 41, 42, 43, or 44, GIVE DETAILS IN 47. For each violation write the *1) date 2) charge 3) place 4) court and 5) action taken*

45 Do any of your relatives work for the United States Government or the United States Armed Forces? Include *father, mother, husband, wife, son, daughter, brother, sister, uncle, aunt, first cousin, nephew, niece, father-in-law, mother-in-law, son-in-law, daughter-in-law, brother-in-law, sister-in-law, stepfather, stepmother, stepson, stepdaughter, stepbrother, stepsister, half brother, and half sister*

If "YES" use **47** to write for each of these relatives their *a) name b) relationship c) department, agency, or branch of the Armed Forces*

46 Do you receive, or have you ever applied for retirement pay, pension, or other pay based on military, Federal civilian, or District of Columbia Government service?

ADDITIONAL SPACE FOR ANSWERS

47 Write the number to which each answer applies. **If you need more space,** use sheets of paper the same size as this page. On each sheet write your name, Social Security Number, and the announcement number or job title. Attach all additional sheets at the top of page 3.

SIGNATURE, CERTIFICATION, AND RELEASE OF INFORMATION

YOU MUST SIGN THIS APPLICATION. Read the following carefully before you sign.

A false statement on any part of your application may be grounds for not hiring you, or for firing you after you begin work. Also, you may be punished by fine or imprisonment (U.S. Code, Title 18, Section 1001).

I understand that any information I give may be investigated as allowed by law or Presidential order.

I consent to the release of information about my ability and fitness for Federal employment **by** *employers, schools, law enforcement agencies and other individuals and organizations,* **to** *investigators, personnel staffing specialists, and other authorized employees of the Federal Government*

I certify that, to the best of my knowledge and belief, **all** of my statements are true, correct, complete, and made in good faith.

48 SIGNATURE *(Sign each application in dark ink)*	**49** DATE SIGNED *(Month, day, year)*

Page **4** ☆ U.S. GOVERNMENT PRINTING OFFICE : 1985 O - 461-275 (20059)

Standard Form 171-A—Continuation Sheet for SF 171

Form Approved: OMB No. 3206-0012

• Attach all SF 171-A's to your application at the top of page 3.

1. Name (Last, First, Middle)	2. Social Security Number
3. Job Title or Announcement Number You Are Applying For	4. Date Completed

ADDITIONAL WORK EXPERIENCE BLOCKS IF NEEDED

☐ Name and address of employer's organization (include ZIP Code, if known)

Dates employed (give month and year) From To

Average number of hours per week

Salary or earnings Starting $ per Ending $ per

Place of employment City State

Exact title of your job

Your immediate supervisor Name Area Code Telephone Number

Number and job titles of any employees you supervised

Kind of business or organization (manufacturing, accounting, social service, etc.)

If Federal employment (civilian or military), list series, grade or rank, and the date of your last promotion

Your reason for leaving

Description of work: Describe your specific duties, responsibilities and accomplishments in this job. If you describe more than one type of work (for example, carpentry and painting or personnel and budget), write the approximate percentage of time you spent doing each.

For Agency Use (skill codes, etc.)

☐ Name and address of employer's organization (include ZIP Code, if known)

Dates employed (give month and year) From To

Average number of hours per week

Salary or earnings Starting $ per Ending $ per

Place of employment City State

Exact title of your job

Your immediate supervisor Name Area Code Telephone Number

Number and job titles of any employees you supervised

Kind of business or organization (manufacturing, accounting, social service, etc.)

If Federal employment (civilian or military), list series, grade or rank, and the date of your last promotion

Your reason for leaving

Description of work: Describe your specific duties, responsibilities and accomplishments in this job. If you describe more than one type of work (for example, carpentry and painting or personnel and budget), write the approximate percentage of time you spent doing each.

For Agency Use (skill codes, etc.)

THE FEDERAL GOVERNMENT IS AN EQUAL OPPORTUNITY EMPLOYER

PREVIOUS EDITION USABLE NSN 7540-00-935-7157 171-205

Standard Form 171-A (Rev. 2/84) Office of Personnel Management FPM Chapter 295

DEPARTMENT OF TREASURY - BUREAU OF ALCOHOL, TOBACCO AND FIREARMS
EXPLOSIVES TRANSACTION RECORD
(NONLICENSEE OR NONPERMITTEE)
(Prepare in duplicate - Type or print in ink)

NOTE: Please read and care fully follow the instructions attached

TRANSACTION SERIAL NO. *(Begin with "1" and number sequentially)*

NOTICE TO DISTRIBUTEE (BUYER)

1. Explosive materials must be stored in conformance with regulations set forth in 27 CFR Part 181. It is unlawful for any person to store any explosive material in a manner not in conformity with these regulations. If the distributee (buyer) will store explosive materials, he should familiarize himself with the store requirements before he stores such materials.

2. Section 842(k), 18 U.S.C. Chapter 40, provides "It shall be unlawful for any person who has knowledge of the theft or loss of any explosive materials from his stock to fail to report such theft or loss within twenty-four hours of discovery thereof, to the Secretary and to appropriate local authorities." To meet this requirement, any theft or loss must be reported within 24 hours by telephone and in writing to the nearest Bureau of Alcohol, Tobacco and Firearms office shown on the attached sheet and to the appropriate local authority. Telephone ATF (Toll-Free) 800-424-9555 to report all losses or thefts of explosives. For Alaska, Guam, Hawaii, Puerto Rico, or Virgin Islands call collect 202-566-7143.

3. Each business entity acquiring explosive materials shall furnish a current certified list of the names of representatives or agents authorized to acquire explosive materials on behalf of such business entity.

SECTION A – STATEMENT OF DISTRIBUTEE OR BUYER

1. DISTRIBUTEE *(Buyer)*
2. HEIGHT
3. WEIGHT
4. RACE
5. SSN *(Mandatory)*
6. DATE OF BIRTH
7. PLACE OF BIRTH
8. ADDRESS *(No., Street, City, County, State & Zip Code)*
9. SHOW WHAT USE WILL BE MADE OF EXPLOSIVE MATERIALS

☐ COAL MINING *(Including construction on coal mining property)*	☐ AGRICULTURE	☐ SEISMOGRAPHIC RESEARCH
	☐ CONSTRUCTION	
☐ OTHER MINING OR QUARRYING	☐ ROAD BUILDING	☐ FIREWORKS DISPLAY
	☐ OIL WELL DRILLING	☐ OTHER *(Specify)*

10. EXPLOSIVE MATERIALS WILL BE USED AT *(Show complete address, including county)*
11. EXPLOSIVE MATERIALS WILL BE STORED AT *(Show complete address, including county)*
12. DATE OF INTENDED USE
13. TYPE OF STORAGE MAGAZINE(S)
☐ INDOOR ☐ OUTDOOR

14. DATA OF CORPORATION OR OTHER BUSINESS ENTITY
a. PRINCIPAL PLACE OR BUSINESS *(Address)*
b. LOCAL PLACE OF BUSINESS *(Address)*
c. EMPLOYER IDENTIFICATION NO.

15. DATA OF AGENT OF CORPORATION OR OTHER BUSINESS ENTITY
a. NAME AND RESIDENT ADDRESS
b. PLACE OF BIRTH
c. DATE OF BIRTH

16. CERTIFICATION OF DISTRIBUTEE *(Buyer)* – An untruthful answer may subject you to criminal prosecution. Each question must be answered with a yes or no.

a. Are you a fugitive from justice?

b. Are you an unlawful user of, or addicted to marijuana or a depressant, stimulant, or narcotic drug?

c. Have you or the corporation or other business entity been convicted in any court of a crime punishable by imprisonment for a term exceeding one year? (Note: The actual sentance given by the judge does not matter – a yes answer is necessary if the judge could have given a sentence of more than 1 year. Also, a yes answer is required even if a conviction has been discharged, set aside, or dismissed pursuant to an expungement or rehabilitation statute).

d. Are you or the corporation or other business entity under charges in an indictment or information in any court for a crime punishable by imprisonment for a term exceeding one year? (Note: "Information" means a formal accusation of a crime made by a prosecuting attorney as distinguished from an indictment presented by a grand jury.)

e. Have you been adjudicated mentally defective or have you ever been committed to a mental institution?

I hereby certify that the answers to the above are true and correct. I understand that a person who answers any of the above questions in the affirmative is prohibited by Federal law from shipping or transporting any explosive in interstate or foreign commerce or from receiving any explosive which has been shipped or transported in interstate or foreign commerce. I also understand that the making of any false oral or written statement or the exhibiting of any false or misrepresented identification with respect to this transaction is a crime punishable as a felony. I also certify that I have a legitimate use for the explosive materials for the purpose stated in item 9 above and that the explosive materials hereby obtained will be use in such lawful activity at the location stated in item 10 and will be stored at the location specified in item 11, and that I am familiar with all published Federal and State laws and local ordinances related to explosive materials for the location in which I reside and in which I intend to use these explosives.

DISTRIBUTEE'S *(Buyer's or agent's)* SIGNATURE	TITLE	DATE

ATF Form 4710 (5400.4) (8-80) EDITION OF 4-79 MAY BE USED Page 1 of 4

Explosives Transaction Record

NOTICE TO DISTRIBUTOR (SELLER)

1. Under 18 U.S.C. Chapter 40 of the Organized Crime Control Act of 1970, explosive materials and certification on this form are designed so that a licensee or permittee may determine if he may lawfully distribute explosive materials to the nonlicensee or nonpermittee identified in Section A of this form, and to alert such distributee (buyer) of certain restrictions on the receipt of explosive materials.

2. Explosive materials shall not be distributed to a business entity on the order of a person whose name does not appear on a certified list required by regulations to be furnished by such business entity and containing the names of representatives or agents authorized to acquire explosive materials on behalf of such business entity.

3. Prior to the delivery at the distributor's premises of explosive materials to an employee of the distributee or to an employee of a carrier transporting explosive materials to the distributee, the distributor so delivering explosive materials shall also obtain an executed ATF Form 4721, Explosives Delivery Record, from such employee before releasing the explosive materials.

4. This form must be kept for not less than five years.

SECTION B – STATEMENT OF DISTRIBUTOR OR SELLER

17. The Person Whose Signature Appears In Section A Is *(Check One)*		18. The Person Whose Signature Appears In Section A Is *(Check One)*	
☐	a. The distributee shown in item 1, Section A.	☐	a. Is known to me
☐	b. Listed as a representative or an agent authorized to acquire explosive materials for distributee shown in item 1, Section A.	☐	b. Has identified himself to me as indicated in items 19 and 20, Section B

19. TYPE OF IDENTIFICATION *(Driver's license, etc. Positive identification is required. A Social security card is not positive identification.)*	20. NUMBER ON IDENTIFICATION

On the basis of: (1) the statements in Section A; (2) the verification of identity noted in Section B; and (3) my knowledge of Federal and State laws and local ordinances relating to explosive materials, it is my belief that it is not unlawful for me to sell, deliver, or otherwise dispose of the explosive materials described in item 21 or on the attached list to the person identified in Section A.

21. IDENTIFY QUANTITY, SIZE AND TYPE OF EXPLOSIVE MATERIALS INCLUDING NAME OF MANUFACTURER AND ALL MANUFACTURER'S MARKS OF IDENTIFICATION, IF ANY. *(If more space is required, attach a list identified by the Transaction Serial Number)*

22. *(Check appropriate boxes)*

☐ THE EXPLOSIVE MATERIALS WERE DELIVERED AT DISTRIBUTEE'S PREMISES.

☐ THE EXPLOSIVE MATERIALS WERE DELIVERED AT DISTRIBUTOR'S PREMISES.

☐ ATF FORM 4721 ☐ WAS ☐ WAS NOT COMPLETED

23. SELLER'S BUSINESS NAME AND ADDRESS	24. SELLER'S LICENSE OR PERMIT NO.

25. SELLER'S SIGNATURE	26. TITLE	27. TRANSACTION DATE

Page 2 of 4

(it is suggested that one copy be given to distributee (buyer) for information)

INSTRUCTIONS

1. ATF 4710 should be prepared in duplicate for each transaction involving the distribution of explosive materials to persons who have not been issued a Federal explosives license or permit.

2. If the distributee (buyer) is a corporation or other business entity, the agent authorized by such corporation or business entity to arrange for the distribution of explosive materials will complete items 1, 8 through 15, and 16c. and d.

3. All signatures required on this form must be in ink on the original and copy. All other entries on the form must be in ink or be typewritten.

4. The distributor (seller) of explosive materials will, in every instance, require the distributee (buyer) to complete and sign Section A of this form.

5. The distributor (seller) will complete Section B of this form. He will then serially number the original and copy, retain the original as his permanent record of disposition, and forward the copy to the nearest Bureau of Alcohol, Tobacco and Firearms office shown on the reverse on or before the close of business on the business day after the transaction occurs.

NOTICE TO DISTRIBUTEE (BUYER)

1. Explosive materials must be stored in conformance with regulations set forth in 27 CFR Part 181. It is unlawful for any person to store any explosive material in a manner not in conformity with these regulations. If the distributee (buyer) will store explosive materials, he should familiarize himself with the storage re-requirements before he stores such materials.

2. Section 842(k), 18 U.S.C. Chapter 40, provides "It shall be unlawful for any person who has knowledge of the theft or loss of any explosive materials from his stock, to fail to report such theft or loss within twenty-four hours of discovery thereof, to the Secretary and to appropriate local authorities." To meet this requirement, any theft or loss must be reported within 24 hours by telephone and in writing to the nearest Bureau of Alcohol, Tobacco and Firearms office shown on the attached sheet and to the appropriate local authority. Telephone ATF (Toll-Free) 800-424-9555 to report all losses of theft of explosives. For Alaska, Guam, Puerto Rico, or Virgin Islands, call collect 202-566-7143.

3. Each business entity acquiring explosive materials shall furnish a current certified list of the names of representatives or agents authorized to acquire materials on behalf of such business entity.

PRIVACY ACT INFORMATION

The following information is provided pursuant to Section 3 of the Privacy Act of 1974 (5 U.S.C. § 552a(e)(3)):

1. **AUTHORITY.** Solicitation of this information is made pursuant to 18 U.S.C. § 842. Disclosure of this information is mandatory.

2. **PURPOSE.** To enable ATF to identify the purchaser and his place of residence, and to determine his eligibility to purchase explosives.

3. **ROUTINE USES.** The information will be used by ATF to make determinations set forth in paragraph 2. In addition, the information may be disclosed to other Federal, State, foreign and local law enforcement and regulatory agency personnel to verify information on the form and to aid in the performance of their duties with respect to the regulation of explosives, unless such disclosure is prohibited by law. The information may further be disclosed to the Justice Department if it appears that the furnishing of false information may constitute a violation of Federal law. Finally, the information may be disclosed to members of the public in order to verify the information on the form where such disclosure is not prohibited by law.

4. **EFFECTS OF NOT SUPPLYING INFORMATION REQUESTED.** Failure to supply complete information will preclude effectuation of the transaction.

The following information is provided pursuant to Section 7(b) of the Privacy Act of 1974:

Disclosure of the individual's social security number is mandatory. Under 18 U.S.C. § 842(f), ATF has authority to solicit an individual's social security number. The number may be used to verify the individual's identity.

ATF FORM 4710 (5400.4) (8-80) EDITION OF 4-79 MAY BE USED Page 3 of 4

ADDRESS AND TELEPHONE LISTING OF ATF DISTRICT OFFICES

IMMEDIATELY REPORT ALL LOSSES OR THEFTS OF EXPLOSIVES BY TELEPHONING ATF (TOLL-FREE) AT 800-424-9555. FORWARD COMPLETED ATF FORM 4710 OR REPORTS OF THEFT OR LOSS OF EXPLOSIVES TO THE NEAREST BUREAU OF ALCOHOL, TOBACCO AND FIREARMS OFFICE LISTED BELOW:

CENTRAL REGION

INDIANA, KENTUCKY, MICHIGAN, OHIO AND WEST VIRGINIA

Special Agent in Charge (ATF)
U.S. Post Office Building
(Mailing Address: P.O. Box 1759)
Cincinnati, Ohio 45201
Phone: 513-684-3756

Special Agent in Charge (ATF)
55 Erie View Plaza
Cleveland, Ohio 44114
Phone: 216-522-3000

Special Agent in Charge (ATF)
371 Federal Building
Detroit, Michigan 48226
Phone: 313-226-7300

Special Agent in Charge (ATF)
600 Federal Place
Louisville, Kentucky 40202
Phone: 502-582-5211

MID-ATLANTIC REGION

DELAWARE, DISTRICT OF COLUMBIA, MARYLAND, NEW JERSEY, PENNSYLVANIA, AND VIRGINIA

Special Agent in Charge (ATF)
701 West Broad Street
Falls Church, Virginia 22046
Phone: 703-557-1650

Special Agent in Charge (ATF)
P.O. Box 327
Union, New Jersey 07083
Phone: 201-687-6100

Special Agent in Charge (ATF)
U.S. Customs House
2nd and Chestnut Streets
Philadelphia, Pennsylvania 19106
Phone: 215-597-7266

Special Agent in Charge (ATF)
400 North 8th Street
(Mailing Address: P.O. Box 10068)
Richmond, Virginia 23240
Phone: 804-782-2871

NORTH-ATLANTIC REGION

CONNECTICUT, MAINE, MASSACHUSETTS, NEW HAMPSHIRE, NEW YORK, RHODE ISLAND, VERMONT, PUERTO RICO, & VIRGIN ISLANDS

Special Agent in Charge (ATF)
John F. Kennedy Bldg.
(Mailing Address: P.O. Box 9115)
Boston, Massachusetts 02114
Phone: 617-223-3817

Special Agent in Charge (ATF)
90 Church Street
(Mailing Address: P.O. Box 3482
Church Street Station)
New York, New York 10008
Phone: 212-264-4658

NORTH-ATLANTIC REGION (cont.)

Special Agent (ATF)
U.S. Courthouse & Federal Bldg.
Carlos E. Chardon Ave.
Hato Rey, Puerto Rico 00919
Phone: 809-753-4084

Special Agent in Charge (ATF)
135 High Street
Hartford, Connecticut 06101
Phone: 203-244-3642

MIDWEST REGION

ILLINOIS, IOWA, KANSAS, MINNESOTA, MISSOURI, NEBRASKA, NORTH DAKOTA, SOUTH DAKOTA, AND WISCONSIN

Special Agent in Charge (ATF)
2115 Butterfield Road
Oak Brook, Illinois 60521
Phone: 312-325-8620

Special Agent in Charge (ATF)
1150 Grand Avenue
Kansas City, Missouri 64106
Phone: 816-374-3886

Special Agent in Charge (ATF)
1114 Market Street
St. Louis, Missouri 63101
Phone: 314-425-5560

Special Agent in Charge (ATF)
U.S. Court House & Fed. Bldg.
316 North Robert Street
St. Paul, Minnesota 55101
Phone: 612-725-7093

SOUTHEAST REGION

ALABAMA, FLORIDA, GEORGIA, MISSISSIPPI, NORTH CAROLINA, SOUTH CAROLINA & TENNESSEE

Special Agent in Charge (ATF)
C&S Bank Building
1 West Court Square
Decatur, Georgia 30030
Phone: 404-221-6526/27

Special Agent in Charge (ATF)
2121 8th Avenue, North
Birmingham, Alabama 35203
Phone: 205-254-1205

Special Agent in Charge (ATF)
222 S. Church Street
Charlotte, North Carolina 28202
Phone: 704-544-7071

Special Agent in Charge (ATF)
Federal Building
901 Sumter Street
Columbia, South Carolina 29201
Phone: 803-765-5541

Special Agent in Charge (ATF)
100 West Capitol Street
Jackson, Mississippi 39201
Phone: 601-969-4200

SOUTHEAST REGION (cont.)

Special Agent in Charge (ATF)
5205 N.W. 84th Ave.
Miami, Florida 33166
Phone: 305-592-9568

Special Agent in Charge (ATF)
4004 Hillsboro Road
Nashville, , Tennessee 37215
Phone: 615-251-5412

SOUTHWEST REGION

ARKANSAS, COLORADO, LOUISIANA, NEW MEXICO, OKLAHOMA, TEXAS, AND WYOMING

Special Agent in Charge (ATF)
P.O. Box 60927
Houston, Texas 77205
Phone: 713-226-5405

Special Agent in Charge (ATF)
1200 Main Street
Dallas, Texas 75202
Phone: 214-767-2250

Special Agent in Charge (ATF)
Hale Boggs Federal Office Bldg.
500 Camp Street
New Orleans, Lousiana 70130
Phone: 504-589-2048

Special Agent in Charge (ATF)
200 N.W. Fifth Street
Oklahoma City, Oklahoma 73102
Phone: 405-231-4877

WESTERN REGION

ALASKA, ARIZONA, CALIFORNIA, GUAM, HAWAII, IDAHO, MONTANA, NEVADA, OREGON, UTAH, AND WASHINGTON

Resident Agent in Charge (ATF)
300 Ala Moana Blvd.
(Mailing Address: P.O. Box 50103)
Honolulu, Hawaii 96850
Phone: 808-546-3196

Special Agent in Charge (ATF)
300 N. Los Angeles Street
(Mailing Address: P.O. Box 1991)
Los Angeles, California 90053
Phone: 213-688-4812

Special Agent in Charge (ATF)
915 2nd Ave.
Seattle, Washington 98174
Phone: 206-442-4485

Special Agent in Charge (ATF)
2721 N. Central Ave.
Phoenix, Arizona 85004
Phone: 602-261-3220

Special Agent in Charge (ATF)
525 Market Street
San Francisco, California 94105
Phone: 415-556-6769

Resident Agent in Charge (ATF)
Federal Bldg.
Anchorage, Alaska 99501
Phone: 907-279-7914

PEACE CORPS

VOLUNTEER APPLICATION

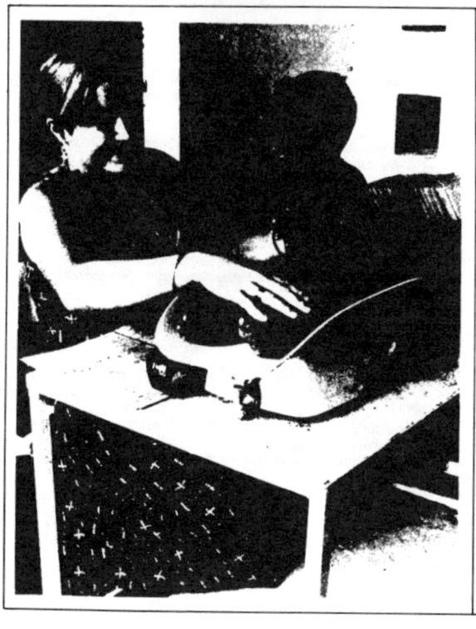

Peace Corps Volunteer Application

INFORMATION FOR THE APPLICANT

To be a Peace Corps Volunteer, you must:

- be a United States citizen
- be at least 18 years old (there is no upper age limit)
- if married, both spouses must serve as Volunteers (there are few exceptions)
- if you have a family which would accompany you, have no more than 2 dependents between the ages of 2 and 18 (and be highly skilled)
- have technical and personal skills that will qualify you for Peace Corps service
- meet legal, security and medical requirements
- be available within the next 12 months

In the host country you will:

- work for a government department, an independent agency or other organization
- be supervised by and work with host nationals
- speak the language of the people
- live as your host country people do and on the living allowance allotted to you
- be subject to local laws
- adjust your vacation and holidays to the local situation

INSTRUCTIONS FOR COMPLETING THE APPLICATION

Fill out your application carefully. Use it to tell us as much about yourself as you can. The application is a presentation of you to the people who will review your skills, your way of life and your experience in an attempt to match you with the needs of a particular assignment. We recommend that you scan through the documents before beginning.

Answer each question as completely as possible. If you need additional space, use section 33 at the back of the application, or attach a sheet of paper. Be sure to identify the number of the question you are answering. If using an attached sheet, make sure your name and social security number appear on it.

Read the instructions for each question carefully. Type or clearly print in black ink. Remove the reference list from this application before you begin.

Your selection of references is very important. Choose people who really know your capabilities and talents. Be sure to let your references know that we will contact them. Urge them to respond promptly once they receive the reference form.

Please remember that you are in no way obligating yourself by submitting this application.

PRIVACY ACT NOTICE

The Agency is required, by provisions of the Privacy Act of 1974 (5 U.S.C. 522a), to advise you of the following information regarding this application:

a) This application is authorized by the provisions of the Peace Corps Act (22 U.S.C. 2501, et seq.) which require the collection of information regarding the suitability qualifications, etc., of applicants.

b) The principal purpose for which the information provided herein will be used is to evaluate your qualifications to serve in a Peace Corps full-time volunteer program.

c) Information in this application may routinely be disclosed as follows:

(1) to sponsoring agencies including agencies of foreign governments for the purpose of determining placement, obtaining visas, and other program related matters;

(2) in appropriate cases, information herein may be divulged to police authorities where appropriate and properly requested;

(3) to the Treasury and other Federal agencies for preparation of support checks and payment of social security and Federal income tax;

(4) to the Office of Personnel Management and other Federal agencies for the purpose of a background suitability investigation;

(5) to other Federal agencies having an interest in employment of the applicant or volunteer, provided that except for information required for authorized security clearances, information provided will be limited to dates of service and a standard description of service;

(6) to a court or other appropriate tribunal upon subpoena or other request;

(7) to a member of Congress upon request indicating that such member has been requested by an individual about whom the record is maintained to obtain such information;

(8) information may be used as a source for management information or preparation for statistical reports (without personal information);

(9) to the National Archives and Records Service, GSA, in authorized management inspections;

(10) when required under provisions of the Freedom of Information Act (5 U.S.C. 552) and Privacy Act (5 U.S.C. 522a);

(11) to the Bureau of the Census for the purposes of planning or carrying out a census of survey or related activity pursuant to the provisions of Title 13; and

(12) to Peace Corps personnel who have a need for the information in the performance of their duties.

d) The completion of this application is voluntary; however, failure to provide information requested may result in Peace Corps' inability to assess the qualifications of an applicant and result in nonselection for the volunteer program applied for.

> IMPORTANT: Remove the PEACE CORPS APPLICANT REFERENCE LIST between pages 4 and 5 before completing this application to prevent damaging the carbon copy. Be sure to return the completed REFERENCE LIST with the completed application.

PC 1502

Form Approved
Office of Management and Budget 0420-0005

PEACE CORPS VOLUNTEER APPLICATION

PLEASE PRINT IN BLACK INK OR TYPE

1. **NAME**

____
LAST FIRST MIDDLE

2. **SOCIAL SECURITY NUMBER**

☐☐☐ ☐☐ ☐☐☐☐

3. **DATE OF BIRTH**

_____ / _____ / _____
NUMERIC MONTH DAY YEAR

4. **SEX**

Female ☐-F Male ☐-M

5. **ADDRESS**

A. Current Mailing Address
(All information will be sent to this address until you notify Peace Corps of a change of address.)

____
NUMBER AND STREET

____
CITY AND STATE ZIP CODE

____
(AREA CODE) HOME PHONE

____
(AREA CODE) BUSINESS OR SCHOOL PHONE

B. Permanent Mailing Address
(Name and address of person through whom you can always be reached.)

____
LAST NAME FIRST NAME INITIAL

____
NUMBER AND STREET

____
CITY AND STATE ZIP CODE

____
(AREA CODE) HOME PHONE

C. Do you expect to move in the next 12 months?

Yes ☐ No ☐

If yes, when _______________
NUMERIC MONTH/DAY/YEAR

6. **AVAILABILITY FOR SERVICE**

Indicate the earliest date you will be available for training.

_____ / _____ / _____
NUMERIC MONTH DAY YEAR

Notify us immediately if your availability date changes.

7. **PREVIOUS APPLICATION FOR PEACE CORPS**

A. Have you applied previously? Yes ☐ No ☐

B. Have you participated in training? Yes ☐ No ☐

C. Have you been a volunteer? Yes ☐ No ☐

If yes to any of the above, please give dates and location. _______________

____

APPLICANT: DO NOT WRITE IN THIS SPACE. OFFICE USE ONLY.

Citizen _____ Marital _____ Spouse Name _____ Spouse SSN _____ Dependents _____

Teach Exp _____ Lang 1 _____ Exp. _____ Lang 2 _____ Exp. _____ Ed Level _____ UG Coll _____ UG Degree _____

UG Major _____ UG Minor _____ G Coll _____ G Degree _____ LDDT _____ Skl 1 _____ Skl 2 _____

Skl 3 _____ Skl 4 _____ Skl 5 _____ Skl 6 _____ Skl 7 _____ Skl 8 _____ Skl 9 _____ Skl 10 _____

Source _____ Status _____ Medical _____ Legal _____ Minority _____ Date _____ Completed by _____

8. CITIZENSHIP—*EVERYONE MUST ANSWER 8A.*

A. Are you a citizen of the United States? Yes ☐ No ☐

Place of Birth ______

B. Naturalization Number if you are a naturalized citizen ______

Only citizens or nationals of the United States are eligible for enrollment as Peace Corps Volunteers.

9. MARITAL STATUS—*EVERYONE MUST CHECK THE APPROPRIATE BOX.*

1. single (never married)
2. plan to marry within one year (date of expected marriage ______)
3. married - living with spouse (date of marriage ______)
4. married - not living with spouse (list below)
5. widowed (list below)
6. divorced or legally separated (list below)

List the names of all former spouse(s) as well as the year(s) of divorce, separation or death

______

______

If engaged or married, do you plan to serve with fiance/spouse? Yes ☐ No ☐

If yes, is his/her application attached? Yes ☐ No ☐

If you are applying for Peace Corps service and your spouse plans to accompany you or join you overseas, he/she must apply to serve as a volunteer before you can be considered for placement.

Indicate name and social security number of fiance/spouse

______ Social Security Number ☐☐☐ ☐☐ ☐☐☐☐

LAST NAME FIRST NAME INITIAL

10. CHILDREN AND OTHER DEPENDENTS—*EVERYONE MUST ANSWER 10A.*

A. Are any persons partially or totally dependent upon you for their support (whether or not they are living with you)? Yes ☐ No ☐

B. List all children under the age of 18 whether or not they are dependent upon you for financial support.

Name of Child	Address	Age	Dependent (Yes/No)	Will Accompany

C. List all dependents not listed above

Name of Dependent	Address	Relationship

D. Do you have adequate means to continue support obligations while serving without salary as a Volunteer? Yes ☐ No ☐

If yes, please specify what arrangements have been made to meet your financial obligations in section 33 at the back of the application. If you need additional space, attach a sheet of paper.

11. LEGAL INFORMATION—*EVERYONE MUST ANSWER 11A, B and D.*

A. Have you ever been convicted of any offense, including both felonies and misdemeanors, by a civilian or military court? (Do not include traffic violations for which you paid a fine of $50 or less, or any offense that occurred before your eighteenth birthday.) Yes ☐ No ☐ (See "C")

B. Are you now under charges for any offense (including charges for traffic offenses), or are any civil suits or judgments now pending against you? Yes ☐ No ☐ (See "C")

C. If you answered yes to either of the above, provide details on a separate sheet of paper. State your name, the date and place of each arrest, suit or judgment. Give the nature of the charge or suit, and current status or disposition including any sentence or fine imposed. Provide a complete explanation of the circumstances. If you wish, place a separate sheet in a sealed envelope including your name and social security number on the outside of the envelope and attach it to this application. Only a limited number of authorized employees will have access to this information and it will be treated in confidence.

D. Do you have any outstanding financial obligations that cannot be satisfied prior to your participation in the Peace Corps? Yes ☐ No ☐

If yes, please specify the nature of these obligations and describe what arrangements will be made to meet them on a separate sheet of paper. Include your name and identify appropriate question number. It may be placed in a separate envelope and attached to this page.

FAILURE TO PROVIDE ALL REQUESTED INFORMATION MAY LEAD TO IMMEDIATE DISQUALIFICATION FOR APPLICANTS AND IMMEDIATE SEPARATION FOR TRAINEES/VOLUNTEERS.

12. INTELLIGENCE ACTIVITIES AND ORGANIZATIONS—*EVERYONE MUST ANSWER 12A AND B.*

A. Are you, or have you ever been, employed by or sought employment with an agency of the U.S. Government, civilian or military, or by a division of such an agency, whose exclusive or principal function is to perform intelligence activities? Yes ☐ No ☐

B. Have you ever engaged in or had any connection with the collection, dissemination or analysis of intelligence information? Yes ☐ No ☐

C. If you answered yes to either of the above, provide details on a separate sheet of paper. Include dates and agency or division for whom the work was performed and/or nature of the connection. If military, give your MOS number and any service schools attended. Include your name, social security number and identify appropriate question number.

2

13. MILITARY STATUS—*EVERYONE MUST ANSWER 13A AND B.*

A. Have you ever served in the Armed Forces? Yes ☐ No ☐

If yes, complete the following:

Branch ______________________ Serial/File number ______________________

Highest rank held ______________________ Dates of Service: From ____________ To ____________

Type of discharge ______________________

B. Are you now a member of the ROTC, National Guard or Reserves? Yes ☐ No ☐

If yes, how do you expect to fulfill your obligation?

____

____

14. PERSONAL HEALTH INFORMATION

Handicapped persons and other individuals with health or medical problems who can, with reasonable accommodation, perform volunteer assignments and who are otherwise qualified, are eligible to serve as Peace Corps Volunteers. To determine whether you are medically qualified for volunteer service and to enable Peace Corps to identify those overseas assignments which are appropriate to any health problems you may have, *you must answer the following questions completely and accurately.* Failure to do so may delay processing of your application.

A. Statistics

Height: ________ ft. ________ in. Weight: ________ (lbs.) Age: ________

Former Peace Corps Volunteer? Yes ☐ No ☐ When? ______________

B. Medical History

Do you suffer from or have you ever been treated for any of the following:

Yes	No	
☐	☐	asthma
☐	☐	diabetes
☐	☐	heart ailments
☐	☐	liver problems
☐	☐	stomach or intestinal problems
☐	☐	cancer
☐	☐	high blood pressure
☐	☐	joint or back problems
☐	☐	kidney problems
☐	☐	epilepsy or other neurological problems
☐	☐	eye problems
☐	☐	lung problems
☐	☐	thyroid problems
☐	☐	skin disease
☐	☐	hernia
☐	☐	pilonidal cyst
☐	☐	alcoholism
☐	☐	drug abuse

Do you need any special medical or dental services?
Yes ☐ No ☐

Have you ever had psychological counseling or therapy?
Yes ☐ No ☐

Have you ever been hospitalized for a psychological problem?
Yes ☐ No ☐

Are you allergic to any medicines (e.g. penicillin, sulfa, etc.), insect stings, foods, animals, or plants?
Yes ☐ No ☐

Have you had surgery other than a tonsillectomy, hernia repair, abortion, appendectomy, or wisdom tooth removal?
Yes ☐ No ☐

Are you now under the care of a doctor or other practitioner for any reason?
Yes ☐ No ☐

Describe nature of problem, treatment, results, and dates for everything checked yes under Medical History. Add any other pertinent medical information you would like to include or think we should know. You may put this information on a separate piece of paper, place it in a sealed envelope which has your name and social security number on the outside and attach it to this page. The information would then be seen only by a limited number of authorized employees.

____

PRACTICAL EXPERIENCE FOR PEACE CORPS (Sections 15-19)

Since the Peace Corps needs—and places—people in many different types of programs, it is necessary to ask a wide range of questions, many of which may not apply to you. In short, the following sections are designed to give you an opportunity to tell us as much about yourself as possible. Be sure to read through each section to see if you do have the type of experience discussed. Your extra efforts in filling out these sections will help us in considering you for placement in that situation which will give you the greatest opportunity of being productive and getting satisfaction from your work. If you find that sections do not apply to you, do not feel that your chances for becoming a Peace Corps Volunteer are lessened.

These questions deal with practical experience in various skill areas. This experience may include actual job experience, summer or part-time work, on-the-job training, field work or other activities associated with academic courses, and hobbies. Detail your level of responsibility; knowledge, skills, and abilities acquired/applied; tools and equipment used; hours worked per week; species of plants/animals worked with; credentials/certificates acquired, etc. Be as specific as possible. If you need more space, use section 33 at the back of the application or attach a separate sheet.

For dates, be sure to include month and year.

15. AGRICULTURE/FISHERIES/FORESTRY EXPERIENCE

If you have any agricultural, fisheries, forestry or conservation experience, please complete this section.

Since the age of 14, have you worked on a farm? Yes ☐ No ☐ If yes, give dates: From __________ To __________.

Type of Experience	Area(s) of Specialization	Amount of Experience		
		Acres/Head	From mo/yr	To mo/yr
A. Agriculture/Home Vegetable Gardening				
Beekeeping				
Beef Production				
Dairy Production				
Farm Machinery				
Forage Production				
Fruit Production				
Grain Production				
Home Vegetable Gardening				
Other crops (rice, etc. Specify)				
Irrigation				
Poultry Production				
Sheep/Goat Production				
Swine Production				
Other animals (rabbits, etc. Specify)				
Veterinary Medicine				
4-H/FFA				
B. Conservation/Fishing/Forestry				
Commercial Fishing/Fish Hatchery				
Conservation/Environmental Education				
Forestry				

Briefly describe your practical experience (include any summer, part-time, academic or club activities). Describe the size of the operation, your specific skills and responsibilities, equipment operated, etc. If not full-time experience, please provide the average number of hours per week. If you need additional space, use section 33 or attach a sheet of paper.

4

16. TRADES AND TECHNICAL SKILLS

If you have any trades or technical skills complete this section.

Type of Experience	Area(s) of Specialization	Amount of Experience		Amount of Training	
		From Mo/Yr	To Mo/Yr	On Job	Trade School
Auto Mechanics					
Carpentry					
Diesel Mechanics					
Electrical					
Electronics					
Machine Skills					
Masonry					
Metalworking					
Plumbing					
Refrigeration, Air Cond., Heat					
Welding					
Other (specify)					

What diplomas, certificates, licenses do you have? ____________________

Do you have journeyman status? Yes ☐ No ☐

If yes, indicate which area(s): ____________________

Describe your experience (including any on-the-job teaching, experience with woods/metals, etc., equipment/tools used, etc.).: ____________________

17. PROFESSIONAL EXPERIENCE

If you have any professional experience, please complete this section.

Type of Experience	Area(s) of Specialization	Amount of Experience	
		From Mo/Yr	To Mo/Yr
Accounting			
Architecture			
Bookkeeping			
Business Administration/Management			
Computer Science (languages:)			
Cooperatives			
Drafting			
Engineering			
Law			
Public Administration			
Surveying			
Urban/Regional Planning			
Other (specify)			

Do you have certification or registration in any of the fields listed above? Yes No
If yes, certification/registration number: ____________ Type: ____________ When Received? ____________

Describe your practical experience (including field work associated with academic courses, classroom or on-the-job training or teaching) ____________________

5

18. HEALTH AND SOCIAL SERVICES

If you have any health and social services experience, please complete this section.

Type of Experience	Area(s) of Specialization	Amount of Experience From Mo/Yr	To Mo/Yr
First Aid			
Homemaking (sewing, cooking, food preservation, etc. Also see Section 28.)			
Home Economics			
Medic			
Med/Lab Technology			
Medical (doctor dentist)			
Nursing			
Nurse's Aid			
Pharmacy			
Public Health (health education, sanitarian)			
Social Work			
Therapy (physical, occupational, etc.)			
Other (specify)			

Do you have certification or registration in any of the fields listed above? Yes ☐ No ☐

If yes, certification/registration number: ____________ Type: ____________ When Received? ____________

If not, when do you plan to take your exam ____________? When do you expect to have results ____________?

Describe your practical experience (including field work associated with academic courses, classroom or on-the-job training or teaching): ____________

19. TUTORING/TEACHING/TRAINING

Please document any formal or informal teaching, tutoring and/or training experience that you have had.

Type of Experience	Area(s) of Specialization (Grade Level/Subject Matter)	From Mo/Yr	To Mo/Yr
Tutoring or informal teaching (please specify hours per week)			
Teacher's Aid			
Practice Teaching Only			
Pre-school or Kindergarten			
Primary (grades 1-6)			
Secondary (grades 7-12)			
College			
Curriculum Development			
Teacher Training			
Supervision of teachers			
Adult Education			
Business Education			
Physical Education			
Special Education			
Vocational Education			
Other (specify)			

Will you have a valid teaching certificate by the time you are available for Peace Corps service? Yes ☐ No ☐

If yes, what type: ____________ When Received? ____________

List any in-service seminars, workshops, etc., in which you have participated. ____________

Are there any grades or subjects, other than those you listed above, which you would feel qualified and comfortable in teaching? ____________

If you have not taught beyond practice teaching, give your Master Teacher/Student Teaching Supervisor's name, full address and telephone in Reference C or D (See Peace Corps Application Reference List).

If you have ever trained anyone to do anything including on-the-job training particularly in the areas of practical experience which apply to you, please briefly describe the nature and extent of this training. ____________

6

20. EDUCATIONAL BACKGROUND

Complete this item if you will have two or more years of college, trade school or equivalent specialized training by your availability date. Include all courses you will have taken by then. This information is needed in addition to any information you provided in the previous "Practical Experience" questions.

Enter the number of *hours* of credit received for each area you have studied as an undergraduate and as a graduate student. List semester credits under "Sem" column and quarter credits under the "Qtr" column. For all areas not listed, specify area and enter appropriate hours under "Other." Please include a transcript, if available.

	Undergrad HRS		Graduate HRS	
Areas of Study	Sem.	Qtr.	Sem.	Qtr.
Accounting				
Agronomy				
Animal Husbandry				
Apiculture				
Architecture				
Arts, Fine/Commercial				
Biology				
Botany				
Business Administration				
Chemistry				
Computer Science				
Conservation/Ecology				
Dietetics				
Economics				
Education				
Engineering (Type:)				
English				
Entomology				
Finance				
Fisheries (Type:)				
French				
Forestry				
Geography				
Guidance/Counseling				
Health Education				
Home Ec (Type:)				
Horticulture				
Industrial Arts				
Liberal Arts (Major:)				
Library Science				
Linguistics				

	Undergrad HRS		Graduate HRS	
Areas of Study	Sem.	Qtr.	Sem.	Qtr.
Marketing				
Mathematics				
Medicine				
Med/Lab Technology				
Nursing				
Nutrition				
Ornamental Horticulture				
Physical Education				
Physics				
Plant Pathology				
Public Health				
Range Management				
Recreation				
Social Science (Major:)				
Social Work				
Soil Science				
Spanish				
Special Education (Type:)				
Speech Therapy				
Statistics				
Therapy (Type:)				
Urban/Regional Planning				
Vocational Education				
Zoology				
Please specify:				
Other:				
Other:				
Other:				
Other:				
Other:				
Other:				

21. LANGUAGES

List language(s) known or studied below.

	For each category below, give us the number of years of experience in the language (i.e., studied or spoken):				Speaking Ability			
Language	H.S.	College	Home	Travel (specify)	Poor	Fair	Good	Exc.
Spanish								
French								
Other (specify)								

22. FOREIGN TRAVEL

List foreign countries in which you have lived and/or travelled and give dates. ______________________

____

____

____

____

7

23. EDUCATIONAL INSTITUTIONS ATTENDED

Check the box for the highest level of education you will have completed by the time you will be available to enter training:

1. ☐ Did not complete high school
2. ☐ High School graduate
3. ☐ One or two years of college completed
4. ☐ A.A. Degree or equivalent
5. ☐ 3rd year of college completed
6. ☐ College graduate
7. ☐ Graduate Study
8. ☐ Graduate degree
9. ☐ Technical school graduate
0. ☐ Other (specify GED, etc. ____________)

Beginning with the most recent, list all schools attended since and including high school. Include any trade or technical schools, military training, etc.

Name of School	City and State	Dates Attended				Areas of Study		Type of Degree or Certificate	Date Received (or expected)
		From		To					
		Mo.	Yr.	Mo.	Yr.	Major	Minor		

24. EMPLOYMENT RECORD

In this section, please include any self-employment, home management, full or part-time, salaried or volunteer employment. *Start with your current or most recent experience,* and go back *TEN* years or until the date of your high school graduation. A summary for the rest of your job history is sufficient. Use additional sheets to reflect a longer work history, using this format. Even if you submit a resume, this section must be completed.

Company/Organization

Name ____________
City & State: ____________
From (mo/yr): ______ To (mo/yr): ______
Salary: $______ Hrs per week: ______

Title: ____________
Duties and Responsibilities: ____________
Reason for Leaving: ____________

Company/Organization

Name ____________
City & State: ____________
From (mo/yr): ______ To (mo/yr): ______
Salary: $______ Hrs per week: ______

Title: ____________
Duties and Responsibilities ____________
Reason for Leaving: ____________

Company/Organization

Name ____________
City & State: ____________
From (mo/yr): ______ To (mo/yr): ______
Salary: $______ Hrs per week ______

Title: ____________
Duties and Responsibilities ____________
Reason for Leaving: ____________

Company/Organization

Name ____________
City & State: ____________
From (mo/yr): ______ To (mo/yr): ______
Salary: $______ Hrs per week ______

Title: ____________
Duties and Responsibilities: ____________
Reason for leaving: ____________

25. TIME GAPS

Please explain periods of time not otherwise accounted for by employment, school, military, etc. Give specific dates for each activity: ____________

8

26. ATHLETICS

Have you ever participated in athletics or formal recreational programs? Yes ☐ No ☐

In which sports did you participate? ____________________

Have you had any coaching experience? Yes ☐ No ☐

If yes, describe level of team and frequency. ____________________

27. COMMUNITY/VOLUNTEER ACTIVITIES

Volunteers must demonstrate leadership, creativity and initiative in their assignments overseas. Please describe any active community, volunteer and organizational work you've done. Be as specific as possible. Some examples might be Hot Line or other counseling services; Scout leader or youth work; church, civic or club activities; political campaigns or voter registration; community organizing; running charity drives; work with senior citizens or other special groups; social and professional organizations; etc. Explain who was helped and how you gained from this experience.

List the most recent activity first. If necessary, use section 33 or attach a separate sheet.

1. Name of Organization: ____________________
   Involvement: From (mo/yr) ________ To (mo/yr) ________ # hours per week ________ per month ________
   Position(s) held: ____________________
   Duties, Responsibilities, Achievements: ____________________

2. Name of Organization: ____________________
   Involvement: From (mo/yr) ________ To (mo/yr) ________ # hours per week ________ per month ________
   Position(s) held: ____________________
   Duties, Responsibilities, Achievements: ____________________

3. Name of Organization: ____________________
   Involvement: From (mo/yr) ________ To (mo/yr) ________ # hours per week ________ per month ________
   Position(s) held: ____________________
   Duties, Responsibilities, Achievements: ____________________

28. HOBBIES, HANDICRAFTS, OTHER SKILLS AND ACTIVITIES

If you would like to be considered for a program utilizing your handicraft/homemaking skills, please complete this section even if information is included elsewhere. Describe below any additional hobbies, activities or other interests not elsewhere included. Check one box to indicate the extent of your involvement. Be as specific as possible.

Description of Skill or Interest	Level of Competence		
	Slight Knowledge	Skilled Amateur	Can Earn A Living
(1)			
(2)			
(3)			

9

29. MOTIVATION STATEMENT

Explain why you wish to be a Volunteer.

30. VOLUNTEER ASSIGNMENT PREFERENCE

In order of preference, please list and describe the type of Volunteer assignments which, as a Volunteer, you would feel most qualified to perform and in which you would prefer to work.

1.

2.

3.

Please list any skills you do not wish to use as a Volunteer:

31. GEOGRAPHIC PREFERENCE

Please indicate the region(s) in which you would prefer to work:

☐ No Preference ☐ Africa ☐ Latin America

☐ North Africa/Middle East ☐ Asia/Pacific ☐ Caribbean

Why:

Please indicate any countries in which you do not want to work and why:

32. CERTIFICATION

I CERTIFY that all of the statements made in this application are true, correct, and complete to the best of my knowledge and are made in good faith. I understand that any misinformation may be cause for disqualification or termination.

DATE SIGNATURE

33. ADDITIONAL INFORMATION

33. ADDITIONAL INFORMATION (continued)

REQUEST FOR RACIAL AND ETHNIC DATA

This information is requested solely for the purpose of determining compliance with federal civil rights law, and your response will not affect consideration of your application. By providing this information you will assist us in assuring that the Peace Corps is administered in a nondiscriminatory manner.

The information requested on this detachable section is covered by the provisions of the Privacy Act as stated on the inside cover of this application.

Instructions: please categorize yourself by placing an "x" in the box next to the proper category.

☐ Black, not of Hispanic origin (a person having origins in any of the Black racial groups of Africa). (1)

☐ Hispanic (a person of Mexican, Puerto Rican, Cuban, Central or South American or other Spanish culture or origin, regardless of race). (2)

☐ American Indian or Alaskan Native (a person having origins in any of the original peoples of North America, and who maintains cultural identification through tribal affiliation or community recognition). (3)

☐ Asian or Pacific Islander (a person having origins in any of the original peoples of the Far East, Southeast Asia, the Indian subcontinent, or the Pacific Islands. This area includes, for example, China, India, Japan, Korea, the Philippines, Samoa, and Viet Nam). (4)

☐ White, not of Hispanic origins (having origins in any of the original peoples of Europe, North Africa, or the Middle East). (7)

☐ I prefer not to respond. (8)

NAME ____
(Last) (First) (Initial)

SOCIAL SECURITY NUMBER ☐☐☐ ☐☐ ☐☐☐☐

IMPORTANT

There is no discrimination on account of race, color, national origin, age, political belief, sex, or religion. All services are administered on a non-discriminatory basis. Anyone who feels he/she has been discriminated against may write to the Peace Corps, Office of Compliance, Washington, D.C. 20526.

When completed, this application and reference list should be mailed to the nearest Peace Corps recruitment office. (See list below.)

If you have further questions about Peace Corps service or would like additional help in completing this application simply contact a representative at the Peace Corps recruitment office nearest you.

Peace Corps Recruitment Offices

This is a list of the area offices where you can reach Peace Corps representatives or you may call Washington, D.C. toll-free (800) 424-8580, Ext. 293.

BOSTON (MA, VT, NH, RI, ME)
Peace Corps Recruiting Office
150 Causeway St., Rm 1304
Boston, MA 02114
617-223-7366

PHILADELPHIA (PA, DE, Southern NJ)
Peace Corps Recruiting Office
U.S. Customs House, Rm. 102-A
Philadelphia, PA 19106
215-597-0744
800-462-1589 (PA)
800-523-0216 (NY, NJ, DE)

WASHINGTON, D.C. (DC, MD, NC, WV, VA)
Peace Corps Recruiting Office
633 Indiana Ave., NW, Rm. 600
Washington, D.C. 20004
202-376-2550
800-424-8580 (ext.226 or 238)

DALLAS (TX, OK, LA, NM, AR)
Peace Corps Recruiting Office
P.O. Box 638
Dallas, TX 75221
214-767-5435
800-442-7294 (TX only)
800-527-9216 (AR, NM, OK, LA)

MINNEAPOLIS (MN, WI)
Peace Corps Recruiting Office
Old Federal Bldg., Room 104
212 Third Avenue, South
Minneapolis, MN 55401
612-349-3625
800-328-8282 (WI only)

NEW YORK (NY, NORTHERN NJ, CT)
Peace Corps Recruiting Office
26 Federal Plaza, Room 1607
New York, N.Y. 10278
212-264-7123

ATLANTA (GA, TN, MS, AL, SC, KY)
Peace Corps Recruiting Office
101 Marietta St., NW, Rm. 2207
Atlanta, GA 30323
404-221-2932
800-241-3862 (Outside GA)

PUERTO RICO (PR)
Peace Corps Recruiting Office
Mercantil Plaza Bldg, Rm 710
Ponce De Leon Ave., Stp. 27½
Hato Rey, PR 00918
809-753-3076

CHICAGO (IL, IN)
Peace Corps Recruiting Office
175 West Jackson St, Rm A-531
Chicago, IL 60604
312-353-4990
800-621-3670 (IN only)

KANSAS CITY (KS, MO, IA, NE)
Peace Corps Recruiting Office
Gateway II Bldg., Room 318
4th & State Streets
Kansas City, KS 66101
913-236-3725
800-255-4121 (IA, NE, MO)

DETROIT (MI, OH)
Peace Corps Recruiting Office
P.V. McNamara Federal Bldg.
Room M-74, 477 Michigan Ave.
Detroit, MI 48226
313-226-7928
800-521-8686 (OH)

DENVER (CO, MT, SD, ND, UT, WY)
Peace Corps Recruiting Office
1845 Sherman Street, Rm. 103
Denver, CO 80203
303-866-1057
800–525–4621 (MT, SD, ND, UT, WY)

LOS ANGELES (Southern CA, AZ)
Peace Corps Recruiting Office
11000 Wilshire Blvd, Suite 8104
West Los Angeles, CA 90024
213-209-7444

SAN DIEGO
Peace Corps Recruiting Office
2022 Camino Del Rio North
Room 501
San Diego, CA 92108
619-293-7088

SAN FRANCISCO (NORTHERN CA, NV, HI)
Peace Corps Recruiting Office
211 Main Street, Room 533
San Francisco, CA 94105
415-974-8754

SEATTLE (WA, OR, ID, AK)
Peace Corps Recruiting Office
1111 Third Avenue, Room 360
Seattle, WA 98101
206-442-5490
800-426-1022 (OR, ID)

MIAMI (FL)
Peace Corps Recruiting Office
330 Biscayne Blvd., Room 420
Miami, FL 33132
305-350-5273

*** As of July 15, 1985**

Peace Corps Applicant Reference List
Instructions – Read Carefully!

List names and COMPLETE mailing addresses of all references. All information provided by your references is confidential and for agency use only. As we must occasionally contact references by phone, list phone numbers in space provided. Contact references and ask them to respond promptly. The references you list will be important in selection for placement. YOU CANNOT BE CONSIDERED FOR PLACEMENT WITHOUT REFERENCES.

Since applicants have different qualifications, it is extremely important to choose individuals who have knowledge of your qualifications for PEACE CORPS service. Therefore, consider each block carefully and use the person who best fits your own history. Be sure to PRINT CAREFULLY because these address blocks will be used as mailing labels. Print your name in the top section of each block. BLOCK A: self explanatory, BLOCK B: self explanatory. BLOCKS C and D: It is necessary to list college references if you attended college within the past three years. If longer than three years, you may use additional supervisors or co-workers. If you did not attend college, use high school teachers. If self-employed, list business contacts or people for whom you have performed work-related services. BLOCKS E, F, G, H are for personal references.

Applicant's Name ____________________

A. Name and address of current job supervisor. (If you do not want this person contacted, list another employer or supervisor.)

SUPERVISOR COMPANY

ADDRESS

CITY STATE ZIP CODE

(AREA CODE) PHONE NUMBER

Applicant's Name ____________________

B. Name and address of job supervisor. (If you are self-employed use business references.)

SUPERVISOR COMPANY

ADDRESS

CITY STATE ZIP CODE

(AREA CODE) PHONE NUMBER

Applicant's Name ____________________

C. Name and address of an instructor, teacher, major advisor, counselor from school within the last three years. (See instructions above.)

NAME SCHOOL

ADDRESS

CITY STATE ZIP CODE

(AREA CODE) PHONE NUMBER

Applicant's Name ____________________

D. Name and address of an instructor, teacher, major advisor, counselor from school within the last three years. (See instructions above.)

NAME SCHOOL

ADDRESS

CITY STATE ZIP CODE

(AREA CODE) PHONE NUMBER

Applicant's Name ____________________

E. Name and address of the one person who knows you best. Do not list a relative.

NAME

ADDRESS

CITY STATE ZIP CODE

(AREA CODE) PHONE NUMBER

Applicant's Name ____________________

F. Name and address of a personal acquaintance, may be friend. coworker, classmate, etc. Do not list a relative.

NAME

ADDRESS

CITY STATE ZIP CODE

(AREA CODE) PHONE NUMBER

Applicant's Name ____________________

G. Name and address of personal acquaintance, may be friend, coworker, classmate, etc. Do not list a relative.

NAME

ADDRESS

CITY STATE ZIP CODE

(AREA CODE) PHONE NUMBER

Applicant's Name ____________________

H. Name and address of a personal acquaintance, may be friend. coworker, classmate, etc. Do not list a relative.

NAME

ADDRESS

CITY STATE ZIP CODE

(AREA CODE) PHONE NUMBER

FOR OFFICIAL USE ONLY

Form approved 0420-0006
Office of Management and Budget

________ date refs sent ________ by whom

USPA USE ONLY

10 11 41 09 12

UNITED STATES PARACHUTE ASSOCIATION
1440 Duke Street
Alexandria, VA 22314
(703) 836-3495

MEMBERSHIP APPLICATION

YOUR USPA MEMBERSHIP BENEFITS INCLUDE: *Parachutist Magazine* monthly, Public Liability/Property Damage Insurance, Representation at all levels of government, Eligibility for USPA and NCPL sanctioned competitions, Discount on NAA Membership, Eligibility for membership in USPA and NCPL affiliated clubs, Eligibility for US/FAI Parachuting Licenses, USPA insignia and credentials, Guidance and assistance in all parachuting activities . . . JOIN NOW!

MEMBERSHIP DUES (Check One)

- ☐ New or Expired US Members (1 Year) $32.50
- ☐ Renewing Current US Members (1 Year) $29.50
- ☐ New or Renewing Members living outside the United States (except APO, FPO) (1 Year) $42 50
  For overseas airmail magazines, add $35.00.
- ☐ 90 day Membership $21.00
- ☐ Lifetime Membership (join forever) $550.00

Annual membership dues include $12.00 for subscription to "Parachutist"

01 FIRST NAME (AND MIDDLE) | LAST NAME

☐ Check here if you do not wish your name to appear on mailing list occasionally sold by U.S.P.A.

02 STREET ADDRESS OR P O BOX

07 DATE OF BIRTH (MO/DAY/YR)

03 ADDITIONAL STREET ADDRESS OR P O BOX

08 SEX

04 CITY | 05 STATE | 06 ZIP CODE | 43 COUNTRY (IF NOT USA OR APO FPO)

PLEASE FILL IN PAYMENT INFORMATION BELOW

U. S. SKYDIVING TEAM CHECK-OFF Help send America overseas! Please check here:
Give ☐ $1 ☐ $3 ☐ $______.
Add your voluntary contribution to your dues payment or credit card.
"Support U.S.!"

▶ Please Check One:

☐ ENCLOSED IS MY CHECK FOR $ ______
☐ I AM PAYING BY CREDIT CARD

☐ VISA ☐ MASTERCARD

CREDIT CARD NUMBER

MASTERCARD INTERBANK NO. (ABOVE YOUR NAME) | EXPIRATION DATE ▶ MO. YR.

Make checks or money orders payable to "USPA".
Payments from outside USA only by valid VISA or MasterCard or by International Money Order/U.S. Postal Money Order/foreign bank check with *U.S. bank name AND bank routing code* printed on money order or check.

PLEASE UPDATE FOR OUR RECORDS

LICENSES (CHECK BOXES) LIC. NUMBER	RATINGS (Use rating renewal form below) If AFF, check here	ISSUED	EXPIRED	USPA AWARDS		
19 ☐ A	☐ JUMPMASTER ○			23 ☐ GOLD WINGS •	29 ☐ 4-STACK •	51 ☐ FALCON •
20 ☐ B	☐ INSTRUCTOR ○			24 ☐ DIA. WINGS •	30 ☐ CCR •	52 ☐ DOUBLE FALCON •
21 ☐ C	☐ INSTRUCTOR/EXAMINER ○			25 ☐ DOUBLE DIA. WINGS •	31 ☐ CCS •	53 ☐ EAGLE •
22 ☐ D	☐ PRO EXHIBITION*			26 ☐ GOLD FREEFALL •	32 ☐ NITE-4 •	54 ☐ DOUBLE EAGLE •
	☐ JUDGE*			27 ☐ DIAMOND FREEFALL •	33 ☐ NCCR •	
				28 ☐ 36-HOURS FREEFALL •	34 ☐ NCCS •	

*Submit renewal information separately as required.

MEMBER SINCE ______ 13

STATISTICAL SURVEY (Fill in as indicated)

TOTAL SPORT JUMPS TO DATE ▶ ______ 38 | NO. OF MALFUNCTIONS IN LAST 12 MONTHS ▶ ______ 40 | DOCTOR VISITS RELATED TO PARACHUTING LAST 12 MONTHS ▶ ______ 39

I certify that all statements in this application are true and correct to the best of my knowledge; and that my credit card charge authorization (if needed) is correct as shown.

X ____________ YOUR SIGNATURE PLEASE

RATING RENEWAL FORM Complete details below, and have certifying official countersign as indicated

IMPORTANT: Jumpmaster ratings must be certified by current USPA I, I/E, or BOD member. AFF Jumpmaster ratings must be certified by current USPA I, I/E or BOD member who also holds an AFF rating. Instructor and Instructor/Examiner ratings must be certified by current USPA I/E or BOD member. AFF Instructor and AFF Instructor/Examiner ratings must be certified by current USPA I/E or BOD member with an AFF rating. Instructor ratings may also be certified by an S&TA who holds the same or higher ratings. (You may NOT certify your own ratings.) To renew your rating(s) please follow these two steps:

- First, list in right column the location(s) and date(s) of those seminars, JCCs, ICCs and/or AFF CCs you attended to meet the renewal requirements in USPA Part 106; and
- Second, after filling in your recertification information, obtain the initials and signature of an appropriately rated certifying official.

APPLICANT MUST FILL IN:
To renew my ☐ JM, ☐ I, ☐ I/E, ☐ AFF JM, ☐ AFF I, ☐ AFF I/E rating I participated in ☐ seminar or ☐ certification course at this location on this date:

Location ______ Date ______

And, if renewing any regular or AFF I or I/E rating, I also participated in JCC or ICC course at this location and date:

Location ______ Date ______

And, if renewing my AFF I or I/E rating, I also participated in AFF renewal course at this location and date:

Location ______ Date ______

I hereby certify that this individual has met all the renewal requirements as listed above and as specified in the current USPA Part 106, and is therefore qualified to perform the duties of:

JM 15 initial | *I* 16 initial | *I/E* 17 initial | *AFF JM* 44 initial | *AFF I* 45 initial | *AFF I/E* 46 initial

☐ Check here - Annual Renewal Fee for any AFF rating ($25.00) enclosed.

CERTIFYING OFFICIAL signature X ______ printed name and USPA rating of Certifying Official ▶ ______

Membership Form for the United States Parachute Association